CONCISE COLLEGE TEXTS

Hotel and Catering Law in Britain

OTHER BOOKS IN SERIES

"A" Level Law, B. Hogan, P. Seago and G. Bennett
"A" Level Law: Cases and Materials, B Hogan, P. Seago and G. Bennett
Banking Law, C. Hamlin
Contract, F. R. Davies
Criminal Law, P. Seago
English Legal System, K. J. Eddey
GCSE and "O" Level Law. W. J. Brown
Grant and Levin: Family Law, Jennifer Levin
General Principles of Law, C. R. Newton
Introduction to Commercial Law, C. Hamblin and F. B. Wright
Labour Law, C. D. Drake
Land Law, W. Swinfen Green and N. Henderson
Law of Arbitration, William H. Gill
Law for Retailers, Jennifer Brave
Patents, Trade Marks, Copyright and Industrial Designs, T. A. Blanco White and Robin Jacob
Press Law, Robin Callender Smith
Sale of Goods and Consumer Credit, A. P. Dobson
Shipping Law, R. Grime
Tort, C. D. Baker

AUSTRALIA AND NEW ZEALAND
The Law Book Company Ltd.
Sydney : Melbourne : Perth

CANADA AND U.S.A.
The Carswell Company Ltd.
Agincourt, Ontario

INDIA
N. M. Tripathi Private Ltd.
Bombay
and
Eastern Law House
Calcutta and Delhi
M.P.P. House
Bangalore

ISRAEL
Steimatzky's Agency Ltd.
Jerusalem : Tel Aviv : Haifa

CONCISE COLLEGE TEXTS

Hotel and Catering Law in Britain

Fifth Edition

by

David Field, B.A.

Solicitor, Head of the Department of Law,
Napier College, Edinburgh

London
Sweet & Maxwell
1988

First Edition 1971
Second Edition 1974
Third Edition 1978
Fourth Edition 1982
Fifth Edition 1988

Published in 1988 by
Sweet & Maxwell Limited,
11 New Fetter Lane, London.
Computerset by Promenade Graphics Limited, Cheltenham.
Printed in Great Britain by
Butler & Tanner Limited,
Frome, Somerset.

British Library Cataloguing in Publication Data

Field, David,
Hotel and catering law in Britain.—5th ed.
1. Great Britain. Hotel industries. Law
2. Great Britain. Catering industries. Law
I. Title
344.103'78647944101

ISBN 0–421–39250–9

PREFACE TO THE FIFTH EDITION

Over five years have elapsed since the last edition of this book went to press, and inevitably, during that period, there have been many legal changes, some large and some small, which necessitate a new edition.

Perhaps the greatest single change has occurred as the result of the Wages Act 1986, which reduced the area of remit of the wages councils, introduced a new system for the deduction of fines from staff wages, and freed the parties to a contract of employment to make such arrangements as they see fit for the form in which wages are to be paid.

Substantial changes in company law have been felt within the catering industry, as has new legislation such as the Local Government (Miscellaneous Provisions) Act 1982, which among other things replaced music and dancing licensing with public entertainment licences, and the Licensing (Restaurant Meals) Act 1987, which did away with the two hour afternoon break in permitted hours in restaurants. Many other minor changes in the law are reflected in this new edition, and several significant cases heard since 1982 in established areas of the syllabus have been included.

At the end of the day, however, it has been the author's wish to retain as much as possible of the style and content of previous editions, which it is believed have now become familiar and acceptable to both students and lecturers alike.

Once again, I cannot let this opportunity pass without recording my grateful thanks to my publishers for their continued faith in the publication, and those readers who took the time and trouble to contact me with comments, criticisms and helpful pointers to improvements in the text. Chief among these, as in the case of the Fourth Edition, was Mr C S Dixon, Senior Lecturer at Norwich

Hotel School, without whose "consumer feedback" no new edition of this book would now be complete.

I have endeavoured, wherever possible, to state the law as it stood on January 1, 1988.

David Field

CONTENTS

TABLE OF CASES

TABLE OF STATUTES

TABLE OF STATUTORY REGULATIONS

CHAPTER ONE

The legal system

In order to understand more fully the chapters which follow, relating directly to the law as it affects the hotelier or caterer, it is necessary for the reader to familiarise himself, in a general way, with some background facts concerning the legal system.

The most important items in this respect are the sources of law and the courts of law, but first, one must grasp the basic distinctions between the *criminal law* and the *civil law*.

Criminal law

Criminal law is, in effect, the law handed down by the State to regulate individual behaviour for the sake of the majority. A "crime" is any act which the Government of the day regards as so injurious to the general wellbeing of the population as to require official prohibition. Some crimes, such as murder and robbery, are obvious, but many "criminal offences" are not acts which one would automatically class as "dangerous" or "offensive." It is particularly important for catering students to grasp this point, since breaches of the Licensing Acts, Food and Drug Acts, Health and Safety at Work etc Act and so on are classed as criminal offences, even though many would not regard such offences as "morally dangerous."

A person who commits a crime is "prosecuted," either by the police or by some public official such as an Environmental Health Officer or Trading Standards Officer, at public expense. In Scotland, prosecutions are conducted by a local civil servant known as the Procurator Fiscal. In court, the person accused is referred to as the "defendant" or, more commonly, the "accused," and his punishment, if convicted, is likely to be a fine, imprisonment or in suitable cases, probation. He may also, in some cases, be ordered to compensate his victim.

Civil law

The civil law is a collection of rules and principles which have arisen to regulate relationships between *private* individuals (including, of course, public bodies, companies, etc.). Thus, the law of contract regulates business dealings between organisations and individuals, while the law of torts (in Scotland, delict) protects the rights of the individual against, for example, trespass, negligence and defamation.

A person who breaks the civil law (*e.g.* refuses to fulfil a contract) is "sued" by the aggrieved party (known as the "plaintiff" or, in Scotland, the "pursuer"), usually at the latter's expense, although costs may be awarded against the party being sued (the "defendant" or "defender" in Scotland). If judgment is given against the defendant, the likely outcome is the award of damages to the plaintiff, although other remedies exist (*e.g.* injunctions, known in Scotland as "interdicts").

The sources of law

The following are the normal categories under which the sources of law are listed.

Legislation

"Legislation" is the word used to describe the laying down of rules of law by authorised law-making bodies. The most obvious of these, of course, is Parliament, and new laws passed by Parliament are known as "statutes" (examples of statutes are the Licensing Act 1964, and the Hotel Proprietors Act 1956). Statutes cover both civil and criminal law, and they are the supreme source of law. Nothing can override or alter a statute except another statute, and except for those matters now handled by the EEC in Brussels, Parliament has no rivals. All legislative power not exercised from Brussels is vested in Parliament, which may if it wishes delegate some of its functions.

This "delegated legislation" may take many forms. Thus, for example, local authorities are given the power to legislate (by issuing "byelaws") for their own particular areas in matters which Parliament does not possess the time or inclination to deal with. But this power is given to them by Parliament, and may be controlled, and if necessary withdrawn, by Parliament. Individual ministers are also given powers to create legislation on matters concerning their own departments; such legislation usually takes the form of a "statutory instrument" (a good example of a statutory instrument is a Wages Council Order, for which see Chap. 10). Again, bodies such as British Rail and the British Airports Authority have the power to enact byelaws covering their own areas of activity. But in all these cases, such powers are closely controlled by Parliament.

Judicial precedent

"Judicial precedent" is the name given to that law which is "handed down," or created, by our courts of law. Basically, the function of a court is to interpret those laws laid down by Parliament or other legislative authorities, and to adjudicate in those matters which have never before come before a court of law. In doing so, of course, a judge may have many opportunities for laying down new principles, or "precedents." Whether or not such precedents will be followed by later courts will depend upon two factors.

First of all, the point of law laid down by the judge must be *essential* to the matter in hand (in technical language, it must be the "*ratio*" of the case). Secondly, the court which is considering the previous decision should be either at the same level or below the level of the court which delivered the judgment. Thus, to refer to the section on the English courts of law, below, a judgment of the Court of Appeal (if it constitutes the "*ratio*" of the case) is binding on the High Court, but a judgment of the Court of Appeal, even if it *is* the *ratio* of the case, cannot bind the House of Lords.

Where a court *is* obliged to follow the precedent set by an earlier court, it is said to be "bound" by that decision, and the decision itself is referred to as a "binding precedent." The House of Lords, since 1966, has not regarded itself as being bound by its own decisions, but if the House of Lords sets an unpopular precedent which it refuses to overrule, the only remedy will be for Parliament to pass a statute overruling it. It should be noted that judicial precedent is often referred to as "case law."

No system of precedent could, of course, work effectively without a speedy and accurate system of reporting, and it is for this purpose that various types of law report are published. Until 1867 our law reports were spasmodic and far from comprehensive, relying mainly on private professional reports, but since that date, the General Council of Law Reporting has issued the *Law Reports*, in various divisions such as Queen's Bench (Q.B.), Chancery (Ch.) and Appeal Cases (A.C.). It also publishes *The Weekly Law Reports* (W.L.R.), while several commercial organisations have begun issuing their own law reports, notably the *All England Law Reports* (All E.R.) and the Industrial Relations Law Reports (I.R.L.R.). Reports of cases also appear in all leading law journals.

Miscellaneous

Between them, legislation and judicial precedent account for an overwhelming proportion of our law, and are therefore rightly regarded as the two most important sources of law. But certain other sources require at least a mention.

For example, custom has, historically, played an important part in the formulation of the law as it is today. The customs of a particular locality or trade have often been used as a basis for the creation of new codes of law covering the whole nation. For example, the unwritten codes of generations of merchants were utilised to good effect when Parliament enacted a set of laws for the whole country in the Sale of Goods Act 1893, now the Sale of Goods Act, 1979.

Of marginal importance, and mainly as a comparison or reference, the laws of other nations have played their part. Thus, the Roman law, which at one time covered almost all Western Europe, never really took hold in England, although certain principles of Roman law have from time to time been adopted by our courts particularly in Scotland. A further source of law has been old books and documents, which in many cases constitute the only evidence we have of what the law was on a particular subject until the fifteenth or sixteenth century.

The courts of law

Because of the division between the English and Scottish legal systems, the law is administered in a different set of courts in each country.

(A) ENGLAND AND WALES

The civil courts

The following, in ascending order of seniority, are the main English courts of law dealing with *civil* cases.

Magistrates' courts

The magistrates' courts have a limited jurisdiction in civil cases, most of their work being the trial of *criminal* offenders (see below). In civil matters, they deal, for example, with cases concerning matrimonial disputes (*e.g.* separation orders and maintenance), and also, of great significance in the context of hotel and catering law, with liquor licensing. A more detailed description of their duties in this context may be found in Chapter 4. Appeal from the decision of the magistrates lies to the appropriate division of the High Court (see below).

County courts

"County courts" are local civil courts, and their name is somewhat misleading since they are not organised on a county basis, and most counties have more than one. They deal with a whole host of minor civil actions, and may in fact handle almost any type of normal civil action, the only limit being the size of the claim involved. Thus, for example, they may deal with any claims in contract or tort which are under £5000 in value. In addition, they may try an action for *any* amount where both parties agree to accept the jurisdiction of the court. The county courts also have extensive jurisdiction in undefended matrimonial causes.

The county courts are staffed by circuit judges and they are divided into districts and "circuits" accordingly. In addition, *each* court has a *registrar*, who may himself try claims for under £500 in value. Both judges and registrars usually sit without a jury, and the procedure is much simpler, and less costly, than in the High Court. A right of appeal lies from the decision of the county court to the Court of Appeal.

The system whereby smaller claims are heard by the registrar has developed in recent years into what has become known as the "small claims procedure," under which a claim for less than £500 will automatically be referred to the registrar for a simple arbitration. The case is not heard in open court, and neither side may claim legal costs against the other. The "award" by the registrar is just as binding on the parties as the "judgment" of a full court, and the small claims procedure is now very popular in "consumer" cases (which might well include, for example, loss or damage claims against an hotelier where the amount claimed is less than £500).

The High Court

The High Court of Justice first emerged in 1875, and has been reorganised since then. It is the highest court of trial in civil matters (the higher courts being appeal courts) and is organised in three divisions:

The Queen's Bench Division. This division is headed by the Lord Chief Justice and staffed by over 40 judges of the Division. As well as having an important role to play in the administration of the criminal law, the Division also deals with the more expensive actions in areas of the law such as contract and tort. Thus, whereas a breach of contract claim of, say, £250 would be tried by a county court, a claim for £2,500 would be tried in the Queen's Bench Division of the High Court.

Actions in the Queen's Bench Division are before a single judge and, normally, do not entail a jury. Since 1970, the entire High Court, including the Q.B.D., has had the right to sit, not just in London, where it sits traditionally, but in any part of the country which is more convenient. The Q.B.D., of course, also hears appeals from magistrates' courts. It should also be noted that a sub-division of the Q.B.D., called the "Commercial Court," exists to hear commercial cases, and has commercial specialist judges to staff it.

The Chancery Division. This division consists of the Lord Chancellor, a Vice-Chancellor and judges of the Chancery Division, and deals primarily with cases involving land, company law and partnership agreements. Again, one judge usually presides, without a jury, and the court may sit in whichever part of the country it wishes.

The Family Division. This division consists of the President and judges of the Family Division, and deals almost exclusively, as its name implies, with family matters, notably defended divorce cases.

Appeals lie from all divisions of the High Court to either the Court of Appeal (Civil Division) or, if both parties agree, and the trial judge grants a certificate to authorise it, the House of Lords directly.

The Court of Appeal (Civil Division)

This court, headed by the Master of the Rolls and staffed by Lords Justices of Appeal, exists solely to hear appeals in civil cases from the High Court and the county courts. The appeal takes the form of a rehearing from the shorthand notes of the trial and from the judge's notes. Judgments are issued in writing, but often read out in open court. There is normally a quorum of three judges.

The House of Lords

The House of Lords, acting in its judicial capacity, consists of the Lord Chancellor and the Lords of Appeal in Ordinary (maximum number 11), and it is the highest court of appeal in civil matters. It hears appeals from the Civil Division of the Court of Appeal by leave of either the Court of Appeal or the House of Lords, and also, in certain cases (see above) from the High Court. Normally, appeals to the House of Lords are on points of law of general public importance. There is a quorum of three, although five Lords often sit.

The criminal courts

The following, in ascending order of seniority, are the main courts of law dealing with *criminal* cases.

Magistrates' courts
The magistrates have a variety of functions with respect to the criminal law. Quite apart from signing warrants, granting bail, etc., the magistrates also take part in the criminal trial process in two ways:

Examining magistrates. Every serious criminal case, regardless of which court is eventually likely to try the case, is first brought before the examining magistrates in order that: (a) the police may prove that they have at least a prima facie case against the accused; (b) the magistrates may decide which court is to try the case. So far as this choice is concerned, the Criminal Law Act 1977, divides all cases into three categories, namely:

1. Offences triable *only* on *indictment* (*i.e.* by jury); *e.g.* murder and rape;
2. Offences triable only *summarily* (*i.e.* without a jury); *e.g.* drunk driving, assaults on police;
3. Offences triable *either* way, *e.g.* common assault, most types of theft, perjury.

It is at the examining magistrates stage that the initial classification is made in the case of those offences which may be tried *either* way; if it is agreed that the case shall be taken summarily, the trial proceeds in the magistrates' court, but if not (*i.e.* if the case is to go before a jury), the examining magistrates complete their involvement with the case, and enter it for trial in the Crown Court (see below). It is also at this stage that matters such as bail and legal aid are considered.

Summary trial. The great majority of criminal actions are tried "summarily" before the magistrates, who may be either "lay" (*i.e.* part-time and unpaid) or "stipendiary" (full-time, salaried and legally qualified), the latter usually sitting alone.

The 1977 Act has increased the maximum penalties which may be imposed following upon a conviction before the magistrates' court. These are now six months' imprisonment, or a fine not exceeding £2000, or both. In many cases, the maximum penalty is much lower, depending upon the nature of the offence and the penalty fixed by the statute creating the offence. In many cases also, the magistrates' court may remit a convicted person to the Crown Court for sentence.

A right of appeal lies from the decision of the magistrates to the Crown Court for a rehearing, or to the Queen's Bench Division of the High Court on a point of law only.

Crown Courts
The conduct of trial by jury (*i.e.* "trial on indictment") is now centred on the Crown Courts, which are organised on a full-time "circuit" basis, and represent, in effect, the Queen's Bench Division on tour. These Crown Courts deal with all serious crimes such as murder, armed robbery, rape, etc., and all other crimes, such as theft and dangerous driving, which are regarded as sufficiently serious as to require trial by jury. But the gravity of the offence which may be tried is in practice decided by the status of the judge available to preside over the hearing. There are, in fact, three types of judge in the Crown Court, and each sits with a jury. They are:

High Court judges, who try what are called "Class One offences"; in practice, these are the most serious of all, *e.g.* murder. They also try "Class Two offences" (*e.g.* manslaughter and rape), unless authority is given for them to be tried by:

Circuit judges and recorders, who may also be given leave by a High Court judge to try "Class Three offences" such as theft and fraud. Circuit judges and recorders also have full powers to try "Class Four offences," which consist largely of offences which may be tried either summarily or on indictment. The main difference between circuit judges and recorders is that the former are full-time, appointed by the Queen on the recommendation of the Lord Chancellor, while the latter are part-time, being solicitors or barristers of at least ten years' standing. Circuit judges and recorders are accompanied in court by two to four magistrates.

The Crown Court for The City of London is the Central Criminal Court, perhaps better known as "The Old Bailey."

A right of appeal lies from the decision of a Crown Court to the Court of Appeal (Criminal Division).

Court of Appeal (Criminal Division)
The Court of Appeal (Criminal Division) is headed by the Lord Chief Justice, and staffed by Lords Justices of Appeal, some of whom specialise in criminal cases. It hears appeals from decisions of the Crown Court, both on points of law and, where the court approves, on a point of mixed law and fact. In practice, the bulk of modern criminal appeals are on questions of mixed law and fact, where there was some irregularity or error in the trial itself. A convicted defendant may also, with the leave of the court, appeal against sentence. There is a quorum of three judges, and there may be either one joint judgment or, where a point of law is involved, separate judgments. There is a right of appeal from a decision of the Court of Appeal (Criminal Division) to the House of Lords.

House of Lords
The composition of the House of Lords, sitting in its judicial capacity, has already been explained (see above), and it is sufficient here to note that the same rules which apply to civil appeals also apply to criminal cases.

(B) SCOTLAND

As explained earlier, the Scots have always enjoyed their own legal system, with its own set of courts. However, the court structure in Scotland is less complex than its counterpart in England and Wales, and may be more simply explained.

The Sheriff Courts
In both criminal and civil cases, the sheriff court is the court in which the vast majority of cases appear. The sheriff courts are organised on a local basis, with Sheriff Court Districts, each containing a number of sheriff courts; the result is that most towns of any size in Scotland have their own sheriff court. The court is presided over by one or more sheriffs, who are normally full-time, and are all lawyers of many years experience.

In criminal matters, the sheriff court will handle all but the most serious cases (the "Crown Pleas," as they are called, which include murder and rape, and which are reserved for the High Court). It is normally the prosecution (represented by the Procurator Fiscal) who decide whether a case in the sheriff court will be tried on *indictment* (*i.e.* before a sheriff and jury, with a maximum sentence of 2 years imprisonment), or *summarily* (before a sheriff alone, maximum sentence six months imprisonment or a £2000 fine).

A sheriff is empowered to hear almost all civil claims, to any value, and it is for the pursuer to decide whether to raise his action in the sheriff court or in the Court of Session. However, each sheriff court only has jurisdiction over cases which arise in its area (which means in effect the area in which the action complained of occurred, or the area in which the defender resides or carries on business), while cases in which less than £1000 is claimed may normally *only* be raised in the sheriff courts.

The District Courts
These are local courts of criminal jurisdiction staffed by "lay" magistrates appointed by the local District Council (in Glasgow there are some stipendiary magistrates). They handle only the most minor offences (*e.g.* breach of the peace), and the maximum sentence imposable by lay magistrates is 60 days imprisonment or a fine of £400.

The High Court of Justiciary

The High Court sits periodically in the major cities of Scotland to hear the most serious criminal cases of all. All cases in the High Court are conducted before a jury and presided over by a High Court judge (drawn from the Court of Session—see below). There is no limit on sentence, and in practice only cases involving murder, rape, serious assault and dangerous conspiracy will be taken in the High Court.

The Court of Session

The Court of Session (which in the exercise of its criminal functions is known as the High Court of Justiciary) is the most senior of the Scottish courts. It is staffed by judges (the "Lords of Council and Session") and in the exercise of its civil jurisdiction it has two divisions, the Inner House and the Outer House.

The Outer House is a court of "first instance" jurisdiction (*i.e.* it hears cases for the very first time), and those pursuers who choose to bring their cases in the Court of Session will find themselves in the Outer House before a single judge (who on rare occasions may sit with a civil jury). The Outer House also deals with "status" actions (*i.e.* actions involving matters such as divorce and legitimacy, which concern a person's status, and which cannot be taken in the sheriff court).

The Inner House is in effect an appeal court in which three judges of the Court of Session hear appeals from the sheriff courts and the Outer House. Appeal *from* the Inner House lies to the House of Lords.

The House of Lords

The House of Lords is still the final court of appeal in *civil* matters for the entire Scottish legal system. At least one of the Law Lords is a Scots lawyer, and by tradition he is always one of the judges who sit in a Scottish appeal. Over the years, many important changes in Scots law have arisen from House of Lords rulings, and many cases which were originally Scots have been incorporated into English law by virtue of this common appeal channel (see, for example, *Donoghue* v. *Stevenson*, in Chapter 15).

Tribunals

No modern outline of the courts of law would be complete without mention being made of "tribunals" which, although they do not occupy a place in the traditional hierarchy of our courts of law, nevertheless play an increasingly important role in the administration of our law. Although officially referred to as "administrative tribunals," they in fact carry out a *judicial* function, in that they determine points of law, and adjudicate on legal disputes between parties.

The growth of such tribunals over the past 20 years may be largely attributed to the increase in specialised areas of the law, notably the law of employment, the sheer volume of which cannot be handled by the ordinary courts, and in which speed and informality are vital factors. There is also a need for specialisation in certain complex areas of the law. For these reasons, successive Acts of Parliament have, whilst establishing new principles and detailed rules of law, at the same time introduced tribunals before which disputes under such Acts can be resolved, as alternatives to the traditional courts of law.

Examples which are of particular relevance to students using this book are the Equal Pay Act 1970, the Sex Discrimination Act 1975 and the Employment Protection (Consolidation) Act 1978. Each of these Acts makes provision for disputes on the subject matter of the Act to be heard before a tribunal. In fact, any hotel manager who becomes involved in litigation concerning employees and their rights is almost certain to find that when the matter "comes to court," it is before such a tribunal, whose proceedings are less formal, and which is staffed not by judges, but by lay experts sitting with a legally qualified chairman.

The decisions of such tribunals, are, so far as the litigants are concerned, just as binding as those of the more traditional courts.

The influence of the EEC

On January 1, 1973, the U.K. became a member of the European Economic Community, and this had several important implications for the independence of its legal system. In particular, neither Parliament nor the House of Lords may now be described as supreme and unfettered in their approach to the law.

So far as legislation is concerned, not all of the documents and statements issued by the Community (via its "Council and Commission") are binding upon member nations, but *Regulations* and *Directives* are. A *Regulation*, in particular, is a direct imposition on all member states of a set of rules and regulations which *must* be obeyed to the letter. Parliament has no direct power to ignore or alter Regulations, which become binding in the U.K. as if they had been passed by our own Parliament. A *Directive*, on the other hand, does not have immediate binding effect but calls upon the Government of each member state to bring about a certain state of affairs by means of legislation of its own.

By these means, for example, Article 119 of the Treaty of Rome (in effect a Regulation which requires equality of pay between the sexes) became translated into the Equal Pay Act, 1970, while certain Directives (*i.e.* those of 1975 and 1976) prodded the Government into broader legislation such as the Sex Discrimination Act 1975, and have led individuals to seek redress in the courts for grievances not directly covered under U.K. law.

So far as the courts themselves are concerned, the European Court stands above the House of Lords as the final court of appeal in all matters which relate to the Community as a whole. Thus, if a U.K. case concerns simply a U.K. issue between U.K. subjects, it will fall to be dealt with in the British courts, and those courts alone. If, on the other hand, it concerns some issue which will affect those in the *other* nations of the Community (*e.g.* the implementation of the Treaty, or some Regulations under it), then the European Court has the final word, and even the House of Lords will be bound by such a ruling. Appropriate cases will be "referred" to the European Court by the English courts.

CHAPTER TWO

Starting the business

Types of business

EVEN before he purchases the land or buildings required for hotel or restaurant development, the business man must decide how his business is to be run, and by whom. Broadly speaking, he has a choice between private ownership, partnership and company formation. Each method has both advantages and disadvantages, and the businessman would be well advised to consult his accountant before choosing one or the other. There are, in addition, considerable legal differences between the three which must be considered before the choice is made.

Private ownership

Unlike many other areas of trade or business, the "one-man firm" is still fairly common in the hotel and catering industry, and many of the large hotel companies in the market today have developed from privately-owned single catering units. The essential feature of the private concern is that it is run by one man (often with private backers) who takes upon himself the risks of the commercial world in the hope of reaping some of its rewards. If the business prospers, he may enjoy all the profits without the need to answer to shareholders or partners. If, on the other hand, it fails, he goes alone to the bankruptcy court, unable to hide behind the convenient shield which is created when a company is formed.

In many cases the "sole trader," as such a man is frequently called, chooses to operate under his own name. If, on the other hand, he chooses to operate under some other name than his own, then by virtue of section 4 of the Business Names Act 1985 he must display his real name clearly on all business letters, written orders for goods or services to be supplied to the business, invoices and receipts issued by the business and written demands for payment of debts arising in the course of the business. He must also include an address in Great Britain at which service of documents may be effected.

The same name and address must also be clearly displayed in any premises where the business is carried on and to which customers or suppliers have access, and must be supplied to any person with whom business is being done or discussed and who demands it. At the same time, by virtue of section 2, no-one may, without the approval of the Secretary of State, carry on business under a name which suggests that the business is connected with the Government or a local authority, or which contains any word or expression forbidden under Regulations issued under the Act.

To fail to comply with any of these requirements is a criminal offence punishable by a fine. What is perhaps even worse is the provision under section 5 of the Act to the effect that if a person who has failed to comply with section 4 raises an action in court under some business contract, and the defendant can show *either* that he himself has a claim against the plaintiff arising under that contract which he has been unable to pursue because of the breach of section 4, *or* that the breach has caused him some financial loss, then the action by the plaintiff will be dismissed unless the court is satisfied that it is "just and equitable" to permit it to continue.

The greatest problem facing the sole trader is, of course, a relative lack of capital. He has only his own resources (and perhaps those of relatives, friends and financial institutions) with which to operate, and however much he "ploughs back" the profits, there must come a time when he must seriously consider joining with others, either in a partnership or in a company, in order that the resulting capital may be used to expand the business on a much larger scale.

Partnership

Partnership may be described broadly as an arrangement whereby two or more persons (there is normally a maximum limit of 20) join together in business with a view to profit. It is a joint venture based upon mutual trust, in which each of the partners contributes something (*e.g.* capital or specialised knowledge) to start the business off, and each shares in any profits which may result. It is usual for the business to adopt the name of the partners, but if some other name is given to it, then the Business Names Act 1985 will apply as it does to sole traders (see above) with certain exceptions in the case of partnerships of more than 20 persons. In Scotland, a partnership is a separate legal *persona.*

There is no legal necessity for a formal written document, but it is in the interests of all the partners that one be adopted, and such a document will be known as the "articles of partnership."(in Scotland, a "contract of co-partnery"). Anyone, except an enemy alien, may be a partner, but a minor who becomes a partner may repudiate such an arrangement either before he becomes 18, or during a reasonable period after the attainment of his eighteenth birthday.

The articles of partnership (if any) regulate the legal rights and duties of the partners as amongst themselves, and they may be altered or varied at any time by the unanimous consent of all the partners. In the absence of such articles, the law will *presume* certain rights and duties. For example, it will be implied that each of the partners has the right to take part in the management of the business, the right to prevent the admission of a new partner, the right to share equally in the profits, and the right to demand the utmost good faith from the other partners.

The most important feature of a partnership so far as the law is concerned is that each and every partner is an *agent* for the business, and his actions will be legally binding upon the other partners unless such actions are outside the scope of the business, or unless the person with whom he dealt must have been aware or was under the impression that he was acting outside the scope of the authority given to him by the other partners. This is the effect of section 5 of the Partnership Act 1890, and is the reason why all partnerships must be regarded as ventures based upon mutual trust. The relationship is one of *uberrimae fidei* or utmost good faith.

All the partners are jointly liable for the debts of the partnership, and the firm's creditors have the right to sue any of the partners to the limit of their personal and business resources. Even if a partner dies, his estate may be proceeded against in settlement of the partnership debts. Any creditor who chooses to proceed against only one of the partners may later proceed against any of the others, and the partner thus proceeded against may call upon the remaining partners to contribute a *pro rata* share of the debt.

A partner who retires will still be liable for debts incurred during the period in which he was a partner unless the other partners release him, and the firm's creditors agree to such a release. A retiring partner may even be liable for partnership debts incurred after his retirement if some third party dealing with the firm is led to believe, if only by implication, that he is still a member of the partnership. Any incoming partner will, in England at least, be free from liability for *existing* partnership debts, but he will be liable for *future* debts in the normal way.

In Scotland, it seems, a partner who comes into a firm which is a "going concern" may well be liable for *existing* debts; for example, in *Miller* v. *Finlay (John), MacLeod and Parker* (1974), Mr. A. carried on business on his own as a solicitor, and in February, 1954, he undertook the winding-up of an estate. In April, 1958, he took on a partner, B, and following A's death in June, 1958, B carried on the firm's business, including the winding-up of the estate. He then took on C as a partner. A had allowed the business to fall into disarray, and eventually the executrix in the estate raised an action against the partnership for an accounting in respect of the estate. B and C. claimed that they could not be held liable for events which had occurred before they became partners, but it was held that they were, since both B. and C. must be taken to have entered into the business accepting all its assets and liabilities; it is a question of fact in each case whether or not a partner may be said to do this.

Partnerships may come to an end in a variety of ways. They may, for example, come to an end after the expiry of the period of time set by the partners at the very start of the venture: such a time limit will normally be specified in the articles. One of the partners may request that the association be terminated, or one of the partners may die or become bankrupt. A partnership will be automatically dissolved if there occurs an event which makes its existence illegal or which renders its business unlawful, and in some cases the court may order the partners to cease business.

The partners may, in the articles, specify the circumstances in which the partnership may come to an end, and frequently the articles provide for the appointment of a new partner, and the creation of a new partnership, upon the retirement, death or bankruptcy of one or more of the partners. When a partnership *does* come to a definite end, the communal property and assets must first be employed for the settlement of outstanding debts. Any surplus which remains may then be divided up among the partners in the proportion to which each contributed the starting capital, up to the limit of that amount. Any further surplus will be divided in the proportion to which each of the partners was, under the terms of the partnership agreement, entitled to share in the profits.

Under the Limited Partnership Act 1907, it is possible to register a firm as a *limited partnership*, whereby certain of the partners are only liable for the partnership debts to the extent of their original capital contribution (in other words, they only lose what they originally put in). Such partners may not take part in the management of the firm and they cannot by their actions legally bind the other partners. They cannot object to the admission of new partners, and their death or bankruptcy does not dissolve the partnership. Above all, not all the members may be limited partners, and there must be at least one who is a partner in the normal way and who may be called upon to pay the firm's debts in full.

Such limited partnerships must be registered with the Registrar of Companies on the standard forms available from his office. It is not a very common form of partnership because of the greater advantages of full incorporation under the Companies Acts.

Companies

Since about 1600, the law has recognised the company as being a separate form of business enterprise. It is in fact a form of "corporation," that is, a separate legal entity all on its own, with an existence which in the eyes of the law is independent of that of the individuals who from time to time make up the company.

There are various types of company. The most famous, historically, were those granted under *Royal Charter*, such as the Hudson's Bay Company and the East India Company. Some companies are established by *Private Act of Parliament*, the best examples of these being local water boards. Yet a third type of company is that formed by *Special Public Act of Parliament*, and the large public corporations such as the British Rail Board and the National Coal Board provide the examples here. But the most numerous, and for our purposes the most important, are those companies which are formed by *registration under the Companies Act of 1985*.

We are concerned, then, only with *registered* companies. But these fall into different categories, and can best be classified as follows:

1. *Public companies*; these are companies limited by shares or by guarantee and having a share capital, which declare themselves in their Memorandum to be "public" companies, and which have complied with the registration provisions of the Acts relating to public companies. In particular, to be a public company, the company must have a minimum authorised share capital of £50,000, and its shares must be available for purchase by the general public.
2. *Private companies*: all other companies which do not fit the definition of a "public" company.

But this is by no means the complete picture, since *private* companies may take one of three forms:

1. *companies limited by shares*, that is, where the liability of each of the members for the company's debts is limited to the

amount (if any) which remains unpaid on his shares; since 1980, this has been the only form which the public company may take.

2. *companies limited by guarantee*, that is, where the liability of each of the members for the company's debts is limited to a specified amount which he has "guaranteed" to pay should the need arise; such companies, are not allowed to register as "public" companies.
3. *unlimited companies*, that is, where each and every member can be made fully liable for the company's debts.

This latter type of company is somewhat rare, since it loses one of the great advantages of incorporation; the right of the members to hide behind the "corporate veil" when it comes to paying debts which the business is unable to meet. This is possible because, as mentioned above, a company is regarded as being a separate legal person (acting through its directors) which has an independent existence. The actual identities of the persons who from time to time make up the company (and who frequently change) have no relevance to the public identity of the company. It lives on as directors and members come and go; outstanding creditors may look only to the company for payment—they may not go beyond the "corporate veil" and sue the members individually except where it is shown that the corporate veil was used to defraud creditors.

A good illustration of the "corporate veil" principle at work—in fact the leading case—is *Salomon* v. *Salomon and Co.* (1897), in which Mr. S. a boot repairer, formed a company with himself as leading shareholder and a few relatives with a handful of shares between them. He loaned money to the company, secured on the assets of the company, and when the company went into liquidation was given priority over ordinary trade creditors with his claim. The principle being illustrated is that S, as a person and a creditor, was a distinct entity from the company, even though, as leading shareholder, he had been its operator and had created the financial problems.

The formation of a registered company

A registered company is a creature created by the law, and it is significant that the "birth" of such a company may only take place after the observance of due legal ceremony. This ceremony occurs when the company is *registered* with the Registrar of Companies, and granted a *certificate of incorporation*.

Before a certificate of registration may be granted, those who wish to form the company (a minimum of two in all cases) will have submitted two important documents for the Registrar's approval. These consist of the following;

(a) The memorandum of association

This is the company's public face, and among its many clauses will be found the name of the company (with "public limited company" or "p.l.c." included in the name of a public company), its objects, the liability of its members (see above), the domicile of its registered office, the breakdown of its share capital, and a statement to the effect that certain named persons wish to form a company on this basis.

Perhaps the most important of these clauses in the memorandum is the "objects clause," which states the purposes for which the company is being formed (*e.g.* for the development of an hotel chain in England and Wales). This objects clause may be as widely phrased as the founders wish and the Registrar will permit, but the important legal point is that in the future, the company may do nothing which is not covered by this objects clause. Any attempted contract for a purpose outside the objects clause will be null and void from the company's point of view, even if the majority of the shareholders later attempt to ratify it.

This was decided in the famous case of *Ashbury Railway Co.* v. *Riche* (1875), in which a company formed with an objects clause which permitted it to make, sell or hire railway wagons and carriages entered into a contract to construct a railway. Fearing that this might be outside the objects clause, the directors obtained the unanimous ratification of the shareholders for what had been done. The House of Lords nevertheless held that the contract was void from the very start because it was beyond the objects clause in the company's memorandum, and not even the unanimous backing of the shareholders could make it valid. However, the effect of section 35 of the Companies Act 1985 is that such a contract may still be enforcible by an innocent outsider trading with the company in good faith and in a contract approved by the directors. Where the company is not yet formed, any person purporting to sign on its behalf will be personally liable on the contract.

(b) The articles of association

These deal with the internal management of the company, regulating the rights and duties of the members as amongst themselves, and laying down rules as to meetings, dividends, accounts and powers of directors. These articles bind each member both with the company and with the other members in a sort of mutual contract, rather like the rules of a club. Both the articles and the memorandum may be altered or varied at a later date if the necessary formalities are observed.

(c) Statutory declaration
To the effect that the formalities of registration have been complied with.

(d) Statutory list
This is a list of the company's first directors and company secretary, together with the full address of the company's registered office.

All these documents will be filed with the Registrar, and may be inspected by any member of the public upon payment of a fee. If the Registrar is satisfied, he will register the company, and issue a "certificate of incorporation," the date of which is the official birthdate of the company.

A company carrying on business under a name which is not its corporate name must comply with the provisions of the Business Names Act 1985 (see p. 13, above).

Control within the Company
As was mentioned above, a registered company acts through its authorised agents, normally the directors and certain senior executives. Their activities are closely defined and limited by the articles of association, and they are answerable to the shareholders (the members) for all that they do. They are legally obliged to use their utmost care and skill, and to act in good faith for the company's benefit at all times. Their duties may be delegated down through the chain of management to the extent permitted by the articles. The most important decisions will be taken at the board meetings, which are usually chaired by the managing director or chairman of the company, and minuted by the company secretary.

This latter individual is sometimes a director, but in all cases he is essentially a servant of the company. Frequently an accountant or lawyer, his main task is to look after the share capital of the company, issue prospectuses and register share transfers, in addition to supervising the company accounts.

Company meetings
It must be clearly understood that ultimate control over a company lies with the shareholders, who in the eyes of the law make up the company. The directors, although invariably shareholders, are answerable to the majority for what they do, and this control by the shareholders is exercised by means of the company meeting, the frequency of which, and the rules concerning which, will be laid down in the articles.

The most important of these is the annual general meeting which must occur at least once every 15 months. The AGM will be convened by the secretary with at least 21 days' notice, and a certain minimum number of the members (called a "quorum") must be present before business may proceed. The chairman will present the annual report, and declare any dividend payable for the year. The auditors will report upon the state of the annual accounts, and the members will proceed to elect or re-elect auditors and directors. Other matters may be raised by the members, and a complete record of the meeting must be filed with the Registrar of Companies, in so far as it relates to special or extraordinary resolutions.

As well as an annual general meeting, the company may hold any number of general meetings, called in accordance with the articles for certain specified purposes. Normally 14 days' notice will suffice, except where the members are being called upon to pass a special resolution (*e.g.* for a change in the company's name), in which case 21 days' notice is required. Most of the everyday company business can be handled by means of an ordinary resolution (*e.g.* the removal of a director, an increase in the share capital, or the appointment of a new auditor). The articles may give details of the method of voting required in each case, failing which a show of hands will suffice, although anyone may demand a poll. Proxies may be appointed, but will only be allowed to vote on a poll.

The dissolution of a registered company

The most important legal aspect of a company is its separate existence in the eyes of the law. A company does not die, for example, when its chairman dies, but continues as before (unlike a one-man business or a partnership). In the same way that a company can only be born in accordance with legal formality, so it may only die in a formal manner. This official death of a company is referred to as a "dissolution," and the company is said to be "wound up." This may occur in one of four ways:

1. *Voluntarily*—where the members decide to dissolve the company by special resolution, or by ordinary resolution if the articles permit this.
2. *By creditors*—where the company is apparently unable to meet its debts and the majority of the creditors agree to petition for the company's dissolution.
3. *By the court*—whenever the court is of the opinion that it is the best course in the circumstances (*e.g.* where there has been fraud or gross mismanagement).
4. *By the Registrar*—where the company is struck off the register for failing to file the necessary records with the Registrar.

Agency

"Agency" is the word used to describe a situation in which one person (known as the "agent") acts on behalf of another (known as the "principal") in order to bring that principal into a contractual relationship with a third party. In popular language, he "acts" for him, and there are countless examples of such relationships in modern business (the estate agent and the theatrical agent being just two of the more obvious ones). The example perhaps best known in the catering industry is the travel agent.

In addition to those agents who refer to themselves as such, there are many more who, by virtue of some other position or office, are acting as agents for someone else. Most professional men (*e.g.* solicitors and accountants) are automatically regarded as agents for their clients, as are specialists such as auctioneers and brokers. But perhaps the most important category of all consists of senior employees, and this is serious enough to warrant further explanation.

Quite apart from those agents who are expressly appointed by their principals, there are some who will be regarded as having been *impliedly* appointed by virtue of the position which the principal has allowed them to occupy—in lawyers' language, the principal has "held out" the agent as being authorised to act for him. This is particularly true of senior management with a degree of independent action, and the manager of an hotel or public house affords a classic example of this process.

Thus, in *Watteau* v. *Fenwick* (1893), the manager of a public house was forbidden by its owner to buy cigars on credit. He continued to do so, and it was held that the supplier, who did not even realise that the manager was not the owner, could recover his money, since the manager had been acting within the normal scope of his implied agency. This case also, of course, illustrates the point that the *implied* authority of an agent extends only to those actions which one would expect from a person in his position.

The main function of an agent, however appointed (and some rare cases of agency can arise from sheer necessity without the parties having ever met), is to negotiate a contract between his principal and the third party. Once this has happened, the agent fades from the picture (no doubt to count his fee or bank his salary), and the two parties to the contract are the third party and the principal. An agent rarely finishes up as a party to the contract, except where he had no authority (express or implied) from the principal in the first place.

In carrying out his duties, the agent owes certain duties to the principal. Primarily, of course, he must carry out the instructions he has been given, and in doing so must display "ordinary skill and diligence." But competence is not enough, and the agent owes his principal a heavy duty of good faith. In particular, he must never allow his own personal interests to conflict with the business interests of his principal, and must account to him for all profits made during the transaction. The principal, in return, must remunerate the agent in the manner agreed, must indemnify him against expenses incurred in the course of his *authorised* activities, and must honour any contract negotiated by the agent within the terms of this authority.

An agency will normally come to an end by virtue of the actions of the parties themselves (*e.g.* by mutual agreement, or when one of the parties indicates that he wishes the agency to terminate). Sometimes the agency is terminated automatically at the conclusion of a particular transaction (*e.g.* when the house is sold or the holiday completed), or the occurrence of a particular event (*e.g.* the death of either party or the bankruptcy of the principal).

Acquiring the premises

Having established some sort of business organisation, the prospective hotelier must now find suitable property for his venture. He may have in mind the acquisition of an already established hotel or restaurant, complete with fittings and clientele. Alternatively, he may choose to purchase a vacant site and erect premises built to his own design. Either way, he has many legal and financial problems to face which are on the whole outside the scope of this book.

There are, however, some points which may usefully be made. The first concerns the choice which faces any businessman acquiring property between buying the property outright, thus becoming the owner, and renting it for either a long or a short term from someone else.

Ownership of property

The state of affairs known under English and Scots law as "ownership" is merely one in which one single individual (called the owner) has more rights over the property than any other single individual or organisation. This does not mean that the owner has *absolute* power over his land; in certain circumstances, others may also have rights over that property, and the owner may not do just as he wishes with it.

For a start, the owner must have due regard for the comfort and convenience of the owners of adjoining property, or he may be sued for "nuisance" if his activities unreasonably interfere with the quiet enjoyment by his neighbours of their property. There may also be others who have certain legal rights, called "easements" (or in Scotland, "servitudes"), over his land (*e.g.* the right to pass to and fro across it, and the right to prevent building so as to block the flow of daylight to adjoining premises). Finally, there may be "covenants" in force over the property, and these are dealt with in more detail below.

Most of the normal restrictions on an owner's activities, however, come from official sources. Historically, the Crown has always exercised a theoretical superiority over all land and these superior rights are occasionally enforced in the public interest. For example, under the Coal Industry Nationalisation Act 1946, the crown asserted its right, through the National Coal Board, to mine for coal wherever it was discovered, upon payment of compensation. Similar rules apply in the case of oil and natural gas. Again, the Crown has for many centuries enforced its claim to treasure trove.

Local authorities have also in recent years acquired certain powers over the use to which property is put, and the way in which it is maintained. Perhaps the most widely known of these powers concerns the granting of planning permission, and this is covered more fully at p. 31, below. Again, they have a variety of powers under the Public Health Acts, and these are dealt with below. Local authorities have now been given fairly sweeping powers of control over the condition and use of business premises under statutes such as the Fire Precautions Act 1971, and the Control of Pollution Act 1974, details of which appear in Chapter 3. Finally, it should be noted that under various Acts of Parliament (notably the Town and Country Planning Acts) many organisations, both official and unofficial, may prevail upon the Secretary of State for the Environment (or the Secretary of State for Scotland), to grant a compulsory purchase order in respect of certain property, where it can be proved that such a step would be in the public interest. Such activities are normally restricted to local authorities and public corporations, and compensation is almost always payable.

Tenancy of property

A *tenant* is a person who occupies property belonging to someone else, who in this context is called the *landlord*. This landlord is usually the owner (although he may, in his turn, be the tenant of someone else), enjoying all the rights of ownership except those which he has granted to the tenant (*e.g.* the right to occupy the premises). Normally, the tenant will be answerable to the landlord for what he does with the property, and his rights and duties, along with those of the landlord, will usually be found in the form of "covenants" in the lease; more information on covenants is given below. At the same time, the tenant, in his capacity as *occupier*, may well be subject to official restrictions on his use of the property in the same way that an owner/occupier may be (see above).

The two most important factors in a tenancy are the size of the rent and the rights of the tenant in respect of security of tenure. The question of the rent of business premises is largely a matter for negotiation, since the network of Rent Acts which has been established in recent years applies primarily to domestic tenancies; in practice, most modern business tenancies contain a "rent review clause" which allows the landlord to raise the rent periodically.

However, since 1927 the tenants of business premises have been entitled to a certain amount of security of tenure, and the law on this subject is now laid down under Part II of the Landlord and Tenant Act 1954, as amended by the Law of Property Act 1969. (These Acts do not extend to Scotland where the relevant legislation is the Tenancy of Shops (Scotland) Act 1949 which covers those premises defined as "shops" under the Shops Act. 1950 (see Chapter 12)).

Business tenants covered by the 1954 Act are, subject to certain exceptions, entitled to a new tenancy at the end of the old one, even if the landlord is unwilling to grant one. It may be that the tenant does not wish to stay on, in which case the lease will come to an end on the date fixed for it, and that will be the end of the matter. But if the tenant is unwilling to move (and he may well be), then he may apply to the local county court (or, in Scotland, the sheriff court) for the grant of a new tenancy based upon the terms of the expiring one.

This protection applies to all business tenancies, whether the tenant is an individual or a company, and whether the lease is an oral one or in writing. It applies to nearly all businesses, but there is an important exception in the case of licensed premises which exist *primarily* for the sale of alcohol; this means that a public-house would not be protected by the Act, but an hotel or restaurant probably would.

It must also be shown that the premises are occupied for "business" purposes. Thus, in *Chapman* v. *Freeman* (1978), the owner of a small residential hotel in Cornwall also rented a cottage fifty yards from the hotel for use as staff accommodation. At the time in question, it was occupied by the head barman and his family, but when the landlord/owner died, her administrator served notice to quit. The hotel owner claimed the protection of Part II of the 1954 Act on the grounds that the cottage was occupied "for the purposes of a business carried on by him." The Court of Appeal held that this was not the case; the cottage was merely occupied for the "convenience" of the staff, and it had not been shown that the occupation was "necessary" for the performance of their duties.

There are certain grounds upon which the landlord may resist the grant of a new tenancy, and so far as England and Wales are concerned, they may be summarised as follows:

1. *Where the tenant has failed to comply with the terms of his tenancy, or has proved to be unsatisfactory*—this will obviously be a question of fact in each case, but it might well cover, for example, the situation in which hotel premises have been degraded by the willingness of the management to allow prostitutes on the premises. It certainly includes the tenant's failure to do such repairs and maintenance as he is liable to do, and also his persistent failure to pay rent.
2. *Where the landlord has offered suitable alternative premises*—again a question of fact, but unless the new premises are in every way comparable with the old, this claim is unlikely to succeed.
3. *Where the tenant occupies only part of the premises*, and the landlord is suffering financially by not being able to let the whole of the property in one single piece.
4. *Where the landlord requires the premises for demolition or reconstruction*. Under the Law of Property Act 1969, the tenant will still be entitled to remain if he gives the landlord a reasonable opportunity to enter the premises to carry out the alterations, or if he agrees to give up that part of the premises which will be affected. In *Betty's Cafes* v. *Phillips Stores* (1959), B owned a cafe in Bradford of which P were the landlords. When B applied for a new tenancy at the expiry of the old one, P replied that they intended to reconstruct the premises. In fact, it was not until the case was before the court that the directors held the meeting at which firm rebuilding plans were put in hand. The court held that the "intention" to demolish need not be held at the time that the renewal is refused, provided that it is held by the date of the hearing. The new tenancy was therefore refused.
5. *Where the landlord intends to occupy the premises himself for business or residence, and he has been the landlord for more than five years*. It is not apparently necessary for the landlord to show that he intends to make actual physical use of the *whole* of the premises he has taken over. Thus, in *Method Development* v. *Jones* (1971), the landlord succeeded on this ground where he declared his immediate need to occupy only

700 sq. ft. of premises extending to 1800 sq. ft. which were currently on lease. It was his intention to take in a further 700 sq. ft. in a year's time, and the remaining 400 sq. ft. at some indefinite time in the future.

This last provision prevents rivals from buying out competitors, at least in the short term.

In Scotland, the grounds upon which the tenant may be removed at the end of the lease correspond with 1. and 2. above. He may also be removed where the landlord has offered to sell the premises to the tenant for an arbitrated price, or on the general ground that greater hardship would arise from the renewal of the lease than from its termination.

If the landlord is unable to make use of one of these exceptions, the court has the power to award a new tenancy for a period not exceeding 14 years (in Scotland, one year). The parties may agree on their own terms for the new tenancy, failing which the court will make terms for them. They will be based very largely on the terms of the old tenancy, although the court has the power to increase the rent payable where it sees fit. It does not, however, have the power to grant a tenancy more extensive than the expiring one.

If the landlord succeeds in removing the tenant under 3. 4. or 5. above, then the tenant in England and Wales is entitled to compensation from the landlord, based upon the rateable value of the premises. This compensation will be equal to the annual rateable value if the previous tenancy was for less than 14 years, and double the annual rateable value if it was for more than 14 years.

The outgoing tenant may also claim compensation for any alterations or improvements he has made in the premises which have increased their letting value. This may occur in one of two ways; first of all, the tenant may well have obtained the prior consent of the landlord to the proposed alterations. This involves giving the landlord notice of the intended alterations, and then waiting for three months. If, within those three months, the landlord does not send a letter of objection, the tenant may assume that such alterations meet with the landlord's approval, and go ahead with them, secure in the knowledge that he can claim compensation for such improvements at the end of the tenancy.

If, on the other hand, the landlord objects, the tenant may apply to the county court for a certificate authorising the alterations on the grounds that they are proper improvements which will add to the value of the premises, and not detract from the value of any other property belonging to the landlord. Upon the granting of this certificate, the tenant may go ahead with the proposed improvements and may claim compensation in the normal way at the end of the tenancy.

It was pointed out above that the provisions of the 1954 Act do not apply to premises which exist primarily for the sale of alcohol. However, provision is made in the Act for the payment of compensation in the case of *off-licensed* premises, and in extreme cases in which compensation cannot be calculated, a new lease *may* be granted. But these provisions do not extend to on-licensed premises such as public houses. However, even a public house tenant will be entitled to compensation where his premises are *compulsorily* acquired under official authorisation (for which see above).

In all cases, claims for compensation must be made either within three months of receipt of notice to quit (which itself must be at least six months before the date set for the expiry of the lease) or from three to six months from the date of the expiry of the lease. Notice of intention to claim must first have been given in accordance with the County Court Rules.

Two final points should be noted. The first is that compensation is payable for goodwill as well as for improvements, and the second is that the provisions of the 1954 Act cannot normally be avoided, even by an express term in the lease.

Covenants

Reference has already been made to the fact that the purchase of property is a complicated business legally, and should be left in the hands of those who are most qualified to deal with it. The vendor's title will need to be thoroughly investigated, any future official plans for the area containing the proposed site will need to be examined, and, above all, it will be necessary to check whether or not the property is burdened with any "incumbrances" such as mortgages or covenants. A little more information on the latter may conveniently be given at this state.

A covenant is an arrangement whereby one person agrees with another to do, or to refrain from doing, something on his land or with his property. Covenants appear most frequently in leases and are legally enforceable as part of the contract between the landlord and the tenant. Covenants frequently encountered in practice in respect of public houses are those in which (i) the tenant agrees to take all his liquor from the landlord, a brewery (although since 1984, the effect of EEC legislation has been to limit this type of tie); (ii) the tenant agrees to do nothing which would hazard the continuation of the licence in respect of the premises; (iii) the tenant agrees to do nothing which would prevent the landlord's quiet enjoyment of neighbouring property.

A good example of a covenant in a lease of an hotel was that in *Egerton* v. *Esplanade Hotels, London, Ltd* (1947), in which the lease of an hotel in Paddington contained a clause to the effect that the tenants covenanted not to do, or allow to be done on their premises, anything which might annoy the landlords or their other tenants. It was proved that the management had allowed rooms in the hotel to be used for the purpose of illicit sexual intercourse. This evidence was the result of a police raid, following upon which the manager and the porter had been convicted of brothel-keeping. It was held that the landlords could evict the management after reasonable notice, on the grounds of breach of covenant.

Another example of a covenant in a lease is the case of *Rowlands (Mark)* v. *Berni Inns* (1985) which is dealt with in Chapter 3.

Originally, there are two parties to the covenant: A, the landlord, and B, the tenant. It may be, however, that A sells his property to C, or that B assigns the remainder of his lease to D, or both. The legal position here is that any covenant which B may have signed with A is still enforceable by either A or C against either B or D, provided that it concerns the protection of the landlord's property rights and that it relates to the use to which the tenant puts the leased property. Similar covenants affecting the tenant's rights are also enforceable by B or D against C or A.

Covenants may also be taken where property is being sold outright and the vendor wishes to exercise *some* control over the use to which the premises are put in the future. Again there is clearly a binding agreement between A, the vendor, and B, the purchaser, since the covenant is one of the terms of the contract of sale, but what is the position years later, when both the original parties have died, leaving their property to others?

The answer in England and Wales is that the covenant may still be enforceable by the successors in title to A against the successors in title to B, provided that—

1. the covenant is a *negative* one; that is, it is an undertaking *not* to do something; and
2. the covenant exists for the benefit of land retained by the original vendor, and passed on to the person who now seeks to enforce it.

This type of covenant (known as a "restrictive covenant") may, however, be extinguished in one of three ways. The parties to it may expressly agree, or the covenantee may passively assent, to its being disregarded, the court may declare the covenant to be no longer operative, or an appeal may be made to the Lands Tribunal, who may discharge or vary the covenant on the grounds that the surrounding district has changed so much as to render the covenant obsolete, or that the covenantee will suffer no detriment from its termination. The equivalent to restrictive covenants under Scots law are "burdens in title" which operate in a similar way but may be bought out or removed after application to the courts.

Restrictive covenants are still encountered in modern business life, as may be seen from *Shaw* v. *Applegate* (1978), in which A had in 1967 bought a plot of land in Withernsea from S. Ltd, which at that time consisted of an open yard and a tearoom. There was a covenant in the conveyance which prevented any part of the property being used as an amusement arcade. At the same time, S. Ltd. conveyed to S. the remainder of the surrounding land, part of which consisted of an amusement arcade, and it was to protect S's business interests that the clause in the conveyance to A. had been inserted. In fact, the benefit of the covenant by A was specifically assigned to S by means of this conveyance by S. Ltd., although A was never informed of this fact.

From 1967 onwards, A began building up a collection of slot machines on his land, and in 1972 he obtained a gaming licence and installed fruit machines. During all this time, S. had been aware of what was going on, but he made no move until 1973, when he formally advised A. that the benefit of the covenant had been assigned to him, and threatened legal action if A. did not cease using his land as an amusement arcade. A. did not cease, and S. sought an injunction. It was held that S. was not barred from seeking to enforce his rights, albeit at a late stage, because he had earlier experienced genuine doubts as to whether or not A's development constituted an "amusement arcade." But because of the delay, it would be inequitable to grant an injunction to prevent A. from continuing, and the court therefore awarded damages instead.

Finally it should be noted that under the Land Compensation Act, 1961, local planning authorities have the power to carry out development schemes of their own over compulsorily acquired land, despite the presence of restrictive covenants, upon payment of compensation to the injured party. With respect to Scotland, the equivalent provisions are contained in the Land Compensation (Scotland) Act 1963.

CHAPTER THREE

Rights and duties in respect of premises

Planning permission

UNDER the Town and Country Planning Acts (and their Scottish equivalents) there is a good deal of official control over the use to which land and property are put. Power is vested in each *local planning authority* and it is the duty of this authority to ensure that all land and property in its area is used for the best possible purposes in the light of the shortage of land and the needs of the community. Under the 1971 Act, every authority has compulsory purchase powers, subject to ministerial approval.

The Acts are concerned with the "development" of land, that is, either (a) building, mining or engineering operations in, on, over or under the land; or (b) the making of any material change in the use of land or buildings. No such development, with certain exceptions, may be carried out without planning permission granted by the local planning authority.

As far as category (a) above is concerned, planning permission is not required for purely internal alterations which do not alter the use to which the buildings are put (unless it is below ground) and which do not materially affect the external appearance of the building. But with any other alterations (even the erection of illuminated signs on the face of the building), the permission of the planning authority must be sought before work is begun.

In category (b), the local planning authority is concerned with the material use to which property is put, in order that the character of the locality (residential, industrial, etc.) may be maintained in accordance with local development schemes. It is often purely a question of degree whether or not the change could be said to be material. For example, it is not a change in material use for a private householder to take in lodgers, but it would be were he to open a guest house on the premises.

The Town and Country Planning (Use Classes) Order 1972 and its Scottish equivalent dated 1973 set out a table of "use classes," the rule being that a change from one use to another *within* a class will not require planning permission, but a change of use from one *class* to another most probably will, depending upon whether or not it is regarded as "material." The planning authority will advise in any doubtful cases. Those use classes which are relevant to the hotel and catering trade may be listed as follows:

1. The use of any building primarily for the sale of goods by retail; this does not include certain shops (*e.g.* a fried-fish shop), nor does it include any part of an hotel. It excludes restaurants, cafés or any premises licensed for the sale of liquor for consumption on the premises.
2. The use of any building as a boarding house or hotel providing sleeping accommodation.
3. The use of any building as an office, for whatever purpose.
4. The use of any building as a public hall, social centre or non-residential club.
5. The use of any building as a theatre, cinema or music hall.
6. The use of any building as a dance hall, skating rink or swimming bath.

It will be noted that public houses, restaurants and cafés are not included in any of these use classes lists. It is in fact impossible to change from any of these to any other use, or vice versa, without seeking planning permission, since these are regarded as being in a class of their own. Thus in *Westminster City Council* v. *MacDonalds Hamburgers* (1986), the famous hamburger chain was obliged to apply (successfully) for permission to convert a shoe shop in the Strand to a restaurant.

The theory behind use classes can now be appreciated. There is, for example, little difference between a theatre and a cinema so far as its effect on the character of the surrounding district is concerned, so that one may switch from one to the other without the need for planning permission. On the other hand, there is a world of difference between an office and an hotel, and so planning permission must normally be sought before such a change may be made. The narrowness of the distinctions which are sometimes drawn in planning cases is well illustrated by the case of *Mayflower (Cambridge)* v. *The Secretary of State for the Environment* (1975) in which the appellants had planning permission to use a seven-storey building for bedsitter units. They in fact used the top three floors for nightly lets and the bottom four for weekly lets. An enforcement notice was served on them, alleging that the premises were being used partly as an hotel, and it was held on appeal that this was indeed the case, and that the appellants were in breach of planning permission. In *Torbay Borough Council* v. *Coughlan* (1986) it was held that a conversion from a guest house to an old people's home required planning permission because it involved a change of use.

On the other hand, in *Blackpool Borough Council* v. *Secretary of State for the Environment* (1980), it was held that there was no "material" change of use when certain rooms in a private house were let out to friends, colleagues at work and "family groups" in return for payment of rent during two months in the summer. It was also held in *Emma Hotels* v. *Secretary of State for the Environment* (1980) that the operation of a public (*i.e.* non-residents) bar in an hotel was a normal "incident" of the use of hotel premises, so that the proprietor did not need to seek planning permission when he opened a public bar in his hotel, since there was no "material change of use." A similar decision was given in *Bradford City* v. *Shellbridge Holdings* (1986).

Whenever planning permission is required, the applicant must approach the local planning officer with full-scale plans and diagrams, preferably after having consulted an architect. Even if the proposed scheme is allowed to proceed, the owner will need to make the premises available for inspection by authorised officials, who will check that the work is being conducted according to the agreed plan. A failure to seek planning permission where it is required can result in the authority serving an "enforcement notice" on the developer, obliging him to return the property to its original state.

There is a right of appeal to the Secretary of State for the Environment (or the Secretary of State for Scotland), both against a refusal to grant planning permission, and against an enforcement notice. In some cases, compensation may be paid upon refusal of planning permission.

It must be borne in mind throughout that each planning authority will adopt different policies, and that facilities for new building will vary from place to place. For example, under the Town and Country Planning Act 1971, no one may demolish or alter a building which is listed as being of special architectural interest without giving six months' notice to the planning authority, who may make a preservation order without ministerial approval.

Rates

The General Rate Act of 1967 (or, in Scotland, the Valuation and Rating (Scotland) Act 1956 as amended), gives to each local rating authority (in effect, each local council), the power to levy rates upon all those who are in "rateable occupation" of premises within its district. These rates, when collected, go towards the maintenance of local authority services such as street lighting, drainage and refuse disposal.

The amount of the rate is expressed as a certain amount in the pound of the "rateable value" of each set of premises. This rateable value is calculated by the local valuation officer (an officer of the Inland Revenue), or, in Scotland, the local valuation assessor who is appointed by the region. He first calculates the "gross value" of the premises, being an estimate of the annual rent which the property could reasonably be expected to command on the open market. In the case of licensed premises, the gross value is normally arrived at by reference to profitability. From this gross value is deducted a sum to represent the estimated annual cost of maintaining the premises in their existing state, to arrive at the "net value." It is this which constitutes the rateable value which, rounded off to the nearest pound, is the figure upon which the rate is actually levied.

These rateable values are entered into local lists (in Scotland, the valuation roll), and any person who disagrees with the valuation placed upon his property may attempt to negotiate with the valuation officer. If this proves unsatisfactory, he may appeal to a local valuation court, and from there to the Lands Tribunal, from whose decision a right of appeal on points of law only lies to the Court of Appeal. The right of appeal in Scotland lies initially to the Valuation Appeal Committee and finally to the Lands Valuation Appeal Court.

Liability for the payment of rates lies upon the *occupier* of premises, unless he can show that someone else (*e.g.* a landlord) has agreed to pay them. So far as empty unoccupied premises are concerned, all rating authorities have a discretionary power to levy rates on property which remains vacant for three months or more. Rates may be reduced where the property is occupied for only a part of any year, and they may be apportioned where occupation of a building is shared between two or more occupiers.

There are facilities under the 1967 Act for the repayment of excess rates, and for the total relief from rates of those too impoverished to pay. Rate relief of varying amounts is available to charities, occupiers of church buildings and registered clubs, which are formed for certain purposes.

For example, in *Meriden RDC* v. *White* (1973), a Miners' Welfare club was registered under statute as existing for "charitable purposes." The club possessed the usual facilities, including a bar, and organised such activities as dances and bingo; 1100 of its membership of 1400 were past or present miners. The club was presented with a rates bill, of which it paid exactly half, claiming that it was entitled to a 50 per cent. rate relief by virtue of the fact that the premises were occupied "wholly or mainly" for charitable purposes. The local authority took legal action to secure the balance, and the case came on appeal to the High Court.

It was held that the club did occupy its premises "wholly or mainly" for charitable purposes, notwithstanding that its bar was its main feature, because of the nature of the club, and the fact that it was registered as a charity. The point might be reached at which a club such as this ceased to be charitable because of the way the bar dominated the premises, but that was not the case here.

Public health

Under a variety of statutes, local authorities have certain rights and duties over property within their areas which are carried out in the interests of public health. These may be best classified as follows:

Control over new buildings

Whenever new buildings are being erected within their area, or whenever alterations are taking place which will alter the use to which any building will be put, the local authority may request that the plans be filed with their clerk, and can prohibit any such building or alteration if it fails to comply with the Building Regulations. These are regulations issued under the Public Health Act 1961 by the Secretary of State for the Environment. In Scotland, the Building (Scotland) Act 1959 conferred powers which are now exercised by district and regional councils. Building Regulations are, of course, a separate issue from planning permission, although in practice such permission will not be granted until the Regulations have been complied with.

Among other things, such regulations deal with the following: the type of construction and the materials used, the minimum space to be left around the building, lighting, ventilation, the dimensions of the rooms, the height of the building, the provision of adequate separate toilet facilities for men and women, the provision of an adequate water supply, and of adequate drainage. Any building which fails to comply with any of these regulations without good reason may, in extreme cases, be pulled down by official order.

The local authority will also be very concerned with the provision of fire escapes, and it has the power to insist that fire escapes be provided for every storey of certain buildings which have a floor more than twenty feet from the ground. Particularly careful attention is paid in this context to hotels, large public houses and restaurants. In practice, control over fire risks is now exercised under the Fire Precautions Act 1971, for which see below.

Control over hazardous buildings

Owners or occupiers of dangerous or defective buildings can be forced to repair or even demolish them (as for example, under s.87 of the Civic Government (Scotland) Act 1982), and local authorities have wide statutory powers of entry into most buildings in order to ensure that all the necessary regulations are being observed. In particular, they may enter and investigate "statutory nuisances" such as the amassing of uncollected garbage, the emission of strong cooking smells, or the creation of unnecessary noise (now regulated under the Control of Pollution Act 1974). Under the Clean Air Act 1956, as amended by the Clean Air Act 1968, provisions may be made for the replacement or repair of heating and cooking equipment in order that the creation of smoke be minimised or eliminated. Control is usually maintained by the service on the occupier of an "abatement notice," followed by a summons if this is ignored.

Finally, local authorities have the same powers of control over toilet facilities on *existing* premises such as hotels, public houses and restaurants as they do over premises under construction.

Water supply and garbage disposal

By virtue of the Water Act, 1973, while responsibility for the actual supply of water is that of the Regional Water Authorities, the local authority retains the overall duty of ensuring that a "wholesome" supply of water is available. At the same time, the Public Health Act, 1936 (and, in Scotland section 124 of the Civic Government (Scotland) Act 1982), continues to look to local authorities for the removal of garbage in their areas. In both connections, however, hotel and catering establishments occupy a special position.

First of all, in the provision of a water supply to "trade" premises such as hotels, restaurants and public houses, the water authority may insist that the flow of such water be recorded on a separate meter, since the supply to such premises is likely to be greater than the supply to normal domestic users.

Secondly, the local authority is only obliged to make a *free* collection of "house refuse," and may charge an additional fee for any "trade refuse" which it has undertaken to collect. The distinction between the two has been said to be that ". . . . that which is produced in a dwelling-house is house refuse; that which is produced in the course of a trade or business is trade refuse."

This distinction was highlighted in *Iron Trades Mutual Employers Association Ltd.* v. *Sheffield Corporation* (1974), in which an insurance company used a converted dwelling-house in Sheffield as an office, and amassed a considerable quantity of refuse, largely paper. It called upon the local authority, under the Public Health Act, 1936, to remove the refuse, which the latter failed to do. The insurance company therefore lodged a complaint against the authority under the Act. It was held that while the local authority was obliged to move "house refuse," the sort of refuse amassed by the insurance company did not fall within that category, since it had not emanated from a house. It was "trade refuse," which the local authority might charge for removing. In *Mattison* v. *Beverley Borough Council* (1977) the Court of Appeal in refusing to order the free collection of refuse from a university hall of residence, said that the test for "house refuse" is twofold, namely (1) whether the refuse in question was produced by a house, and (2) whether it was of the type expected of a house occupied as a house.

Similar provisions to those under the 1936 Act are contained in the Control of Pollution Act, 1974, ss.12–14. Section 13 in particular empowers the local authority to serve a notice on the occupier of any premises upon which is collected "commercial" or "industrial" waste which is likely to cause a nuisance or prove detrimental to the amenities of the area, requiring him to provide suitable receptacles for it on the premises.

Notifiable diseases

Under the Public Health (Control of Disease) Act 1984 local authorities are responsible for preventing the spread of infectious diseases, and they have acquired wide powers in the case of "notifiable diseases" (*e.g.* cholera, smallpox and typhus). In particular, every doctor must notify the local "Community Physician" (formerly the Medical Officer of Health) of any patient believed to be suffering from such a disease, with details of where he has been living. Hoteliers are no longer obliged to notify the authorities of guests with notifiable diseases, but as a matter of caution, they would be well advised to notify the Community Physician at once, if the doctor attending has not already done so. An hotelier must also give all other residents and intending guests due warning of what has happened, and under no circumstances should he relet the room without having arranged for it to be thoroughly disinfected beforehand. To do so is a criminal offence.

It should finally be noted that doctors are under the same obligation to notify Community Physicians of food poisoning as they are to notify them of "notifiable diseases."

Fire precautions

The Fire Precautions Act 1971, which applies throughout Great Britain, was passed in an effort to improve fire safety standards, particularly in premises frequented by the general public. The first Order issued under the Act came into effect on June 1, 1972, and applies to all premises "used for providing, in the course of carrying on the business of a hotel or boarding house keeper, sleeping accommodation for staff, or sleeping, dining room, drawing room, ball-room or other accommodation for guests." Certain hotel premises were exempted from this first Order (*e.g.* where they did not provide sleeping accommodation for more than six persons, either staff or guests), and of course, all restaurants were exempted, but the point became somewhat academic after the passing of the Health and Safety at Work etc. Act 1974. Section 78 of this statute amended the 1971 Act so as to bring all premises "used as a place of work" within the auspices of the 1971 Act. It then only required an Order from the Secretary of State to require any place of work to seek an immediate fire certificate.

This came in 1976, when regulations passed in that year brought certain "shop" premises under the control of the fire protection authorities, with the result that all catering premises which may be classed as "shops" (see p. 171) now require fire certificates if they employ more than 20 persons on the premises at any one time, or more than 10 elsewhere than on the ground floor. Further regulations laid in the same year also state that even in the case of those "shop" premises which are not covered by the above (*e.g.* if they have less than 20 employees), the occupier (*i.e.* the employer) must supply adequate fire-fighting facilities, and maintain them, readily available for use, and must also ensure that doorways to the outside are unobstructed and easily opened.

In addition to this, the 1974 Act also requires that all premises which come under the auspices of the Offices, Shops and Railway Premises Act 1963, shall be equipped with such fire escape facilities for persons employed therein as may reasonably be required. Premises requiring a fire certificate must obtain one before they may continue in business.

These fire certificates are obtained from the local fire authority, and the applicant will be called upon to provide details concerning the use to which the premises are put, and, if so required, plans of the premises. It is then the duty of the fire authority to inspect the premises in question with regard to (a) the means of escape in the event of fire; (b) the type of fire-fighting equipment; (c) the facilities which exist for warning persons of the outbreak of fire. If the inspection proves unsatisfactory, the fire authority must inform the applicant of that fact, and of the steps necessary to remedy the defect; in addition, a time limit will be set within which such alterations must be carried out if a fire certificate is to be granted.

If a fire certificate *is* granted, it will specify (a) the use or uses of the premises which the certificate covers; (b) the means of escape in case of fire which are provided; (c) the type, number and location of fire-fighting appliances on the premises; (d) the means by which persons using the premises are to be warned in the event of fire. Where necessary, plans may be included. Fire certificates may impose requirements on all the above points, and may in addition require that persons working on the premises be properly trained in fire drills, and that records be kept of that training. The certificate may also limit the number of persons who may be on the premises at any one time, and all these requirements may be applied to either the *whole* of the premises, or one or more parts of them. Responsibility for complying with all the above conditions rests with the occupier, who is also responsible for ensuring that the details specified in (a) to (d) above do not alter. All fire certificates must be kept on the premises. Two specific requirements to be found in the normal fire certificate granted for hotels, and other premises which receive guests, are those which insist on self-closing (and often fire-resistant) bedroom doors and automatic fire warning/detection systems (*e.g.* sprinklers).

Fire authorities may maintain regular inspections of all premises covered by a fire certificate, and the occupier must notify the authority before carrying out any material alterations or extensions to the premises; the authority must also be warned in advance of any excessive quantities of explosive or highly inflammable substances kept on the premises. In either case, the authority may insist on additional steps being taken to maintain adequate fire precautions.

If the fire authority is of the opinion that fire precautions have become inadequate in respect of any premises, they may insist upon the amendment of the old certificate, or the issue of a new one. An even stronger measure is the power given to the authority to apply to a court of law for an order preventing certain premises from being put to certain specified uses until steps have been taken to reduce unreasonable fire risks to persons using the premises. Finally, Building Regulations have been passed to take account of the new legislation, while the Secretary of State is given the power to pass Fire Regulations for all types of premises covered by the Act.

The penalties for operation without a fire certificate where one is required are a fine of £2000 (maximum) or two years' imprisonment, or both. In *Berry* v. *Smith* (1983) the proprietor of an Edinburgh boarding house was convicted of operating without a fire certificate after the local sheriff court ruled that the provision of a "breakfast" of tea, toast and marmalade constituted "board" for the purposes of the 1972 Order. He was also convicted of an offence under the Immigration (Hotel Records) Order 1972, which is considered in Chapter 14.

An interesting case involving the fire authority and its relationship with the hotelier and his guests arose in *Hallett* v. *Nicholson* (1979), in the wake of the tragic Oban hotel fire in 1973. Relatives of a couple who died in the fire sued the hotel management for negligence, on the grounds of their failure to take reasonable care in the matter of fire precautions. The hoteliers denied liability, and asserted that it was the responsibility of the local fire authority to ensure the safety of guests once the management had applied for a fire certificate under the 1971 Act. In particular, it was argued that once they had inspected the premises, the fire authority knew the extent of the risk, and should either have ordered the premises to be closed, or else specified the improvements which had to be carried out immediately.

It was held that nothing in the 1971 Act imposed a *duty* on the fire authority to recommend interim measures, and they also had a total discretion as to whether or not to close the premises. Unless there was evidence that they had failed to make *bona fide* use of that discretion (and there was none here), then they were not liable to third parties. A statutory authority is only liable to third parties for *improper* exercise of its duties, and there was no evidence of that in this case. They were also under no legal obligation to give *additional* advice to hoteliers, and were not liable if hoteliers ignored the advice which *was* given.

Insurance

Insurance has grown as a commercial phenomenon during the past century, until today it governs nearly every aspect of business life. Its influence in legal matters has been considerable, since it is now possible for an injured party to sue someone of modest means, with a reasonable chance of receiving damages since there may well be some insurance company standing behind the defendant, waiting (albeit unwillingly) to pay his damages.

An insurance policy is a form of contract whereby A (called the "insured") agrees to pay B (called the "insurer") a certain sum of money (called the "premium") in return for B's assurance that he will pay to A a certain sum by way of compensation if a given event occurs (or, in some cases, does not occur). It is, in effect, a sort of legalised gamble on the future, and it is possible today to insure one's business against almost anything.

The importance of insurance cannot be overrated, particularly by the businessman, whose every action could result in his being sued, however careful he may be in the conduct of his affairs. The sum involved may be many thousands of pounds, and without insurance very few businesses could survive such a financial blow. The following are generally regarded as being the most important insurance policies which should be taken out by an hotelier.

Property insurance

Fire

Fire is the greatest risk which faces any property owner, and the hotelier is no exception, since, in addition to his own losses, he may in certain cases be called upon to compensate guests for the losses which they have sustained. Fire insurance is therefore of the utmost importance.

Most fire insurance policies are based upon the situation in which something is ignited which was not intended to be ignited. This appears to be the only basic requirement, and it makes no difference that the actual ignition occurred in a place where ignition is normally expected to occur.

Thus, in the leading case of *Harris* v. *Poland* (1941), the facts were that a lady, when leaving her flat for a holiday, hid certain valuables in the fire grate. On her return, forgetting what she had done, she lit the fire, with the consequent loss of her valuables. It was held that she was entitled to recover compensation under the insurance policy which she had taken out on them since all that the policy required was that they be ignited. This had occurred, and it made no difference that the ignition had taken place where one would normally expect it to happen.

This case also illustrates the point that, under most insurance policies, the actual cause of the fire is irrelevant. The insured will, for example, be entitled to recover even if the fire is caused by his own negligence, since the purpose of most policies is to protect the insured against the consequences of any unintentional fire, however caused. The policy will *not* apply, of course, where the fire is *delib-*

erately started by the insured; he may even, in these circumstances, be committing a criminal offence.

There are, however, certain potential fire causes which are not covered by the normal insurance policy. These are called "excepted perils," and the most important of these are (a) *riot*, which in this context is given its strict legal meaning; (b) *enemy hostilities*, which normally will only occur in a declared state of war; and (c) *explosion*.

The third of these requires a little more explanation. The problem with explosions is that they cause damage in one of two ways—by fire and by concussion. Where the damage in respect of which compensation is claimed was caused by *fire*, even if that fire was caused by explosion, then the policy will apply, since the damage will have been caused directly by fire.

The problems begin where the actual damage was by way of concussion. If the explosion itself was not caused by fire, then clearly the policy will not apply, since fire is not involved at any stage. If the explosion *is* caused by fire, then one must inquire into the location of the damaged property. If it is situated on the same premises on which the fire occurred, then the policy will apply; if the explosion, and hence the damaged property, occurred *elswhere* than on the premises on which the fire occurred, then the policy will not apply.

In many modern policies, loss by pure concussion is covered under a fire-only policy in two special cases; explosion in a domestic boiler, and explosion caused by gas appliances used for domestic lighting and heating.

Before any claim may be made under a fire insurance policy, the damage must have been a direct and probable result of fire, or, to put it another way, the fire must have been the "proximate cause" of the damage. This is not an easy test to apply, but examples may help. Thus, damage to valuable curtains through the use of chemical extinguishers to put out a fire would be proximate enough for a claim to be made under a fire policy, as would any theft of property during the confusion caused by an outbreak of fire. But the loss of business profits through the need to hire alternative premises during the period of restoration would not.

An interesting case involving fire insurance was *Rowlands (Mark)* v. *Berni Inns* (1985) in which the lease of restaurant premises contained a clause obliging the tenant to pay the premiums on a fire insurance policy taken out by the landlord. When the premises were damaged by a fire which was alleged to have been caused by the negligence of the tenant, it was held that the landlord should reimburse himself from the insurance proceeds rather than sue the tenant.

Theft

Theft is another serious risk faced by an hotelier, since he has not only his own property to protect, but also that of his guests. A broad policy covering theft in all its forms would, however, be both complicated and expensive, and it is often advantageous to limit such policies to certain forms of theft. The problem here used to be that each phrase such as robbery, fraud, and so on, was interpreted in its technical sense, but the introduction of broader definitions under the Theft Act, 1968 has partly solved this problem. In general, the Theft Act, 1968 is not applicable to Scotland, where the term "theft" is used in a more general sense anyway.

A common form of theft policy is one which covers theft after violent and forcible entry, in which case such matters as theft by staff on duty would not be covered. In most cases theft by staff would in any case need to be covered under a separate policy, since theft by the insured's staff or family is normally one of the excepted perils.

Theft policies invariably contain long and strict provisions concerning the safety precautions and security checks which the insured must carry out before the policy will be valid. In addition, there is frequently no cover under a theft policy for certain items of property (such as plate glass windows) which are damaged in the course of the theft. Such items should normally be insured separately, as described below.

Finally, it should be noted that although an hotelier may, if he wishes, take out a theft policy on his guest's property, a straightforward theft policy may not necessarily cover this automatically. In any case, such an occurrence is perhaps best covered under "liability insurance," for which see below.

Special property insurance

There are certain items of property which are usually regarded as being too valuable, or too high a risk, to be covered under a routine policy such as the ones described above. In such cases, the hotelier will need to take out separate policies at higher premiums, and a good example of the type of property in question is provided by plate glass. It is now possible to take out a special policy to cover plate glass against most of the accidents which are likely to occur to it, both in transit and after it has been fitted. Similar policies may be obtained in respect of items such as silver and works of art.

It is also possible to take out a policy against excepted perils, and against unlikely events such as earthquakes and tempests. One can in fact insure against almost anything, if one is prepared to pay the premium, and an hotelier would be well advised to insure against such things as the loss of his licence and a poor season due to bad weather.

Insurable interest

Before anyone may take out any form of property insurance policy, he must first have an "insurable interest" in the property. In most cases this interest is an obvious one (for example, the interest of an owner or a hirer), but many people possess an insurable interest in property without being aware of the fact, since an insurable interest is nothing more than some interest in the property not being destroyed. Thus, it would cover an innkeeper (for the definition of which, see Chap. 13, *post*), whose potential right of lien over the property of his guests is sufficient to give him an insurable interest in the property which would form the basis of a theft policy in his own name, *in addition to* the liability insurance to cover the possibility of his having to pay damages to the guest for its loss or destruction.

Since there are often several persons with insurable interests in the same item of property, it is not unusual to find more than one policy in force in respect of the same item. In any case, an insurable interest may change hands with the property, although normally the insurer needs to be informed.

Utmost good faith

A contract of insurance is said to be a contract requiring utmost good faith; that is, the person taking out the insurance is required to state all those material facts which are likely to have a bearing on the risk involved, and hence the premium payable. This is normally implied in any case, but most policies invariably contain a clause which requires the insured to make certain express declarations.

What may be regarded as a material fact will obviously vary from case to case, but it would include, for example, statements concerning security precautions made prior to the taking out of a theft policy, and statements about the number of claims made on previous policies. Misleading statements are just as serious as total silence, even if made innocently, unless they are expressly described as mere opinions.

In *Glicksman* v. *Lancashire and General Assurance Co.* (1927), for example, G was a tailor with a small business who insured his stock in trade with L, against burglary. When he signed the insurance proposal form, he was asked if any other company had refused to take on his proposal. He replied that the Yorkshire Insurance Co. had accepted, but that he had decided not to take up the policy, omitting to mention that the Sun Insurance Co. had refused to accept his proposal. G's property was burgled, and L. refused to pay, claiming that a "material fact" had been concealed at the time of the proposal. It was held by the House of Lords that the refusal of a previous company to insure G was a "material fact" which should have been disclosed, and that the policy was therefore void.

The making of a misleading statement, or the non-disclosure of a material fact, will often result in the policy being void. This point is also usually expressly stated in the contract.

Average clause

Many policies contain what is referred to as an "average" or "subject to average" clause. The effect of this is that if there is a claim under the policy, and it transpires that the property is insured for less than it is worth, the insurance company will pay out proportionately less in compensation in the event of a *partial* loss.

For example, if a hotel fire causes £250 worth of damage to kitchen equipment valued for insurance purposes at £500, and the loss adjusters estimate that it was in fact worth £1,000, the management will receive only 50 per cent. of the claimable loss, *i.e.* £125. In short, the claim is reduced by the proportion to which the property was under-insured in the first place.

In the case of a *total* loss of under-insured property, the company will simply pay out the *insured* value; alternatively, if the property is worth *less* than it is insured for, the company will pay the *true* value. In other words, the insurance company will normally only pay on the basis of the *real* value or the *insured* value, whichever is *less*.

Liability insurance

In addition to the need to insure himself against loss or damage to property the cautious hotelier will also insure himself against events which are likely to lead to his having to pay damages to someone. That someone will usually be the guest, and an hotelier's liability to a guest can arise in a variety of ways (dangerous premises, incompetant staff, impure food, etc.). Note also the onerous provisions of the Hotel Proprietor's Act 1956, explained in Chapter 13. Most liability policies would not apply if the "statutory notice" under the 1956 Act were not displayed.

Liability insurance may be approached in one of two ways; first, the hotelier may insure himself against a certain *type* of liability, howsoever it is caused (*e.g.* all damage to guest's property). Alternatively, he may insure himself against all liabilities incurred by him in a particular *capacity* (*e.g.* his capacity as an innkeeper, which would cover not only loss or damage to guest's property, but also liability for defective premises).

A variety of factors will have to be taken into account when working out the premium to be paid on a liability policy. Such factors include the state of the premises, the location of the hotel, the type of clientele, the number of staff, and the previous frequency of claims.

One important set of liabilities hitherto unmentioned is the hotelier's liabilities as an *employer*. The actual nature of such liabilities is dealt with in a later chapter, but it must be noted at this stage that the Employer's Liability (Compulsory Insurance) Act 1969, requires every employer to take out an approved insurance policy to cover all possible claims by employees in respect of bodily injuries or disease. Failure to do so is punishable as a criminal offence, and employer's liability insurance is thus placed on a par with compulsory third party motor insurance.

As a general rule, most liability policies do not cover damage, loss, etc., arising from incidents involving boiler explosions and lift accidents. These should be covered under separate "engineering" policies. Note that a coffee-making machine is classed as a "boiler" if it works under steam pressure.

Also excluded under normal liability policies are liabilities entered into by the hotelier or restauranteur under contracts of, *e.g.* hire, leasing, and franchise.

CHAPTER FOUR

Liquor licences

The licensing system

IN England and Wales, modern licensing laws are governed by the Licensing Act 1964, section 160 of which makes it a criminal offence to sell, or to expose for sale, any intoxicating liquor without the authority of a "justices' licence." Intoxicating liquor is defined in the Act itself as "spirits, wine, beer, cider and any other fermented, distilled or spiritous liquor." There are severe penalties for such illegal retail sales; in addition to these, a second offence can lead to disqualification for a maximum of five years, and a third or subsequent offence to disqualification for life, or some shorter period imposed by the court.

In Scotland, the appropriate legislation is the Licensing (Scotland) Act 1976, and matters are controlled by a licensing board. Intoxicating liquor is called "alcoholic liquor" and similar penalties apply for sales without the authority of a licence.

There are, however, certain situations in which the authority of a justices' licence is not required for the retail sale of liquor; the most important of these are as follows:

1. The sale of liquor in a theatre which is licensed by the local authority under the Theatres Act 1968 for the public performance of theatrical works, where the clerk to the licensing justices has been informed in writing of the intention to sell liquor.

   In Scotland, theatres built after 1903 must observe the same permitted hours as other licensed premises and must obtain an "entertainment licence" from the licensing board.

Even those built before 1903 must comply with "permitted hours."

2. The sale of liquor on board an aircraft or vessel which is on a journey, or the sale of liquor on a railway passenger vehicle in which passengers may be supplied with food. Ships, aircraft and railway carriages making use of such exemptions are not even classed as licensed premises (as are theatres), so that not even the normal licensing hours need to be observed. *N.B.* that on Sundays in Scotland, some vessels have to observe permitted hours.
3. The sale of liquor in naval or military canteens, in which such sales are normally confined to servicemen.
4. The *supply* of liquor to the members of a registered club; as will be explained in a later chapter, a *registration certificate* suffices here.

The licensing system in England and Wales is controlled by groups of local licensing justices; that is; committees of between five and 15 members of the local bench of magistrates. It is their function to grant, renew, remove and transfer justices' licences for their district, and the most important event in their calendar is the annual licensing meeting, sometimes referred to as "brewster sessions." This meeting must be held in the first two weeks of February each year, on a date fixed by the justices at least 21 days in advance and advertised in a local newspaper. In addition to this annual meeting, the justices must also hold between four and eight transfer sessions each year, spaced as evenly as possible. It is at these meetings that the functions of the licensing justices are carried out; they are all very much the same in content, except for the fact that the granting of renewals and the fixing of permitted hours may normally only take place at the annual meeting. In Scotland, licensing boards are required to meet in January, March, June and October of each year, on a date fixed at least eight weeks in advance, and on any other such date as appears to the board to be appropriate.

As part of his normal duties, the clerk to the licensing justices or licensing board is required to keep a register of licences, being a detailed list of all the licences in force for the district, with information as to the licensees, the premises and so on. Details of convictions, forfeitures and disqualifications are entered into this register, which local residents may inspect upon payment of a nominal fee.

Application for a licence

In England and Wales there is a standard procedure for applying for all justices' licences, whatever their nature (the different types are explained below). Reduced to a slightly simplified form, it is as follows:

1. Not less than 21 days before the day fixed for the hearing, the applicant must give notice in writing of his intended application to the clerk to the local justices, the local chief officer of police, and the appropriate local authority. A copy must also be sent to the authority responsible for the administration of the local fire service, and the copy which is sent to the clerk must be accompanied by a plan of the premises; this must conform to any standards set by the justices.
2. During the period of 28 days prior to the date of the hearing, the applicant must display a copy of his notice of intended application on or near the premises to be licensed in a place where it can be conveniently read by the public. This notice must be displayed for at least seven days.
3. In the period from 28 to 14 days prior to the date of the hearing, the applicant must publish a copy of his notice of intended application in a local newspaper, or a newspaper circulating in the district. The licensing justices will normally stipulate when this should be done.

All these notices may be made on standard forms supplied by the clerk to the justices on request. In any case, they should all be signed by the applicant or his authorised agent, and should state his name and address, the location of the premises, the type of licence which is being applied for, and the applicant's occupation for the past six months. The justices may postpone the hearing if any of these requirements is not fulfilled. They also have a discretionary power to postpone the hearing if, for good reason, any of the time limits is exceeded.

Invariably, where the owner of the premises in question is a company, it is the proposed manager who applies for the licence.

In Scotland applications are made on the prescribed form, completed and signed by the applicant or his agent and must be lodged with the clerk to the licensing board not later than five weeks before the sitting. If the application is for a new certificate the applicant must also submit a plan of the premises. The applicant must also arrange for a notice in the prescribed form to be displayed at the premises in question for at least 21 days before the start of the hearing. The clerk must also publish, in a newspaper circulating in the district, a list of further applicants for new licences, and this publication must take place not later than three weeks before the start of the sitting. In practice, this advertisement will be in standard form.

Under the 1976 Act, for the first time in Scotland, it is possible for a licence to be granted to a company or a partnership in its own name, together with the name of the person exercising day to day control over the business.

Procedure at the hearing

Licensing sessions are held in public, and the applicant is almost invariably required to attend in person, although he is entitled to legal representation. The justices have the power to demand that all evidence be given on oath, and witnesses may be forced to attend and compelled to give evidence.

The main point to be proved in all licence applications is that the applicant is a fit and proper person to hold a licence, in terms of character, health and temperament. Infancy is not necessarily a bar, nor is bankruptcy or nationality. The justices are also concerned with the suitability of the premises for the purpose for which the licence is required, as well as the state of the premises. There are also additional matters which must be proved according to the type of licence which is being applied for, and these are dealt with below under "Types of Licence."

Certain persons are disqualified entirely from holding a justices' licence, and they may conveniently be listed as follows:

1. a sheriff's officer, or any public officer executing the legal process;
2. any person convicted of forging a justices' licence, or of making use of one, knowing it to have been forged;
3. any person convicted of permitting licensed premises to be used as a brothel;
4. any person disqualified for selling liquor without a licence.

In addition, there are certain circumstances in which the premises may be disqualified, as for example where—

5. within a period of two years, two separate licensees have forfeited their licences for the same premises; the premises are disqualified from receiving a justices' licence for the 12 months following the second forfeiture; or
6. the premises are part of a motorway service area.

Any licence inadvertently issued to disqualified persons or premises is void.

A justices' licence may sometimes be granted subject to certain conditions, such as the restriction of sales to certain types of liquor, or certain parts of the premises. The licensee may be required to provide more exits, better fire-fighting equipment, or easier access to the premises. Other possible restrictions are dealt with below (see "Types of Licence"). Breach of such a condition would not in itself be an offence, but it could indirectly lead to the commission of an offence (*e.g.* sales without licence), and would in any case prejudice the chances of a renewal of the licence.

It is not possible to attach conditions to off-licences, but, in the past, licensing justices have achieved the same effect by requiring the licensee to give certain "undertakings." Recent developments in the courts have suggested that this may become a thing of the past, but as yet this is uncertain.

In England and Wales, anyone may object to the grant of a justices' licence without notice, although the justices may postpone the hearing in order to permit the applicant to prepare his defence. The grounds for such objections will vary; sometimes the objectors are local licensees worried about loss of business. Sometimes they are local residents, and sometimes they are members of the local temperance league. In choosing between the case put forward by the applicant and the objectors, the justices may use their own knowledge of the district.

Both the applicant and any objectors have the right of appeal to the Crown Court against the decision reached by the justices, and against any condition imposed upon the grant of the licence. Notice of intention to appeal must be served upon the clerk to the justices within 21 days of the hearing.

In Scotland, the classes of persons who may object are those who own or occupy property in the neighbourhood, any local church body, any local community council, or the Chief Constable. Objections must be in writing, specifying the grounds of objection, and lodged with the clerk not later than seven days before the first day of the sitting. Intimation must be made to the applicant by the board.

Appeals may be made from the licensing board to the sheriff court within 14 days after the procedings appealed against.

Provisional licences

In England and Wales, where the licence application is in respect of premises which are about to be constructed, or in the process of being constructed, or are about to be altered or extended, then the justices may grant a provisional licence when they have examined and approved the plans.

Such a licence is granted on condition that the completed premises conform to the original plans, plus any alterations to them which the justices have authorised. The grant will be made final when the work is complete, and the justices are satisfied that the applicant is a fit and proper person, and that he is not disqualified from holding a licence. The licence is not effective until it has been declared final. A similar provision is available in Scotland.

Duration of licences

A justices' licence comes into force upon the date of its grant, and is valid until April 4 next, by which date it must have been renewed (see below). Licences granted before April 4 in one year continue in force until April 4 of the following year. In the case of a provisional licence, it comes into force on the day upon which it is declared final. In Scotland, a new licence comes into effect when it is granted, or, where there were objections at the hearing, after the expiry of the time limit for lodging appeals, or after the hearing of any appeal. It is valid for three years, and must be renewed at the quarterly meeting of the licensing board three years after the meeting at which it was granted.

Licensing planning

Following the destruction caused by the Second World War, the government established licence planning committees in 33 areas of England and Wales which had suffered extensive damage. Since 1981, they have been phased out and the only remaining planning area as such is London, which still has a licensing planning committee.

The function of this committee is to plan the distribution of licensed premises in its area, and an applicant for a *new* full on-licence or off-licence must obtain a "certificate of non-objection" from the licence planning committee before his licence application may be granted by the justices; there is no right of appeal from a refusal to grant such a certificate.

In addition, in the case of "new towns," there is also a licensed premises committee, whose function it is to determine the number, nature and distribution, of licensed premises in the area. The licensing justices cannot grant or "remove" (see below, p. 65) any licence which is not in accordance with those proposals of the licensed premises committee which have been confirmed by the Secretary of State for the Environment. Nor may the justices change the type of any existing licence without the consent of the licensed premises committee. *N.B.* however, that since 1980 the new town planning legislation has not applied to off-licences.

Scotland also has licensed premises committees, constituted in the same way as their English counterparts and chaired by a representative of the Scottish Office, which carry out functions in the new towns of Scotland. No licensing board may grant or renew any certificate which is not in accordance with those proposals of the committee which have been confirmed by the Secretary of State for Scotland. Nor may any certificate be altered or varied without the consent of the licensed premises committee.

Temperance polls

In Scotland, one-tenth of the electors of a particular area could, under the previous law, petition the clerk to the local authority for the taking of a "poll" in November or December of that year in order to consider the future of licensing in that area. If the area already contained licensed premises, the result of the poll would be one of the following:

1. No change.
2. Limiting Resolution (a majority of those voting, constituting not less than 35 per cent. of the total electorate). This resulted in a 25 per cent. reduction in the number of certificates in force for the area under a scheme drawn up by the licensing court for implementation at the half-yearly meeting, after consultation with those affected.
3. No-licence Resolution (a 55 per cent. majority of those voting, constituting not less than 35 per cent. of the total electorate). This resulted in no new certificates being granted in the future (except for hotel certificates in "special circumstances"), and existing licences ending on May 27 next following.

As a result of the 1976 Act, no new temperance polls may be held. But the Act makes provision for the continuance of any "limiting resolution" or "no-licence" resolution for a further three years, or longer if the district council so resolve. Before making such a resolution, the district council must consult with the local community council. In such cases the licensing board may, for five years following the making of the resolution, refuse to grant any new licences.

But in all cases, the licensing board may grant licences, if they wish, in "special circumstances" to hotels or restaurants. The effect of these provisions is likely to be that temperance areas in Scotland will become a thing of the past.

Types of licence

So far, no distinction has been made between the types of justices' licence available to the hotelier or caterer; they are as follows.

Full on-licence

In England and Wales, a full on-licence enables the holder to sell liquor for consumption on or off the premises to any member of the public who is allowed by law to consume it. Such a licence will normally authorise the sale of all forms of liquor, but sometimes it will be restricted to certain types (*e.g.* beer, cider and wine only). A full on-licence is the broadest type of justices' licence, and is the type in force in respect of a public house.

The justices have a complete discretion as to whether or not they grant a full on-licence, the main consideration being whether or not there is a public need for another such licence in the district in question. Other factors are also taken into consideration (see above), and the applicant himself may request that his licence be restricted in some way; the three most common restrictions are:

1. *A six-day licence*—no sale to the general public on a Sunday; sales on Sundays may still be made to residents of an hotel.
2. *Early closing licence*—permitted hours to end one hour earlier than the general permitted hours for the district.
3. *Seasonal licence*—a licence which only operates during certain months of the year. This type of licence is not uncommon in coastal resorts with a seasonal trade, or in remote areas which suffer severe winters.

None of these restrictions may be imposed except at the applicant's request, and can be revoked at his request upon renewal, transfer or removal of the licence (for which see below). A breach of any of these conditions, once imposed, would not in itself be a criminal offence, but it might lead indirectly to another offence (*e.g.* sale outside permitted hours).

The justices need give no reason for their refusal to grant a full on-licence (they frequently do). Upon refusal, the applicant may request that the justices treat his application as being one for a residential licence, a restaurant licence, or a combined residential/restaurant licence (see below). If the justices refuse to grant any of these licences, they must give their reasons in writing.

It is also possible for a licence to be granted for beer, cider and wine only or for any one or two of these. Such a licence is not a full on-licence.

The Scottish equivalent of the full on-licence is the "public house licence" which gives the same powers of sale as the full on-licence. Lack of space precludes fuller detail on application procedures.

Off-licence

An off-licence, as its name implies, permits the sale of liquor for consumption off the premises. Such a licence is frequently combined with the business of a general store, and in recent years off-licences have become very common in supermarkets. There are only two possible types of off-licence; (a) for the sale of all types of liquor; (b) for the sale of beer, cider and wine only. In neither case may wines or spirits be sold in open vessels.

The licensee commits a criminal offence if liquor sold by him is consumed on or near his premises with his "privity or consent."

The Scottish equivalent to the off-licence is the "off-sales licence."

Residential licence

Bona fide = In good faith

The title is almost self-explanatory; a residential licence authorises the sale of liquor to residents of an hotel, that is, "premises bona fide used, or intended to be used, for the purpose of habitually providing for reward board and lodging, including breakfast and one other at least of the customary main meals." Off-sales may be made to residents where they will accompany meals (*i.e.* packed lunches), and residents may entertain private friends at their (the residents') own expense.

The justices must be satisfied that the premises are suitable for use as a licensed hotel, and two important conditions are always attached to the grant of a residential licence, the first by implication and the second by express statement in the licence. These are that (a) other beverages, including water, must be equally available with meals; and that (b) adequate seating facilities must be provided in a room in the hotel which is not used for sleeping or for the service of food, and in which there is no supply *or consumption* of liquor. This latter condition is occasionally dispensed with where the justices see fit.

If the premises qualify in the manner indicated above, then the justices may only refuse to grant a residential licence on one or more of the following grounds:

1. that the applicant is under 18, or not a fit and proper person

to hold such a licence, or that either he or the premises are disqualified;

2. that the premises are not suitable and convenient for the purpose;
3. that within the past 12 months, an on-licence for the premises has been forfeited, or either of conditions (a) and (b) above has been broken, or the premises have been ill-conducted;
4. that a large proportion of the clientele is habitually made up of unaccompanied persons under eighteen;
5. that reasonable attempts at an inspection of the premises by the local authority, the police or the fire authority have failed.

The Scottish equivalent of the residential licence is the hotel licence which may be normal, six-day, or seasonal, and which authorises sales to all persons for consumption on or off the premises. *N.B.* that sales are not limited to residents only. The only way in which a hotel licence differs from a public-house licence is that the premises covered by it are those of an hotel.

Restaurant licence

A restaurant licence is granted for the sale of liquor to be consumed within a restaurant, that is, "premises structurally adapted and bona fide used, or intended to be used, for the purpose of providing the customary main meal at midday or in the evening, or both, for the accommodation of persons frequenting the premises."

Sales under such a licence are automatically limited to persons taking table meals, where the sale of drink is an ancillary to the service of the meal. A table in this context can include a counter or some similar fitting, and there is nothing to prevent the consumption of aperitifs before the meal, and liqueurs afterwards, in another part of the premises, provided that such sales are associated with a meal, and that the meal is taken seated.

The condition mentioned under "residential licence" above, concerning the availability of other beverages, including water, with meals, applies equally in the case of a restaurant licence. The permitted hours for premises with a restaurant licence will of course be limited to those during which table meals are being served, although the holder of a restaurant licence may now serve liquor throughout the day as the result of the Licensing (Restaurant Meals) Act 1987 considered in Chapter 5, regardless of the limits of the general permitted hours for the district.

The licensing justices may only refuse to grant a restaurant licence on certain grounds, in addition to the one concerning other beverages. The first *four* of these, are identical to those listed as 1.

2. 4. and 5. under "residential licence," above, and the remainder are:

6. that within the past 12 months, an on-licence for the premises has been forfeited, or the condition concerning other beverages has been broken, or the premises have been ill-conducted;
7. that a substantial part of the applicant's trade is not the provision of the type of refreshment to which this type of licence is intended to be linked.

It should also be noted that in the case of both the residential and the restaurant licence, application may be refused where the service of liquor is by means of the self-service system.

The Scottish equivalent of the restaurant licence is also called a "restaurant licence," and is granted to establishments which are qualified in the same way as their English counterparts, but have no bar counter. Such a certificate authorises the sale of liquor to those taking table meals to which the sale of liquor is ancillary.

Residential and restaurant licence

This is a useful combination of the residential licence and the restaurant licence, and it is granted to premises which qualify for both. It has the effect of authorising the sale of liquor to residents generally and to members of the general public who are taking table meals. It is obviously of great use to the proprietor of an hotel which possesses a public restaurant; if he wishes to add a public bar, of course, then a full on-licence must be obtained.

The grant of a combined residential and restaurant licence is subject to all the conditions listed under the separate licences above, and can be refused only on the same grounds.

It should be noted that there are certain criminal offences, the commission of which could result in the holder of a residential, restaurant or combined licence, or his premises, being disqualified for a period not exceeding five years. They are (i) the breach of any condition concerning the provision of other beverages or the provision of seating accommodation in a "dry" room, (ii) permitting drunkenness on the premises; (iii) permitting unlawful gaming on the premises; (iv) allowing prostitutes to assemble on the premises; (v) allowing the premises to be used as a brothel; and (vi) allowing illegal betting transactions to occur on the premises. These possible reasons for disqualification are of course in addition to those listed earlier in connection with licences in general. Disqualification also has the effect of disqualifying the applicant and premises from holding even a late night refreshment licence under the 1969 Act (see Chap. 8).

The Scottish equivalent of the combined licence is the "restricted hotel licence."

Occasional licence

An occasional licence is granted to a person who already holds an on-licence for one set of premises, and who wishes to sell liquor at some special event to be held on premises which are normally unlicensed; two frequent examples are local fêtes, and dances in university halls of residence. In *R.* v. *Bow Street Magistrates* (1983) it was held that an occasional licence may be applied for by a licensee who has missed the final date for applying for a renewal of his licence, in order to cover the gap in time before he secures his renewal.

Such a licence can only authorise the sale of the kinds of liquor which the licensee is entitled to sell under his existing licence, although the other conditions imposed upon his licence will not apply. In any case, the holder of a restaurant licence will only be allowed to sell liquor along with substantial refreshment, and the holder of a residential licence may not even apply.

Application for an occasional licence is made to the local magistrates (*N.B.*—not the licensing justices), and the applicant must state his name and address, the location and nature of the event, and the number of hours for which the licence will be required. He must give at least 24 hours' notice to the local police of his intention to apply, and they have the right to attend the hearing and object.

An alternative (and preferable) method of application is for the applicant to send two copies of the application to the clerk to the justices at least 28 days before the chosen date of the hearing. The clerk will send one copy to the police, and if they have not voiced an objection within seven days, the magistrates may grant the licence without calling the applicant for a hearing. If the police do object, the applicant will be sent a copy of the objection, which he must answer in person at the hearing.

The magistrates have a complete discretion as to whether or not they grant the licence, and may refuse for any reason. The licence, if granted, may be for any number of hours which the magistrates see fit, and this number will be stated on the licence itself. It may also cover several days or weeks, although there is a statutory maximum of three weeks. An occasional licence may not be granted for Christmas Day, Good Friday, or any day of public thanksgiving or fasting, nor may it be granted for a Sunday in the "dry" counties of Wales.

Premises for which an occasional licence is in force become licensed premises, and the normal rules of good conduct therefore apply.

In Scotland, a licence holder may obtain an "occasional licence" under the 1976 Act in much the same way as his English counterpart. Application is to the licensing board.

Occasional Permissions

By virtue of the Licensing (Occasional Permissions) Act 1983, it is now possible for an "officer" of "an eligible organisation or of a branch of such an organisation" to apply to the licensing justices for an "occasional permission," the effect of which will be to permit that organisation to sell liquor "during a period not exceeding twenty-four hours" at a function held by that organisation or branch in connection with their activities. The applicant in such cases will obviously be some person or body not normally licensed to sell liquor.

Application is made in writing to the justices (supplying two copies of the application form) at least a month in advance of the function, and the application will be heard at the next licensing sessions, after a copy has been sent to the police for any comments they may have. The purpose of the occasional permission is to permit organisations "not carried on for private gain" to raise funds by selling liquor at some social function organised by them. The main benefactor of the system will be organisations such as Oxfam, although occasional permissions may be, and frequently are, granted to members' clubs. The "place" covered by the permission will not necessarily be restricted to unlicensed premises, and could include something like a sports field.

However, the justices must be satisfied, before granting the permission, that the "officer" is a fit and proper person, and he must be resident in the licensing district in which the function is to be held. The "place" in which it is to be held must also be "suitable," and the justices must be satisfied that no disorderly conduct, or disturbance or annoyance to neighbours, will thereby be created. The justices also have the power to limit the hours during which the liquor may be sold, and may also limit the kinds of liquor which may be sold. They may also attach any other condition which they think proper. One of these may well concern the persons to whom the liquor may be sold at the function, and almost certainly will exclude persons under 18 although such sales are prohibited under the 1983 Act anyway.

No more than four occasional permissions per twelve months may be granted in any one licensing district to the same organisation or branch. Nor may such a permission be granted for a Sunday in a "dry" county of Wales (for which, see Chapter 5).

Renewal of licences

(A) ENGLAND AND WALES

As has already been explained, all justices' licences must be renewed before April 4. Renewals of justices' licences may only be granted by the justices at their annual licensing meeting, although the applicant need not attend in person unless he is called upon to do so. He need send no formal notices of his intention to apply for a renewal, which is taken for granted, but his actual application must reach the clerk on or before the date set for the hearing. In exceptional cases, later applications may be heard at the next transfer sessions, and in these cases, the applicant is required to serve certain notices. As a matter of caution, all notices and applications should be sent by registered mail or recorded delivery.

No one may object to the renewal of a licence unless he has given the applicant at least seven days' written notice, stating in general terms the grounds for his objection. Otherwise the justices will postpone the hearing until both parties have had time to prepare their arguments. In either case, all evidence will be taken on oath.

One of the main factors which the justices will consider on a renewal of an on-licence is the actual structure of the premises. They may (and frequently do) require that plans of the premises be submitted along with the application, and they may then order that structural alterations be carried out, if they feel it necessary for the proper conduct of the business. They may fix a time limit for these alterations, and if it is not met, the licensee could face a fine for every day over the limit. If an order is given and complied with, the justices may not issue another order in respect of the same premises for five years. The applicant has a right of appeal to the Crown Court.

The consent of the justices is also required for any structural alterations to on-licensed premises which will (a) increase the drinking facilities in the public part of the premises; or (b) conceal the public drinking area from the observation of the licensee; or (c) affect the communication between the public drinking area(s) and the rest of the premises, or any street or other public place. The penalties for proceeding without the justices' consent are possible forfeiture of the licence, and an obligation to restore the premises to their original state. There is a right of appeal to the Crown Court in the normal way, and the owner of the premises for which the licence has been forfeited may apply for a "protection order" (for which see below). The justices cannot, however, raise any objection where the alterations have been carried out at the request of the local authority (see Chap. 3).

With the exception of the above, the only other conditions which may be imposed upon the renewal of a licence are those concerning six-day, early closing and seasonal licences, and "dry" rooms in hotels.

When considering the grounds upon which the justices may refuse to renew a justices' licence, we must make certain vital distinctions.

Premises licensed after August 15, 1904

In the case of these "new on-licences," and in the case of *all* off-licences, regardless of their age, the justices have a fairly wide discretion as to whether or not they choose to grant a renewal, and they may refuse on any of the grounds for which they may refuse an initial grant (see above). There is no question of any compensation being paid for this refusal, although both the applicant and any objector have the normal rights of appeal to the Crown Court.

Premises licensed before August 15, 1904

Licences which have been in existence (with renewals) since before the above date are referred to as "old on-licences," and they are given certain protection.

Licensees of premises with these old on-licences were until 1981 obliged to contribute to a mutual insurance scheme known as a *compensation fund*, administered by a compensation authority. This contribution system was abolished under the Licensing (Alcohol Education and Research) act 1981, but premises licensed before August 15, 1904 may still only be refused a renewal of their licences for one of the reasons in respect of which renewal could have been refused under the pre-1981 system, which gave the licensee the right to compensation. No such compensation is now payable, but the limited grounds for refusing a renewal continue in force.

These grounds are:

1. That the premises have been ill-conducted, or are structurally deficient or unsuitable. This can include a failure to observe any undertaking given by the licensee, which he cannot be *compelled* to give anyway;
2. that the applicant is not a fit and proper person;
3. that such a renewal would be void (*e.g.* the applicant is disqualified);

4. that the applicant is recorded in the register of licences as having been convicted of bribery in elections.

In all these cases, the normal rights of appeal apply. The justices may not oppose the renewal of the licence on any other grounds.

Premises licensed before May 1, 1869

Premises in respect of which a beerhouse licence was in force on May 1, 1869, and which are still the subject of an on-licence today, are referred to as "old beerhouse premises," and are in a class of their own when it comes to the question of renewal. They can in fact only be denied a renewal of the licence by the justices in the following cases:

1. where the applicant has failed to produce satisfactory evidence of good character; the onus would appear to be on him to produce it;
2. where the premises in question, or any adjacent premises, owned or occupied by the applicant, are of a disorderly character, or frequented by thieves, prostitutes or persons of bad character;
3. where any licence previously held by the applicant has been forfeited, or he has been disqualified;
4. where the applicant is recorded in the register of licences as having been convicted of bribery in elections.

As with a refusal to renew an old on-licence, the justices must give their reasons in writing, and they may request the applicant to give certain undertakings, although they may not compel him. The normal rights of appeal to the Crown Court apply.

One final point to be noted in connection with renewals is that there can only be a renewal of an existing licence, so that the applicant for a renewal must be able to show that there is a valid licence in force for the premises which is capable of renewal.

(B) SCOTLAND

The procedure to be followed upon a renewal of a licence in Scotland is essentially the same as for a new licence, except that the applicant is excused from making a personal appearance, unless specifically cited to attend by the licensing court. Also, the applicant is not required to submit any plan of the premises.

Licences must be renewed by the end of their three year duration (see p. 52, above).

Transfer of licences

(A) ENGLAND AND WALES

Justices' licences are granted to a specified person in respect of specified premises (*e.g.* to John Smith for the Seaview Hotel), and it follows from this that any change in the identity of either must be given official sanction. The change from one licensee to another is called a "transfer," and it may be granted either at one of the "transfer sessions," or at the annual licensing meeting.

Application for a transfer

The applicant for a transfer will be the person who intends to take over the licence, and he must give notice of his intention to apply almost as if he were applying for a new licence; that is, his notices must contain the same details, and copies must be sent to the clerk to the justices, the local authority and the local police. No copy need be sent to the fire authority. An extra copy must be sent to the present holder of the licence, although there is no need to display copies either on the premises or in a newspaper. The same time limits apply as for an application for a new licence.

The applicant, the present licence holder, and any witnesses can be compelled to appear in person, give evidence on oath and produce any important documents relating to the taking over of the business. Objectors may speak without prior notice, and the justices have the same discretion as to whether or not to grant transfers as they do in the case of renewals. This is true even in the case of an old on-licence or an old beerhouse licence, except that the justices may refuse to transfer either type on the additional ground that the applicant is not a fit and proper person. Once again, there are rights of appeal to the Crown Court from a decision of the justices.

Persons to whom transfers may be made

Quite apart from the question of the justices' discretion over whether or not they choose to grant the transfer, there are only certain specified situations in which a transfer may be granted at all, and then only to specified persons; these may best be listed as follows:

1. On the death of the licence holder; to his personal representatives or the new tenant or occupier of the premises.
2. When the licence holder becomes incapable, mentally or

physically, of carrying on the business; to his assigns, or the new tenant or occupier.

3. On the adjudged bankruptcy of the licence holder, or upon the appointment of a trustee in bankruptcy; to the trustee or the new tenant or occupier.
4. Where the licence holder has, or is about to, give up occupation of the premises or the carrying on of the business; to the purchaser or the new tenant or occupier.
5. Where the licence holder, on the point of quitting the premises, has wilfully omitted or neglected to apply for a renewal of the licence; to the new tenant or occupier.
6. Where the owner, or his agent, has obtained a "protection order" in respect of the premises; to the owner or his agent.

A transfer can (and should) be granted before the date of the proposed changeover, and it may be postdated in order that there is no break in the licence. On April 4 next, the licence will be renewed in the normal way, and the new licence holder will therefore have slipped neatly into the system.

Protection orders

It sometimes happens that there is an urgent need to transfer a licence before the date fixed for the next transfer sessions, or that the justices need to adjourn a hearing for a transfer until a later date. In such a case, the applicant may apply for a "protection order," which is, in effect, a temporary transfer until something more permanent can be arranged.

In the event of the death or bankruptcy of the licence holder, his heirs, personal representatives or trustee in bankruptcy may take over the management of his business without the need to obtain a protection order, until such time as a formal transfer may be arranged.

In all other cases, application for a protection order is made to the local magistrates, with seven days' prior notice to the police, giving the same details as are required on application for a new licence; in urgent cases, this may be dispensed with if the magistrates agree. The applicant may be questioned on oath, and the magistrates must satisfy themselves that the applicant appears to be eligible for a transfer. The protection order is then granted, and it lasts until the end of the second transfer sessions after the hearing, unless superseded by another protection order, a transfer or a removal. The order permits the holder to behave in all ways like the previous licence holder.

Protection orders may also be used in a special way where the licence is forfeited by the licensee, or he becomes disqualified. The owner of the premises, or his agent, may in these cases apply for a protection order until another licensee is installed, or another licence obtained. This procedure is obviously of great value to an hotel company whose manager falls foul of the law; by this method, a new manager (licence holder) may be installed with the minimum delay. This method obviously cannot be used by an owner/licensee, since it would not be in pursuance of a transfer, unless he intended to call upon someone else to manage the business for him.

(B) SCOTLAND

In Scotland, transfers may take place at any meeting of the licensing board; and are granted to the new tenant or occupant in a similar manner to the procedure in England and Wales. However, in *Chief Constable of Tayside* v. *Angus District Licensing Board* (1980), it was held that where a husband and wife had conducted a hotel business together for many years, the husband could not transfer the licence to his wife as a "new tenant or occupant."

On the death or bankruptcy of the holder before the expiry of the certificate, the licensing board may grant a transfer until the next meeting.

The transferred licence must be renewed in the normal way when it expires.

Removal of licences

When it is desired to change the identity of the licensed premises (*i.e.* move the licence from one set of premises to another), the licensee may make use of a system known as "removal." There are two types of removal.

Ordinary removal

This is a removal from one set of premises to another, whether inside the same licensing district or not, application being made to the justices in whose district the new premises will be situated. The applicant must give the same notices to the same persons as if he were applying for a new licence, although he need not state his occupation for the past six months, nor need he give details of the type of licence for which he is applying. However, a copy of these notices must be sent to the owner of the existing premises, and a copy of the plans of the new premises must be sent along with the notice to the clerk to the justices.

Any member of the public may oppose the removal, without giving notice. The licensing justices have the same discretion over whether they decide to grant the removal as they have over a grant of a new licence, and they must be satisfied that there is no objection from the owner of the existing licensed premises, or any other person whom the justices feel has the right to object. An off-licence may be removed, and there is no reason why an old on-licence (or old beerhouse licence) may not also.

A provisional removal may be granted, and a removal may be combined with a transfer, although this is not very common. However, a residential, restaurant or combined licence may not be removed, and the applicant must make an application for a new licence in the new district. The usual rights of appeal exist.

Special removal

A special removal may be obtained where premises in respect of which an old on-licence or old beerhouse licence is in force are about to be pulled down or occupied for some public purpose (*e.g.* a new road scheme), or where they are rendered unfit by some unforeseen calamity such as fire.

A special removal may, however, only be from one set of premises to another *within the same licensing district*. Application is made as for an ordinary removal, with the exception that plans of the new premises do not have to be submitted. The justices may only refuse a special removal on one of the grounds upon which they may refuse a renewal (see above).

N.B. Scots law does not provide any procedure for the "removal" of a certificate.

CHAPTER FIVE

Permitted hours

SECTION 59 of the Licensing Act 1964 and section 54 of the Licensing (Scotland) Act 1976, make it a criminal offence for any person, either personally or through an employee or agent, to sell or supply intoxicating liquor on either licensed premises or premises registered as a club, except during permitted hours. It makes no difference whether the sale or supply is for consumption on or off the premises, and any customer will also be committing a separate offence if, outside permitted hours, he either consumes liquor on the premises, or takes it away from the premises. The offence is punishable with a fine, and in addition, such an offence may hazard the licence.

Sections 59 and 54 do not, however, apply to liquor sold or supplied under the authority of an occasional licence, nor do they apply in any of the situations in which the Acts provide for an extension to normal permitted hours. Similarly, it will not be an offence for residents of licensed or registered premises (a term which includes not only the licensee himself, but also his family and his staff), to purchase or consume drinks on the premises after hours, or for them to entertain their private friends after hours at their own expense. They must all, however, be bona fide residents, if only for a short while. In Scotland, the licence holder may entertain his private friends after hours, even if he does not reside on the premises. Residents may also make off-sales purchases outside normal permitted hours.

There are also other situations in which sections 59 and 54 do not apply. Thus, liquor may be ordered and paid for outside permitted hours, provided that it is not delivered for consumption until the start of the next period of permitted hours at the earliest. It may also be sold by a supplier outside the permitted hours to the occupier or manager of licensed premises, to a registered club, or to any canteen or mess. In England and Wales, persons employed, but not resident, on licensed premises, are permitted to consume liquor outside permitted hours, where such liquor is supplied to them by their employers or his manager at his own expense. In addition, in the case of an occasional permission (for which see Chapter 4), the permitted hours will be those fixed under the permission itself.

Section 84 of the 1964 Act also makes it an offence to supply or consume liquor outside the permitted hours at "bottle parties," that is, parties which are organised for gain, and which take place on premises habitually used for the holding of parties at which intoxicating liquor is consumed, where the premises are not licensed or registered, or do not form part of any mess or canteen, or are not covered by an occasional licence.

It must be noted that sections 59 and 54 only make it an offence to sell liquor outside permitted hours; there is nothing illegal in licensed premises or registered clubs remaining open outside such hours, provided that no drinks are sold or supplied. There are, of course, obvious risks involved in doing this.

At the same time, there is no statutory requirement that licensed or registered premises remain open during permitted hours. Here again, however, there are hidden dangers; a licensee who refused to open during permitted hours would run a serious risk of losing his licence on the ground that he was not fulfilling a public need, while a registered club which did not open could be accused of not being a bona fide club established for the social convenience of its members.

It can be seen, therefore, that the legal requirements with respect to permitted hours are important, and that anyone concerned with the sale or supply of intoxicating liquor must be fully conversant with the permitted hours as they affect him. The actual permitted hours can best be dealt with in two parts: (a) general permitted hours; (b) extensions to permitted hours.

General permitted hours

There can be no such thing as a universal code of permitted hours for all establishments which sell or supply drink. There are, for example, quite different limits for licensed premises and for registered clubs, while local magistrates possess the power to vary the limits for their own particular area. There are also, as will be seen below, special hours which apply to restaurants. Nevertheless, there are certain general rules which can be laid down.

Licensed premises in England and Wales

Section 60 of the Licensing Act 1964 lays down general provisions for the permitted hours in licensed premises in England and Wales. They are as follows:

On-sales	*Metropolis*	*Elsewhere*
Weekdays, other than Christmas Day and Good Friday	11 a.m. to 3 p.m. 5.30 p.m. to 11 p.m.	11 a.m. to 3 p.m. 5.30 p.m. to 10.30 p.m.
Sundays, Christmas Day and Good Friday	12 noon to 2 p.m. 7 p.m. to 11 p.m.	12 noon to 2 p.m. 7 p.m. to 10.30 p.m.

These figures, however, must not be taken as necessarily representing the actual hours which will be observed in any given area. They are intended as a basic framework, and the licensing justices for each area are given certain powers to alter the permitted hours for their district.

They may, for example, in those areas in which the permitted hours would otherwise end at 10.30 p.m., add half an hour to the permitted hours in the evening, so as to make closing 11 p.m. They may also vary other hours, provided that the total number of hours remains exactly nine (or nine and a half in those areas in which 11 p.m. is the end of evening hours), that the hours chosen do not begin before 10 a.m. or end after 10.30 p.m. (11 p.m. where this is chosen), and that there is a single break of at least two hours in the afternoon.

These powers of variation of permitted hours may only be exercised by the licensing justices at their annual licensing meeting, and variations of this sort may only be made for periods of at least eight weeks in duration (although they need only be for specified days of the week, *e.g.* Friday and Saturday). Also, such powers are only exercisable where the justices are of the opinion that the requirements of the district render such a change desirable; examples of this would be the special needs of coastal resorts or conference centres.

As a result of these variations, in many districts the permitted hours during the lunch period end at 2.30 p.m. However, the effect of the Licensing (Restaurant Meals) Act 1987 is that when drink is served as an "ancillary" to "table meals" (for which see below) in "a part of the premises usually set apart for the service of "such meals (*i.e.* premises which qualify for a "supper hour certificate"—see below), then such service may continue throughout the afternoon, with no obligation for the premises to close for the normal two-hour break.

Off-sales

In premises licensed for the sale of liquor for consumption off the premises only, the permitted hours are as follows:

	Metropolis	*Elsewhere*
Weekdays, other than Christmas Day and Good Friday	8.30 a.m. to 11 p.m.	8.30 a.m. to 10.30 p.m.
Sundays, Christmas Day and Good Friday	As for on-sales	As for on-sales

Thus, the permitted off-sales hours begin earlier than on-sales hours, and there is no break in the afternoon. The licensing justices for each area outside the Metropolis, where they make an order extending evening on-sales hours until 11 p.m., will automatically be doing the same thing for the off-sales hours.

On premises where both "on" and "off" licences are in force (that is, where the licensee is entitled to sell liquor to the public for consumption both on and off the premises), these extra off-sales may only be enjoyed by the licensee where the off-sales part of the premises is kept strictly separate from the rest, and there is no direct internal customer access to or from the on-licensed part of the premises.

Licensed premises in Scotland

The hours during which the sale, supply and consumption of alcoholic liquor are permitted in licensed premises are set out under section 53 of the Licensing (Scotland) Act 1976, and are as follows:

Weekdays	11 a.m. to 2.30 pm 5 p.m. to 11 p.m.
Sundays	12.30 p.m. to 2.30 p.m. 6.30 p.m. to 11 p.m.

Public houses, and premises covered by a refreshment licence, are only permitted to open on Sundays where the licensing board has granted an application to that effect. Other licensed premises, and the premises of a registered club, may open on Sundays without the authority of the licensing board. Christmas Day and Good Friday are not special cases for licensing in Scotland. Off-sales are permitted from 8 a.m. to 10 p.m. on weekdays, with no permitted hours on Sundays.

Registered clubs

Section 62 of the 1964 Act lays down the general rules for the fixing of permitted hours in registered clubs in England and Wales. The hours may in fact be fixed by the club itself by means of the club rules, provided that the clerk to the magistrates is notified in writing of such rules, and provided that the hours thus fixed comply with the following conditions:

1. The total number of hours may not exceed the total number of permitted hours for the district as a whole.
2. The hours may begin no earlier and end no later than these general permitted hours.
3. There must be a break of at least two hours in the afternoon. On Sunday, Christmas Day and Good Friday, this break must include the hours from 3 p.m. to 5 p.m., and there may not be more than three and a half hours after 5 p.m.

It would seem that any registered club which fails to fix its permitted hours under its rules is not entitled to serve drinks at all, since there is no provision in the 1964 Act which states that the general licensing hours for the district shall apply in the absence of any hours fixed by the club.

In Scotland, the permitted hours in registered clubs are the same as for licensed premises, other than public houses or refreshment houses, with the exception of certain athletic clubs which may observe the hours 11 a.m. to 2 p.m. and 4 p.m. to 10.30 p.m. for the months October to March inclusive. Alternatively, the club may observe the above hours on weekdays, with permitted hours on Saturday being the continuous period from 1 p.m. to 10.30 p.m. On Sundays, the hours in such clubs may be 12.30 p.m. to 2 p.m. and 4 p.m. to 9 p.m.

Limitations

The fact that each licensing district has a set of permitted hours is in itself no guarantee that any given set of premises will be observing those particular hours at any given time. There may, for example, be a condition in the licence which requires that the establishment close one hour before the end of normal permitted evening hours; for further details on this early closing licence, see page 54, above. Alternatively, there may be a condition in the licence stating that the premises must remain closed on a Sunday; this six day licence is also explained on page 54, above.

Section 66 of the 1964 Act states that there shall be no permitted hours on Sundays for licensed premises (*N.B.*—not registered clubs) in Wales and Monmouthshire, except in those counties or boroughs in which a majority of the local electorate decide by ballot that there shall be. These polls are held every seven years, provided that at least 500 of the local electorate demand them, and if successful, the normal Sunday hours will be adopted. Such polls may also be held to abolish Sunday hours in those areas where they have been operating.

But by far the greatest number of exceptions to the general permitted hours occur where the establishment in question has succeeded in obtaining one of the various extensions to permitted hours which are made available under the 1964 and 1976 Acts. These are examined in detail below.

Extensions to permitted hours

There are obviously many situations in which the general permitted hours described above would be inadequate. Parliament has therefore designed a network of extensions which may be claimed by both the licensee and the club official in certain closely defined circumstances.

Drinking-up time

Section 63(1) of the 1964 Act allows for a certain amount of time at the end of general permitted hours, during which liquor purchased before time may be consumed. This drinking-up time is permitted at the end of both the lunchtime and the evening period, but at the end of these extended periods, all consumption of liquor must cease, otherwise both the licensee (or the club) and the customer (or the club member) will be committing an offence under section 59 of the Act (for which see p. 67, above).

These extended periods are; (a) 10 minutes in normal cases, (b) 30 minutes where the liquor was served along with a meal, and they apply in addition to any of the other extensions to permitted hours described below. Thus, whatever the time at which the actual *supply* of liquor must cease, these extra periods for *consumption only* may be added on at the end. In Scotland, the equivalent period allowed under section 54 of the 1976 Act is 15 minutes, or 30 minutes where a drink is taken with a meal.

General order of exemption

Section 74 of the 1964 Act provides for the grant, to either licensed premises or a registered club, of a general order of exemption, where such establishments cater for persons who either (a) attend a local market at times during which licensed premises would normally be closed, or (b) follow a "common trade or calling" which results in the need for refreshment during hours in which the sale of liquor would normally be prohibited.

The effect of the general order of exemption is to extend the permitted hours to whatever time the licensing authority sees fit, either on one particular day of the week, or several days, or throughout the week. The actual hours will therefore vary from establishment to establishment, and can only be ascertained by reference to the order itself.

But before such an order may be made, the premises in question must be in a position where they can serve a genuine need of the type specified. Thus, in the case of *R.* v. *Bungay Justices* (1959), it was held that a mere meeting between dealers and farmers in a certain public-house every Thursday afternoon did not constitute a public market so as to warrant the grant of a general order of exemption to serve the needs of the market.

In fact for many years it was believed that the presence of a public market was the only reason for which a general order could be granted, and that the public-houses around markets such as Covent Garden and Smithfield were the only ones which would be granted such an extension. But in the case of *Young* v. *North Riding Justices* (1965), it was decided in the High Court that there was no reason in theory why the exemption should not be granted to a social club attached to a large industrial firm whose staff finished work at 5 p.m. and were unable to purchase alcoholic refreshment until 6 p.m. under the club rules. The members of the club followed a common trade or calling, and the extension was genuinely required for their needs.

Procedure for application

Application for a general order of exemption is made to the appropriate licensing authority, that is—

(a) in the *City of London*, to the Commissioner of Police for the City of London;
(b) in the *Metropolitan Police District*, to the Commissioner of Police for the Metropolis;
(c) in *all other areas*, to the local magistrates' court.

There is little formality involved in any of these cases, and the only matter which must be proved is that the extended hours are required for the benefit and convenience of those who would otherwise have nowhere to go for refreshment.

In all three cases, the licensing authority is not bound to grant the order, and need only do so at its discretion. No such order may be granted for *off-licensed* premises, although once an order is granted for *on-licensed* premises, off-sales may be made during the new hours if the original licence permits off-sales during normal permitted hours.

The licensing authority may at any time (and, it seems, for any reason) revoke or vary any order; otherwise it remains in force indefinitely, and does not require renewal. A fee is payable upon the granting of the order, and the holder must display a permanent notice on the premises stating the effect of the order. This notice must be displayed in a prominent place.

In Scotland, section 64 of the 1976 Act provides for the grant of "occasional" or "regular" extensions to permitted hours by the licensing board where the "social circumstances of the locality" or "activities" taking place in that locality" make it "desirable" for such regular extensions of hours; and this has the same general effect as the general and special orders of exemption in England and Wales.

Special order of exemption

This exemption, also available by virtue of section 74 of the Licensing Act 1964, allows both licensed premises and registered clubs to remain open beyond permitted hours for the celebration of some special occasion. There is no hard and fast rule as to what constitutes a "special occasion," and it is entirely a matter for the licensing authority to judge for itself.

Among the more common special occasions are dances, dinners, carnivals and events of local or national significance. The exemption may cover, for example, Christmas Day or New Year's Eve, and there is no reason why it may not be granted for a Sunday if all the other conditions are satisfied. Most special occasions, however, do not last for more than a few days, and a special order of exemption will not be granted for any event which appears to be a regular or frequent occurrence.

Thus, for example, in the case of *Lemon* v. *Sargent* (1972), the licensee of a large hotel organised public dances on Wednesday and Saturday of each week, and the question arose as to whether or not such functions merited the grant of a special order of exemption. It was held that whereas a dance as such might well constitute a special occasion, even if a series of dances was held on consecutive nights for a special purpose, the dances in this case could not qualify under section 74 because (a) they were too frequent; (b) they were not connected with any local or national occasion.

In *R.* v. *Llandidloes Justices* (1972), on the other hand, the licensee of a public house applied for a special order of exemption for the period between 5 p.m. and 6 p.m. on a Saturday, in order to provide refreshments for the players and officials in the home games of the local football club. During the previous season, 34 such orders had been granted for home games, and the police appealed against the decision of the local justices to grant another. It was held, applying the principle in *Lemon* v. *Sargent*, that the court would not interfere with the decision of the justices, since the "event" was not organised by the licensee, and the home games were not as frequent as the dances in *Lemon* v. *Sargent*. But the court regarded it as an extreme case for the grant of an order.

However, those for whom the extension is granted must actually be *participating* in the event in question, as may be seen from *R.* v. *Leicester Justices* (1978), in which a special order of exemption was refused to a licensee whose patrons merely wished to watch the World Cup on the television.

Procedure for application

Application for a special order of exemption is made to the same licensing authority as for a general order of exemption (see above).

Where the application is to the local magistrates, two copies of the application for the special order must be sent to the clerk to the magistrates at least one month before the date upon which the special event is to occur or to begin. The only objection to the application may come from the police; if there is an objection, the applicant will be required to attend the hearing in person. In the absence of any such objections, the application may be granted without a hearing.

As with the general order of exemption, the actual hours during which liquor may be sold under the authority of the special order of exemption can only be ascertained by reference to the order itself, since they are set by the granting authority at its own discretion.

A special order of exemption may not be granted in respect of off-licensed premises, although where the order is granted in respect of premises which are licensed or registered for both on-sales and off-sales, off-sales may be made during the extended hours.

The licensing authority is not bound to grant a special order of exemption, and need only to do so at its discretion. They will also in most cases restrict sales during the extended hours to those who are attending the special function in respect of which the order is being granted. A fee is payable upon the granting of the order.

Supper hour certificate

Also known as a "restaurant certificate," this extension, granted by virtue of section 68 of the 1964 Act (in Scotland, ss.57 and 58 of the 1976 Act), allows certain licensed establishments and registered clubs to remain open beyond the end of normal permitted hours for the sale of liquor where it is supplied along with table meals taken in a part of the premises which is usually set aside for the service of such meals.

A decision in the High Court has helped to clarify the law on this last point. In *Norris* v. *Manning* (1971), a club in respect of which a supper hour certificate was in force consisted of one large room with one entrance, a large portion of which was roped off and designated a "dining area" by a notice. On the day in question, only the "dining area" was in use, and no food was served until 10.30 p.m. (the end of the normal permitted hours), at which time a meal was distributed to everyone present, whether they wanted it or not, and the sale of drink continued. M. was charged with serving liquor after hours, the prosecution claiming that the supper hour certificate was invalid under the circumstances. It was held that the so-called "dining area" was not "usually set apart" for the service of table meals to which the sale of drink was ancillary, bearing in mind its use throughout the rest of the day. A supper hour certificate is only available for those who serve meals as an ordinary part of their trade in an area set aside for that purpose and which is available at the normal times of the day when meals are served.

Clearly, then, service of meals to which the sale of liquor is ancillary must take place in a part of the premises always set aside for the service of meals, even during normal permitted hours, and it may not occur, for example in a lounge bar in which the customers may also just purchase drinks if they wish. The drinks, however, need not be supplied strictly with the meal, so that the serving of aperitifs and liqueurs will be perfectly in order, provided that they are associated with the service of a meal. Also, the phrase "table meals" signifies no more than the fact that the customer must be seated at some sort of counter. The meal must also, according to the section, be "substantial." This term is not defined, but has been taken to include a large sandwich accompanied by pickles (*e.g.* a "ploughman's lunch").

The effect of a supper hour certificate in England and Wales is now to extend permitted hours for one hour at the end of normal permitted hours in the evening (*e.g.* until midnight in central London). In addition, as has already been noted, the effect of the Licensing (Restaurant Meals) Act 1987 is to allow premises which qualify for a supper hour certificate to remain open for the service of drink as an "ancillary" to a meal throughout the afternoon. This Act applies only to England and Wales. But such extended hours only apply in those parts of the premises set aside for the service of meals, and the other parts of the premises must be closed down in the normal way. In Scotland, the effect of section 57 of the 1976 Act is to extend permitted hours in the afternoon by a further one-and-a-half hours, while section 58 extends the evening hours by a further two hours.

Procedure for application

Application for a supper hour certificate for licensed premises in England and Wales is made to the licensing justices at one of their normal meetings (*i.e.* annual meeting or transfer sessions) and notice of intention to apply must be sent by the licensee to the clerk to the justices at least seven days before the sessions are to begin; at the same time, a copy must be sent to the local police. Both these notices must be on a standard form which is available either from the clerk to the justices or from the Solicitors' Law Stationery Society. Both these notices must be signed by the applicant, and the copy which is sent to the police must specify the date upon which the certificate, if granted, will be first used. This date may not be less than 14 days from the service of the notice.

In the case of a registered club in England and Wales, application for a supper hour certificate is made to the local magistrates' court, and the procedure upon application is the same as that for the grant of a registration certificate (for which, see p. 96).

In both cases, the applicant will almost certainly be called upon to appear in person, and the main matter which he will have to prove is that the premises are structurally adapted, and bona fide intended to be used, for the purpose of habitually providing substantial refreshment, to which the sale of liquor is ancillary.

Once the suitability of the premises and the quantity and quality of the refreshments offered have been found to be sufficient, the licensing justices have no authority to take any other matter into consideration, and they cannot refuse to grant the certificate.

A supper hour certificate may be withdrawn if the premises at any time cease to qualify in the manner explained above, but otherwise it will remain in force indefinitely without the need for a renewal. The holder may renounce his claim to the certificate at the end of the licensing year (April 4), provided that he notifies the police at least 14 days in advance.

A fee is payable upon the grant of a supper hour certificate, and the holder must display upon his premises a notice stating the effect of the certificate, and indicating the days upon which it operates. In Scotland, sections 57 and 58 of the 1976 Act may be invoked merely by the licence holder or club secretary giving 14 days' notice to the chief constable.

Extended hours certificate

This extension, (which has no Scottish equivalent), is granted by virtue of section 70 of the 1964 Act, and exists for the benefit of premises which qualify for a supper hour certificate (see above), and which also habitually provide musical or other entertainment along with substantial refreshment, and in which the sale of liquor is ancillary to both the refreshment and the entertainment.

The "entertainment" in question must take the form of persons actually present and performing on the premises (so that, for example, a radio or juke box will not suffice), and the premises will not qualify for the certificate unless the refreshment and entertainment are provided for a substantial period of time before the end of normal licensing hours. The entertainment must also be one which is provided regularly on a certain day or days every week for at least 50 weeks of the year.

Once again, the refreshment and entertainment must be provided in a part of the premises "habitually" set aside for the purpose, and in addition, the special provisions apply only in respect of persons who enter the premises either before midnight or at least 30 minutes before the scheduled end of the entertainment, whichever is the earlier.

The extended hours certificate has the effect of extending permitted hours up to 1 a.m. (including Sunday morning). Previous restrictions applying to Easter Eve, Maundy Thursday and Good Friday were removed by the Licensing (Amendment) Act 1985. The service of drink must cease when either the refreshment or the entertainment ceases, although there are the usual periods of drinking-up time allowed, including a period of 30 minutes after the end of the entertainment for the consumption of drinks purchased during the entertainment.

Procedure for application

Application for an extended hours certificate in the case of licensed premises is the same as for an initial application for a justices' on-licence (for which, see p. 48, above). In the case of a registered club, application is to the local magistrates, and the procedure is the same as that for an application for a registration certificate (for which, see p. 96, below).

In both cases, the applicant will almost certainly have to attend the hearing in person, and the main thing which he will have to prove is that the premises are structurally adapted and bona fide intended to be used for the service of substantial refreshment and the provision of musical or other entertainment to which the sale of liquor is ancillary.

If granted, the certificate will usually be limited to certain evenings in the week, and may even require that the permitted hours end before 1 a.m. It appears that the licensing authority has a complete discretion as to whether or not it grants the certificate, even if all the above conditions are fulfilled. The certificate may be revoked at any time where, after a complaint by the police, it appears that the premises no longer qualify, or that the use of the certificate has led to noisy, unlawful or disorderly conduct.

The certificate comes into effect as soon as it is granted; however, the holder must, within 14 days of the granting of the certificate, give notice of its grant to the police, enclosing a copy of the certificate, and the holder must display a notice on his premises indicating the effect of the certificate, and the days upon which it will operate.

An extended hours certificate will expire whenever the licence or certificate expires, and it must be renewed along with it.

Special hours certificate

This extension, (which has no Scottish equivalent), is granted under sections 77 and 78 of the 1964 Act, and exists for the benefit of establishments in which the sale of liquor accompanies, and is ancillary to, the service of substantial refreshment and the provision of music and dancing. In the case of licensed premises, there must also be an entertainments licence in force in respect of the premises, but in the case of a registered club, it is sufficient that the club is one which would qualify for such a licence if one were required for the premises (on entertainments licenses, see p. 101).

The effect of a special hours certificate is to extend permitted hours up to 2 a.m. (3 a.m. in the Inner London area) on all days except Sundays. Previous restrictions on hours during Good Friday, Maundy Thursday and Easter Eve were removed by the Licensing (Amendment) Act 1985. But the lunchtime hours may not begin before 12.30 p.m., while the evening hours may not begin before 6.30 p.m., and if the music and dancing ends between midnight and 2 a.m., then so must the sale of drink, subject only to a 30-minute drinking-up period, whether the liquor was supplied along with a meal or not.

By virtue of the Licensing (Amendment) Act, 1980, any licensing authority outside the Inner London area, when granting the certificate, may impose a condition limiting its operation to certain hours, where they are satisfied *either* (1) that the bona fide use of the premises is likely to end earlier than 2 a.m., *or* (2) that such a restriction is necessary in order to reduce any annoyance or disturbance to neighbours, or to combat any disorderly conduct on the premises themselves. The police may make an independant application for this to be done, but the condition cannot be imposed so as to require the hours to end any earlier than midnight.

The premises must be such as habitually provide refreshment and music and dancing to which the sale of liquor is ancillary, and the fact that such facilities are provided on certain special occasions will not entitle the management to claim a special hours certificate. In addition, the certificate may only be obtained where all three facilities are being offered at the same time, although it would seem that once such facilities are available, the holder of the certificate is under no obligation to ensure that all those on the premises make full use of all three facilities.

Thus, in *Richards* v. *Bloxham*, (1968) the local police were applying for the revocation of a special hours certificate which had been granted to the proprietor of a licensed ball-room, on the grounds that very few of the persons attending the dances were taking the cooked meals which were available, but were making do with sandwiches. It was held that so long as the holder of the certificate was making such facilities available, the certificate was being put to a valid purpose, and it made no difference in this case that all three facilities were not being put to their fullest use.

Procedure for application

Application for a special hours certificate in the case of licensed premises is made to the local licensing justices at any of their licensing sessions; but at least seven days before the date of the hearing, the applicant must give notice of his intention to apply for the certificate to both the clerk to the justices and the local police. The applicant will almost certainly have to appear in person, but the only matter which he may be called upon to prove is that the premises are qualified in the manner described above. Once this has been proved, the justices have no further say in the matter, and they must grant the certificate.

In the case of a registered club, application is to the local magistrates, and the procedure is the same as that for an application for a registration certificate (for which, see p. 96, below). In both cases, a fee is payable upon the grant of the certificate, which will remain in force until either relinquished or revoked.

The certificate will, of course, be limited to those days upon which the necessary facilities are offered, and the licensing authority may restrict the certificate to certain days of the week or periods of the year. The holder must display a notice on the premises, indicating the effect of the certificate, and stating the days upon which it is in operation. In any case, the certificate will not be effective until at least 14 days' notice has been given to the local police; this difficulty can, of course, be overcome in practice by sending both notices of intended application and notice of the date upon which the certificate, if granted, will first be used, at least 14 days before the hearing instead of seven.

A special hours certificate may be revoked at any time where it appears that (a) the premises no longer possess an entertainments licence; (b) the certificate has not been used, or has been used for the wrong purpose; (c) during the period in which the certificate has been held, the premises have been conducted in a disorderly or unlawful manner. It is the duty of the police to lodge the necessary complaints in these last two cases.

By virtue of the Licensing (Amendment) Act, 1981, the police may also apply for the revocation of the certificate where the premises have been the scene of "disorderly or indecent conduct": once these grounds are established, the justices or magistrates *must* revoke the certificate.

These are the different types of extension to permitted hours which it is possible to obtain in the case both of licensed premises and registered clubs. There is nothing to prevent different parts of the same premises being operated in different ways. Thus, it is legally possible to manage an establishment in which there is a normal public bar closing at 10.30 p.m. (or 11 p.m.), a licensed restaurant open for the sale of liquor with meals until midnight, and a separate ballroom with catering facilities operating under a special hours certificate until 2 or 3 a.m.

CHAPTER SIX

The conduct of licensed premises

THERE are many rules concerning the conduct of licensed premises, and space does not permit a detailed examination of all of them. However, what follows below is a brief description of the most important, grouped loosely into categories. Most of them are contained in the Licensing Act 1964 and the Licensing (Scotland) Act 1976, and references are given to the relevant sections of these Acts. Other Acts are mentioned by name.

1. General sales

(a) No licensee may sell, or expose for sale, any liquor for the sale of which he is not licensed. As explained at page 47, this offence can lead to disqualification for life (section 160 of the 1964 Act, and section 90 of the 1976 Act). The actual sale may, of course, be made by a member of the licensee's staff; nevertheless, the licensee may still be convicted if the act of the employee may be taken to be the act of the licensee. He will not, of course, be liable if the employee was acting beyond the general scope of his employment. The employee may be convicted of aiding and abetting only if he acts "knowingly." The penalty for a first offence is imprisonment and/or a fine; second and later offences may lead to forfeiture of the licence, and disqualification.

The section creates an offence of "absolute liability," so that an offender may be convicted of an offence which he did not intend to commit, as in *French* v. *Hoggett* (1968), in which the steward of a registered club was convicted of an offence under section 160 after selling drinks to a plain-clothes police officer whom he genuinely but mistakenly believed to be a member.

(b) No licensee may "knowingly" sell liquor to any person to whom he is not permitted to sell under the conditions of his licence (section 161 of the 1964 Act, and see generally Pt. VI of the 1976 Act). The same rules concerning sales by employees apply here as apply under section 160 (see above), except that the law requires that before he may be convicted, the licensee must act "knowingly." But he may be liable where he may be said to have "delegated" his responsibilities to a member of staff, even if he has no *personal* knowledge of some offence committed by that member of staff. Thus, in *Vane* v. *Yiannopoullos* (1964), the defendant held a restaurant licence, one of the conditions of which was that liquor was only to be sold as an ancillary to a meal. While the defendant was on the premises, but without his knowledge, one of his waitresses served liquor to two persons who were not taking a meal. The defendant exercised general supervision over his staff, and the waitress's actions were in fact contrary to her express instructions. The defendant was charged with an offence under section 161, but he was acquitted on the grounds (a) that he had not delegated his responsibilities to the waitress; and (b) that he could not have been expected to have known what was happening.

In *R.* v. *Winson* (1969), on the other hand, W was the licence-holder of a proprietary club, and it was a condition of his licence that no drink could be sold to any person until he had been a member for two days. The premises were run by a manager, M, and admission procedures were in the hands of a doorman, J. Two police officers gained entry to the club upon the payment of 25p, were admitted without any waiting period, and were sold drinks immediately. M. was in another part of the premises at the time, and claimed that he had no knowledge of what was going on, and that in any case, he had delegated his responsibilities to J, as under-manager.

It was held that if a licensee absents himself wholly from the premises, he cannot dispose of his responsibilities under section 161 simply by delegating to a manager. If the latter knowingly contravenes the section, his knowledge must be imputed to the licensee, who cannot set up his own ignorance as a defence to the charge. If, on the other hand, the licensee retains control, and the employee does something unlawful behind his back, the licensee will not be liable. In this case, W. was convicted. The penalty is a fine and/or imprisonment.

(c) No licensee is legally obliged to serve anyone demanding liquor unless he is an innkeeper and the customer a bona fide traveller (see p. 186). In all other cases he may refuse without reason, although two points must be borne in mind. The first is that it is unlawful to discriminate on racial and sexual grounds (see p. 195), and the second is that by continually refusing to serve large sections of the public the licensee may be accused of not fulfilling a public need, and lose his licence.

(d) Neither the licensee nor his staff may sell liquor on credit (section 166 of the 1964 Act, section 87 of the 1976 Act); both the employer and the employee may be convicted in the normal way (see (a) above). The penalty is a fine only, except in Scotland where disqualification may occur. There are, however, two exceptions to this general rule: (i) liquor supplied with a meal may be paid for at the end of the meal, as part of the table bill; (ii) liquor supplied to a resident may be paid for as part of the final accomodation bill.

(e) It is a serious offence for any person to sell liquor on unlicensed premises, and can lead to disqualification for life (s.160). However, the owner of a restaurant, or his staff, may act as the customer's agent, and go out and purchase liquor for him, provided that payment is made in advance. Residents may, of course, consume their own liquor on unlicensed premises, and premises may become licensed under an occasional licence (see p. 58).

2. Sales to persons under 18

The general rule is that no licensee may sell liquor to persons under 18 (section 169 of the 1964 Act, and section 68 of the 1976 Act). Nor may he permit a person under 18 to consume liquor in his bar, or allow anyone else to sell liquor to him in his bar. It is also an offence for any person to buy, or attempt to buy, liquor for the consumption of any person under 18 (including himself). However a person under 18 only commits an offence if he attempts to make the purchase in a "bar" and in *Woby* v. *B. and O.* (1986) it was held that such a person commits no offence if he waits outside the premises while someone else makes the purchase for him. A licensee may not even deliver liquor for the consumption off the premises of any person under 18, unless it is either to his home or his place of work, nor may anyone send a person under 18 to obtain intoxicating liquor. The penalty is a fine, and further offences (in Scotland, even a first offence) by the licensee or his servant may lead to forfeiture of the licence.

Either the licensee, or his servant, or both, may be convicted, and the normal rules concerning the liability of a licensee for the acts of his servants (including the "delegation" principle) apply here. In

England and Wales, however, the offence must be committed "knowingly," and the leading English case on this matter is now *Wallworth* v. *Balmer* (1965), where the defendant was charged with knowingly supplying liquor to two youths under 18. She claimed that the two youths had told her that they were over 18, and that she assumed that they were telling the truth. It was held that the appearance of the youths was clearly an important factor, and the magistrates were entitled to form their own opinion after seeing them in court. If they were of the opinion that they looked under 18, and that the defendant should have realised that they were, then they were entitled to convict the defendant, as they had done.

However, it should be noted that as the result of the Criminal Law Act 1977, Sched. 12, a licensee may not be convicted of an offence under section 169 on the basis of the fault of one of his staff where it is shown that he personally had no knowledge of what was happening, and where he used all diligence to prevent the offence occurring.

In Scotland, section 71 of the 1976 Act states that no person charged with an offence under section 68(1) of the Act (sales to persons under 18) may be convicted if he proves that he used due diligence to prevent the occurrence of the offence and that he had no reasonable cause to suspect that the person named in the charge was under 18.

Notwithstanding the general rule, a person under 18 but over 16 may purchase beer, porter, cider or perry for consumption with a meal in a part of the premises normally set aside for the service of meals (*i.e.* not in a normal bar) (section 169(4) of the 1964 Act and section 68(4) of the 1976 Act the latter of which also permits the consumption of wine in the circumstances described). A "meal" in this context means a table meal, and the drinks must be consumed during the actual meal (*e.g.* no aperitifs).

3. Presence of persons under 14 on licensed premises

The general rule is that no licensee may allow any person under 14 years of age to be in the bar of licensed premises during permitted hours (section 168 of the 1964 Act, and section 69 of the 1976 Act). In England and Wales, the term "bar," however, does not include any part of the premises normally set aside for the service of table meals, even if liquor is supplied to persons taking meals there, and in Scotland, section 70 of the 1976 Act states that persons under 14 may be in premises operated under a "refreshment licence" if he or she is accompanied by a person over 21, and it is before 8 p.m. This is an offence which may only be committed by the licensee, but he may make use of two defences: (i) that he used all due diligence to prevent the commission of the offence; (ii) that the person in question appeared to be over 14; *Wallworth* v. *Balmer* (above) will no doubt apply here, although both Acts specifically state that where the child in question appears to the court to be under 14, it will be assumed that he/she *is* under 14 until the contrary is proved. The penalty is a fine only.

Notwithstanding the general rule, a person under 14 may be in the bar of licensed premises during permitted hours where (i) he is the licensee's child; or (ii) he is a resident; or (iii) he is merely passing from one part of the premises to another, and it is the only convenient way.

4. Employment of persons under 18 on licensed premises

The general rule is that no licensee may employ any person under 18 in the bar of licensed premises at any time during which the bar is open for the sale or consumption of liquor (section 170 of the 1964 Act and section 72 of the 1976 Act). The penalty is a fine only, although in Scotland, disqualification may result. A person may be employed even though he receives no wages, and, once again, if the person appears to be under 18, the court may assume that he/she is, until the contrary is proved. In Scotland, the effect of section 73 of the 1976 Act is that a person under 18 may be employed in premises operated under a "refreshment licence" provided that he or she is not actually employed to serve alcoholic drinks to customers.

In England and Wales, notwithstanding the general rule, an employee under 18 may work in the dispense bar of a part of the premises normally set aside for the service of meals.

In both countries, staff under 18 may enter the normal bar in order to deliver or receive a message, or pass through the bar, where to do so is the only convenient means of communication between one part of the premises and another.

5. Drunkenness and disorderly conduct

(a) It is an offence for a licensee to permit drunkenness on his premises, and in the case of a residential, restaurant or combined licence it can lead to disqualification. It will rest with the licensee to prove that he took reasonable care to prevent the occurrence, and he will be liable for the acts or omissions of his staff in the normal way (see p. 82). The same provisions apply to violent or disorderly conduct (section 172(1) of the 1964 Act), but the burden of proof of lack of care rests on the prosecution.

(b) It is also a separate offence for a licensee to sell liquor to a person who is drunk; the licensee will as usual be liable for the acts of his staff, and it is no defence that he did not know that the person was drunk (section 172(3) of the 1964 Act).

The strictness of the law in this area is well illustrated by *Commissioners of Police for the Metropolis* v. *Cartman* (1896), a case decided under an earlier Act with identical wording, in which E, who was obviously drunk, entered C's public house. A police constable drew the doorman's attention to the fact that E was drunk, and the doorman told the barman. The barman nevertheless sold E a glass of beer, and C was charged with selling drink to a drunken person. His defence was that he had been nowhere near the bar at the time, and that he had given precise instructions that drunks were not to be served. It was held that this particular law was designed to ensure public order, and that since the great bulk of a licensee's business is carried by other persons (*e.g.* barmen) on his behalf, the licensee must be held liable for their actions in the course of their employment. It makes no difference if the employee concerned has been given precise instructions forbidding the behaviour complained of, otherwise the object of the law would be entirely defeated. This is particularly true where (as here) the section in question does not make the employee liable, and only the licensee may be prosecuted.

(c) It is also an offence for any person to buy, or attempt to buy, liquor for a person who is drunk, or to assist a drunken person to obtain or consume it (section 173 of the 1964 Act).

(d) A licensee may refuse admission to a drunkard, or anyone who is violent or disorderly, and the licensee may also eject such a person (section 174 of the 1964 Act). Any such person refusing to leave is committing an offence, and the police may be called to assist in his removal, making use of the minimum force necessary.

Conviction under any of these headings is punishable by a fine, and conviction under section 173 of the 1964 Act carries an alternative sentence of imprisonment.

Similar provisions exist under Scots law by virtue of sections 74 to 80 of the 1976 Act.

(e) A notable addition to both English and Scots law occured with the passing of the Licensed Premises (Exclusion of Certain Persons) Act, 1980, which empowers both English and Scots courts, when convicting anyone of an offence of violence or threatened violence on licensed premises, to make an "exclusion order" banning that person from the licensed premises specified in the order for a period of between three months and two years.

The order may cover any number of premises, and a fine or imprisonment may be imposed on anyone entering licensed premises in breach of the order. The police may be called to remove such a person, or the licensee may remove him himself, in either case simply once he is under "reasonable suspicion" of being covered by an order banning him from the premises in question.

6. Prostitutes

No licensee may allow his premises to be the habitual resort of persons reputed or known to be prostitutes, although they may remain on licensed premises for as long as is necessary for them to obtain refreshment (section 175 of the 1964 Act). The penalty is a fine. A failure to comply with these rules in the case of a residential, restaurant or combined licence could lead to disqualification.

No licensee may permit his premises to be used as a brothel; the penalty is automatic forfeiture of the licence in *all* cases, and disqualification in the case of those licences mentioned above (section 176 of the 1964 Act).

In Scotland, section 80 of the 1976 Act makes it an offence for a licensee to "knowingly suffer" prostitutes or reputed prostitutes to meet or assemble on the premises, even apparently for an innocent purpose. The penalty is a fine, plus possible disqualification, and under both English and Scots law, the licensee is normally liable for the acts of his staff.

7. Thieves

No licensee may allow his premises to be used to harbour thieves, or as the regular meeting place of thieves, or as a depository for stolen goods. The penalties are fines and possible forfeiture of the licence, and automatic disqualification plus forfeiture for a second or subsequent offence (Prevention of Crimes Act 1871). The Scottish law on this subject is contained in section 80 of the 1976 Act, and is the same as for prostitutes.

8. Unlawful gaming

No licensee may permit his premises to be used for unlawful gaming (section 177 of the 1964 Act, and section 81 of the 1976 Act); the penalty is a fine and possible disqualification in the case of a residential, restaurant or combined licence. The licensee will be liable for the acts of his staff in the normal way, and he may in addition be guilty of an offence under the Gaming Act 1968. See section 12, below, for details of gaming in public houses.

9. Police

(A) ENGLAND AND WALES

(a) The police may enter licensed premises in order to prevent or detect the commission of an offence by virtue of the Licensing Act 1964, s.186, as amended by the Licensing (Amendment) Act 1977; this is in addition to their common law right to enter in order to prevent or suppress a breach of the peace. But in *Valentine* v. *Jackson* (1972) it was held that they must have "reasonable suspicions" before doing so. This led to the passing of the Licensing (Amendment) Act 1977, which states that the police may enter at any time during the following hours:

1. Licensed premises, or licensed canteens (other than those merely covered temporarily by an occasional licence)—the permitted hours and the first half-hour after the end of any period forming part of those hours.
2. Occasional licensed premises—the permitted hours specified in the licence.
3. Premises operated under a special hours certificate under section 78 of the Act—the hours from 11 p.m. to 30 minutes after the end of the hours permitted by the certificate.

In order to be able to enter licensed premises lawfully at any *other* time, a constable must have reasonable cause to suspect that an offence is being or is about to be committed there. Refusal to grant admission to the police in either of these cases is an offence.

In *Hinchcliffe* v. *Sheldon* (1955), H was the son of a licensee of an hotel who returned home at 11.17 p.m. to find several police officers outside, suspicious of two cars in the carpark. H shouted two warnings to his father, who was inside the premises, and it was a further eight minutes before the father opened the door to the police, who found no evidence of any offence under the Licensing

Act. H was charged with wilfully obstructing the police, in that he had effectively delayed them in detecting what might have been an offence, and he was convicted. He appealed on the grounds that he could only be convicted of wilful obstruction if it were shown that the licensee had committed an offence. It was held that the police have the right to enter licensed premises if they suspect that a licensing offence is taking place, and that if they are detained in their efforts to do so, then clearly they are obstructed, since it gives the licensee time to remove the evidence. H was convicted of obstruction.

(b) The police may also obtain a search warrant in respect of any premises upon which they suspect that illegal liquor sales are taking place (section 187 of the 1964 Act). This warrant entitles them, in England and Wales, to enter and search the premises, seize and remove any liquor which they suspect is being sold illegally, and arrest anyone under suspicion who refuses to give his name and address when requested.

(c) No licensee may (i) knowingly permit a police officer on duty to remain on the premises longer than it is necessary for him to perform that duty; (ii) supply liquor or any other refreshment to such an officer except by the authority of a senior officer; (iii) bribe, or attempt to bribe any police officer (section 178 of the 1964 Act). The licensee may be liable for the acts of his staff in the normal way.

(B) SCOTLAND

(a) By virtue of section 85 of the 1976 Act, a constable may at any time enter and inspect any premises covered by any licence other than an off-licence; in the case of off-licensed premises, he must have reasonable cause for believing that an offence has been or is being committed on the premises. Obstructing a constable in such matters is in itself an offence.

(b) A constable may enter and inspect any *unlicensed* premises where food or drink are sold for consumption on the premises, or in which he has reasonable cause for believing that alcoholic liquor is being unlawfully trafficked in. Officers below the rank of inspector must first obtain the written authority of either such an officer or of a J.P., and must then exercise the power within eight days, in accordance with its terms (section 86 of the 1976 Act). Obstructing a constable in the exercise of these powers is in itself an offence.

(c) No licensee may (i) knowingly permit a police officer to remain on the premises longer than necessary for him to perform that duty; (ii) knowingly supply liquor or any other refreshment to such an officer except by the authority of a senior officer (section 84 of the 1976 Act). The licensee may be liable for the acts of his staff.

10. Weights and measures

(a) The Weights and Measures Act 1963, (Intoxicating Liquor) Order 1984, which applies throughout Great Britain, states that:

1. Draught beer or cider may only be sold by retail in quantities of one-third pint, one half-pint, or multiples of one-half pint. An exception is made where the liquor in question is sold as a constituent of a mixed drink (*e.g.* shandy). Unless the approved measuring equipment is used (see below), all beer and cider sold in draught form must be served in "capacity" measured glasses. When assessing the "quantity" of any beer or cider for the purposes of this order, the gas comprised in any foam on the beer or cider will be disregarded; this is the effect of the Weights and Measures Act, 1979, s.19. As an alternative, the licensee may if he wishes make use of stamped measuring equipment, delivery from which is readily visible by the customer.
2. Gin, rum, vodka and whisky may only be sold (otherwise than in pre-packed, "securely closed" containers such as miniatures) for consumption on the premises in quantities of one-quarter, one-fifth, or one-sixth of a gill, or multiples thereof. The chosen measure must be the same for all such drinks consumed in all parts of the premises, and a notice must be displayed informing customers of the one chosen. An exception is made where the liquor in question is a constituent of a mixed drink containing more than three constituents (*e.g.* cocktails). A further exception is made where the customer himself requests a certain quantity of the liquor in question as a constituent of any mixed drink.
3. All liquor sold in sealed containers must be clearly marked with the quantity. The one exception is wine.
4. Wine sold for consumption on the premises, whether pre-packed or not, shall be sold only in quantities of 25 cl., 50 cl., 75 cl., or 1 litre, or 10 fl. oz., or 20 fl. oz., *unless* it is pre-packed in a securely closed bottle or sold by the glass or other vessel.

   Furthermore, the licensee must display for the information of customers, and include on every wine list and menu, a notice stating the quantities in which such wine is for sale for consumption on the premises.

(b) Dilution of liquor is unlawful unless the customer is clearly informed of the fact of dilution, and made aware of the actual strength. Even then, dilution may not take place in the case of proprietary spirits in respect of which excise duty has already been calculated.

Despite the steady encroachment of metrication, it still remains lawful for imperial measures to be used as described above.

The licensee will be liable for all acts committed by persons under his "control," however much he may have endeavoured to prevent breaches of the Act occurring; thus, in *Pickover* v. *Smith* (1975) the accused was the licensee of premises used for the training of licensed trade staff, and a trainee manager, while being trained as a barman, sold a double whisky to a Weights and Measures Inspector which was under-measure, due to spillage. It was held that the accused must be convicted, even though he had done all that he could in the way of taking reasonable precautions and exercising due diligence.

A licensee may still, however, avoid liability by "impeaching" the person whose real fault it was. In addition, in *Bellerby* v. *Carle* (1983), it was held that an employee of a brewery who held the licence for them could not be convicted of "being in possession" of inaccurate measuring equipment which had been installed by the brewery, and which he had been instructed not to touch.

In *Evans* v. *Clayton Inns* (1987) it was further held that the owner of the equipment *can* be convicted, even though the person responsible for using such equipment (the employee) is the licensee.

11. Miscellaneous

(a) The full holder of a justices' licence other than a residential licence must display a notice in a conspicuous place on the premises as directed by the justices (section 183 of the 1964 Act). This notice must state: (i) his name; (ii) the word "licensed"; (iii) the nature of his business; (iv) whether his licence is "on" or "off"; (v) the type of liquor for which he is licensed; (vi) whether the licence is full, six-day, seasonal or early closing. In the case of a residential licence, no notice need be displayed, while in the case of a restaurant or combined licence, the nature of business clause need only state that the licence is for sales of liquor with meals.

(b) The following meetings may not be held on English licensed premises: (i) a coroner's inquest (section 190(3) of the 1964 Act); (ii) a district or parish council meeting (Local Government Act 1972 Sched. 12); in both the above cases, such meetings may be held if there are no suitable alternative premises available; (iii) committee meetings for parliamentary or municipal elections (Representation of the People Act 1949); (iv) petty sessions or, in general, licensing sessions (section 190(1), (2) of the 1964 Act).

(c) An English licensee must produce his licence if it is demanded by a police officer or magistrate (section 185 of the 1964 Act).

(d) The licensee is not required to live on the premises unless the justices so direct, nor need he notify the police when he is on holiday.

(e) All premises (with very few exceptions) upon which food or drink is offered for consumption must now display a price list which may be easily read by the consumer before he makes his purchase. Further details appear on page 220.

12. Gaming on licensed premises

"Gaming" is defined under the Gaming Act 1968 (which applies equally to England and Wales and to Scotland) as "the playing of a game of *chance* for winnings in money or money's worth, whether any person playing the game is at risk of losing any money or money's worth or not." Thus it may be appreciated from the start that games of *pure skill* such as darts or snooker will not be classed as gaming. Games of mixed skill and chance, however, are so classified, with the result that popular games such as pontoon and dominoes come under the broad control of this Act.

Under this Act, there are severe limits on gaming without either a *gaming licence* or a *gaming certificate*, and normal licensed catering establishments such as public-houses, hotels and restaurants will not, on the whole, qualify for either of these. In fact, sections of the Act place a general ban on all gaming in places to which the public have access, whether upon payment or not. To this ban there are two exceptions:

(a) Under section 6 of the Act, in public-houses (*N.B.* not hotels or restaurants), the playing of dominoes and cribbage for money is permitted, and also any other game which is authorised by order of the licensing justices upon application by the licensee. In all cases, the justices (in Scotland, the licensing board) may impose conditions in order to ensure (i) that the stakes are not too high; (ii) that the gaming is not the main attraction of the premises. No person under 18 may participate in such gaming, and the games permitted by the justices may not include any game which involves a bank, or in which the chances are not equal among the players. The licensee may not charge for the privilege of playing, nor may he charge any levy on either the stakes or the winnings. A licensee may apply to the justices for permission to make available, on the same terms and conditions, games other than dominoes and cribbage.

(b) By virtue of section 41 of the Act, in all premises (whether licensed to sell liquor or not), gaming may be organised where it takes the form of "an entertainment not held for private gain." The game in question may not be one which involves playing against a bank, and the chances must be equal among all the players. But under this provision, for example, a licensee could organise a charity whist drive or bingo session, where all the profits were donated to an established charity. The main conditions to be observed are as follows:

1. In respect of all the games, no player may be called upon to make more than one payment (whether as an entrance fee, stake or whatever), and that one payment may not exceed £2,
2. The total value of all the prizes may not exceed £200,
3. The whole of the proceeds, after the deduction of prizes and expenses, must be put to purposes other than private gain.

On premises which are not open to the public (*e.g.* the "residents only" lounge of an hotel), in addition to (b) above, any gaming may be allowed, provided that it does not involve a bank, and that the chances are equal among all the players. The proprietor may not charge for the privilege of playing, and he may not charge any levy on either the stakes or the winnings.

Gaming machines

A "gaming machine" is defined under the Gaming Act 1968, s.26, as being "any machine which is constructed or adapted for playing a game of chance, and which has a slot or aperture for the insertion of money or money's worth in the form of cash or tokens." These machines, sometimes also referred to as "fruit machines" or "one-arm bandits," are strictly controlled under the Act, and the only type of such machine which may be made available for play in any premises other than those of a registered club is one which is covered by a *local justices' permit* (in Scotland, the licensing board's authority) under section 34 of the Act.

Such a machine (of which there may be any number, unless a limit is set by the local justices), must comply with the following requirements.

(1) The charge for playing a game once by means of the machine shall be one or more coins or tokens inserted in the machine to a total value not exceeding 10p.

(2) The only prize, reward, benefit or advantage which any

player may receive as the result of playing one game by means of the machine shall be one and one only of the following:

1. a money prize not exceeding £1.50, or tokens exhangeable only for such a money prize;
2. a non-monetary prize or prizes (*i.e.* one other than money or tokens exchangeable for money) to a total value of £3, or tokens exchangeable only for such prize or prizes;
3. a money prize of a value not exceeding £1.50, together with a non-monetary prize which does not exceed in value £3 less the value of the money prize, *or* a token exchangeable only for such a combination of prizes;
4. one or more tokens which may be used for playing one or more further games by means of the machine, or if not used for further games, may be exchanged for non-monetary prizes in such a way that the total value of prizes thus obtained does not exceed £3 and the total number of tokens thus exchanged does not exceed the maximum number which may be won by playing one game by means of the machine;
5. Any number of free games, provided that as a result of all the games thus played, no player may win anything other than a money prize not exceeding £1.50 in value.

Application for a section 34 permit may be made by the licensee at any time, and the licensing justices have a complete discretion as to whether or not to grant the permit, and as to how many machines it shall cover. The permit may be granted for any period not less than three years in length.

CHAPTER SEVEN

Registered clubs

REGISTERED clubs enjoy a unique position under English and Scottish licensing law, by virtue of the fact that they are not commercial enterprises in the normal sense of the term. They consist in fact of groups of individuals who join together for social purposes, and whose main object is mutual recreation. They are not necessarily concerned with making large profits, and their clubs are not necessarily run along commercial lines. The most common examples are working-men's clubs, British Legion clubs and miners' welfare associations.

The most significant legal factor concerning a registered club is that the club property (including all the liquor) is owned in equal shares by all the members, and any profits are put to purposes other than private gain (*e.g.* club funds, recognised charities and the promotion of sporting events). Because all the members possess this equal share in the liquor which is served over the club bar, there is in the eyes of the law no "sale" of such drink where it is made to a member or his guest. It is regarded instead as being merely a "supply" of liquor, and the club does not therefore require a justices' licence (although in Scotland, the approval of the licensing board, indicated by the signature of two of its members, is required) before such transactions may take place. What is required is that the club be registered.

1. Application for registration

An English club becomes registered by applying under section 40 of the Licensing Act 1964 to the local magistrates, on a standard form signed by the chairman or secretary of the club. Several copies must be supplied, in order that the clerk may send them to the police, the local authority and the local fire authority; in addition the applicant must *either* display a copy of this form on or near the premises for the period of seven days beginning with the date of application, *or* publish a copy in a newspaper circulating in the district on one of these days.

These forms are available from the clerk to the magistrates, and they require all manner of detail, including, among other things, a description of the club, the names and addresses of all committee members, a copy of the club rules (which must comply with certain requirements, for which see below), and details of the interest which the club has in the property which it occupies (*i.e.* whether it is the owner or tenant, and so on).

In Scotland, application for registration, under the Licensing (Scotland) Act 1976, must be made to the sheriff clerk, together with a certificate signed by two members of the licensing board. The procedure is laid out in sections 103 to 110 of the 1976 Act.

The club must, of course, be qualified for registration, and this will in fact be established by reference to the information given on the application form. The main requirements are that:

1. the club must be established and conducted in good faith as a club, and it must not have less than 25 members;
2. the rules must provide that no person may be admitted to the privileges of membership until at least 48 hours have elapsed since his application; (This period is two weeks in Scotland.)
3. all liquor provided in the club must be supplied only by the club;
4. the purchase and supply of liquor must be under the control of the members themselves, or a committee appointed by them;
5. there must be no arrangement whereby any person is to receive at the expense of the club any commission on purchases of liquor, or whereby any person directly or indirectly derives any pecuniary benefit from the supply of liquor.

In deciding whether or not the club is established and conducted in good faith, the magistrates may consider:

1. any arrangement which restricts the club's freedom to purchase liquor;
2. any arrangement whereby club funds are used otherwise than for the benefit of the club as a whole, or for charitable, political or benevolent purposes;
3. the means by which members are informed of the club's finances;

4. the nature of the premises occupied by the club.

Within 14 days of the making of the application, the local authority, the fire authority and the police all have the right to inspect the premises, although the last-named only for special reasons (which are not specified in the Act). They must each give at least 48 hours' notice, and must call at a reasonable time of the day.

Objections to registration may be lodged by any of the above, and also by anyone who has an interest in other premises (*e.g.* potential neighbours or local licensees). These objections must be lodged with the clerk within 28 days (in Scotland, 21 days) of the making of the application, and must state the grounds for objection. In fact, the following are the only grounds upon which objection may be made:

1. that the application is invalid;
2. that in the circumstances the premises are not suitable;
3. that the club is not qualified, that the premises in question are licensed premises, or that the character of some person concerned with the control of the club is not suitable;
4. that the club is conducted in a disorderly manner, or for an unlawful purpose, or that the rules are disregarded in some material respect;
5. that the premises in question are habitually used for an unlawful purpose, or for indecent displays, or as the resort of criminals or prostitutes, or are the scene of frequent drunkeness, or that in the past 12 months illegal sales of liquor have taken place there, or that persons not qualified to be supplied with intoxicating liquor have been habitually admitted for the purpose of obtaining it.

A copy of the objection must be sent by the clerk to the applicant. In England and Wales, the magistrates must refuse registration after a valid objection on the grounds of 1. 2. and 3. above, unless satisfied that it will not happen again. In the other two cases, they have a discretion. In Scotland, the Sheriff appears to possess a discretion in all these matters.

The hearing of the application will be dealt with by the magistrates at one of their normal meetings, and all those concerned have the right to be heard. If granted, the registration certificate will be valid for 12 months, after which it must be renewed. On any subsequent renewal, the certificate may be renewed for any period not exceeding 10 years as the magistrates see fit. In Scotland, the initial grant, and any subsequent renewals, are for a period of three years. Procedure for applying for a renewal is basically the same as that for applying for original registration and, in both cases, there is a right of appeal.

The clerk to the magistrates (in Scotland, the sheriff clerk) keeps a register of all registered clubs in the area, and this may be inspected by any member of the public for a nominal fee.

2. The conduct of registered clubs

The effect of registration is to authorise the club to supply liquor to all those specified in the rules. Normally, this will be restricted to members and their guests, but it is possible for the rules to authorise the sale of liquor to other specified persons, such as the members of visiting sports teams. Off-sales are normally permissible only to a member in person, although the certificate does authorise the supply of liquor to members and their guests on premises which the club is using on some special occasion.

On the whole, clubs are subject to the same broad rules of conduct as licensed premises (although they are not classed as such); for example, they must observe the permitted hours as laid down in the club rules; they may not permit drunkenness, disorderly conduct, indecent displays, unlawful gaming and so on. At the same time, there are some rules which apply only to licensed premises. Thus, for example, the normal rules concerning persons under 18 do not apply to registered clubs in England and Wales.

Above all, registered clubs must be conducted according to their own rules. Observance of these rules is vital to the club's continued existence, and any alterations in them must be communicated to the clerk to the local authority and the chief of police within 28 days. In Scotland, any change in the rules must be communicated to the sheriff clerk immediately.

The police have no right of entry into a registered club without a warrant, since such clubs are regarded as being private premises. However, they may enter under warrant whenever they have reasonable grounds for believing that illegal sales of liquor are taking place, or that events are occurring which entitle the magistrate to cancel the club's certificate. This warrant entitles the police to enter the premises and seize any documents relating to the club's affairs. In practice, the great majority of cases involving clubs arise as the result of police "raids."

A club's registration certificate may be cancelled at any time if, following a complaint, it appears that the club is no longer qualified, or is conducted in a disorderly manner, or for an unlawful purpose, or that the rules are habitually flouted. The club's name will then be erased from the register.

A registered club (sometimes also referred to as a *members' club*), must not be confused with a *proprietary* club, where the club property (including the liquor) is owned by some private individual or company who take all the profits. This type of club will require a justices' licence (or, in Scotland, a licence from the licensing board) before liquor may be sold (even to its members), and a common form in England and Wales is that made available under section 55 of the 1964 Act, which is a standard justices' licence limited so that sale may only be made to members and guests, and often only members. It is the means by which many famous and popular nightclubs flourish, and although the two types of club may appear on the surface to be very similar, they are legally very different indeed.

CHAPTER EIGHT

Additional licences

1. Entertainment licences

The Local Government (Miscellaneous Provisions) Act 1982 swept away the old music and dancing licensing system, and replaced it with a comprehensive system of licensing for all "public entertainments" covered by the Act, which will apply in all areas of England and Wales except the Greater London area. This is still governed by the London Government Act 1963, which had always dealt with music and dancing in a similar manner to the system now applicable to the rest of the country under the 1982 Act. It is for each local authority outside Greater London to implement the new licensing system as and when it chooses.

Both statutes deal primarily with "public" music and dancing, and this section of this chapter concentrates solely on this limited application of the legislation.

The term "public" in the context of music and dancing refers to whether or not the event is limited to a restricted class of persons (*e.g.* the members of a club or the guests at a private dinner/dance). If it is, then it is not public, and no entertainment licence will be required. If, on the other hand, the general public is freely invited to attend (*e.g.* a public dance), then a licence will be required; it makes no difference whether a charge is made for admission or not. Nor does it appear to make any difference how the music is produced, or whether the dancing is by those attending or by entertainers.

In *Severn View Social Club* v. *Chepstow Licensing Justices* (1968), a registered club which applied for a Special Order of Exemption for a cabaret evening for its members and their guests was refused on the grounds that the club did not hold a music and dancing licence, whereas in fact one was required under previous legislation in respect of such a function. The club appealed, and it was held that bona fide guests of members of a reputable club such as this were not "members of the public" such as to necessitate the club acquiring a music and dancing licence, and the extension could be granted without one. The same principle is believed to apply to entertainment licences.

In *Beynon* v. *Caerphilly Lower Licensing Justices* (1970), it was held that the test of whether or not an entertainment is open to "the public" is whether or not any reputable member of the public may, upon payment of the necessary admission fee, come in and take part in the entertainment.

A licence will be required for music alone, and it does not have to be combined with dancing. However, by virtue of s.182(1) of the Licensing Act 1964 a licence will not be required where the event in question takes place on liquor-licensed premises, and consists of music by means of radio, television, records or live performers not exceeding two in number. Any dancing to such music would presumably require a licence.

Under the Private Place of Entertainment Act 1967 (which also does not apply to Scotland), each local authority which maintains a licensing system for *public* entertainments may require that licences be taken out for *private* events which are organised for private gain, a term which does not include things such as club funds and organised charities. In any case, the Act does not apply where there is a public entertainment licence in force for the premises, nor does it apply to licensed premises or the premises of a registered club. It is now necessary to consider Greater London and the rest of England and Wales separately.

London Government Act 1963, Sched. 12

In that area of London previously governed by the Greater London Council, every set of premises upon which public music and dancing is provided now requires a licence from the District Council. Application must be with at least 21 days' notice, and a copy of the application must be sent to the Commissioner of Police. Such licences are renewable annually with 28 days' notice, and conditions may be imposed upon grant or renewal.

Licences are transferable, and they may be granted for single specified occasions with 14 days' notice to the District Council only. Clearly, in all these cases, the District Council will be concerned mainly with the suitability of the premises (both as to their structure and their location) and the character of the applicant. Both the District Council and the police have a right of entry onto licensed premises, and failure to comply with the Act can lead to a fine or imprisonment, or both. Most London boroughs have adopted the 1967 Act.

Local Government (Miscellaneous Provisions) Act 1982

Under this Act, it is for each district council to adopt the system whereby application is made to them for an entertainment licence; research suggests that most of them have already done so. The only exceptions to the need to apply arise when the "entertainment" in question is not public (see above, but *N.B.* the 1967 Act), or where the music in question occurs in connection with a religious service, a pleasure fair (separately licensed anyway) or an entertainment held "wholly or mainly in the open air" (which again may be separately licensed if the local authority wishes).

The procedure by which application is made for an entertainment licence, the fees to be charged, and the manner in which the application will be considered, are all matters left to the discretion of the individual local authority, with the result that no further detail can be supplied here. It is, however, known that district councils vary considerably in the fees which they charge, and the conditions which they impose before an entertainment licence will be granted.

In particular, it will be recalled from p. 79 that the actual *possession* of an entertainment licence is essential before licensed premises will be granted a special hours certificate. In the case of a registered club (which will not normally require an entertainment licence for its musical activities), it is sufficient that the club would qualify for one were one required. Many district councils have taken to imposing "early closing" conditions on the grant of entertainment licences, which in the case of proprietary establishments means that their special hours certificates become in effect useless after such time in the evening as the entertainment licence ceases to apply. The strict legality of this device is still a matter of some contention.

In Scotland, the equivalent scheme for public entertainment licences appears in section 41 of the Local Government (Scotland) Act 1982.

2. Copyright licences

Copyright is a legal right which a person possesses in respect of some creation or invention. In particular, it is the term used to describe the proprietary rights of the owner or composer of an artistic work. Thus, the composer of a tune may either retain "the rights" to it himself, or sell them to a publisher or recording company.

Either way, until 50 years after the death of the composer, someone somewhere will possess the copyright to every piece of music, and under the Copyright Act 1956, he has the right to sue anyone who causes that music to be performed publicly without his permission.

The term "public" in this context has a much wider meaning than it does in the context of entertainment licences, and it covers any performance except that given in a private house to the householder and his private guests. Clearly, then, copyright extends to hotels, restaurants, registered clubs and public-houses, and it makes no difference whether the performance is live or by means of records, radio, television, or tapes. If it is public, and if it is without the authority of the copyright owner, it is said to be a "breach of copyright," and legal action for damages may result.

In *Performing Right Society* v. *Rangers F.C. Supporters Club Greenock* (1974), for example, it was held by the Court of Session that the performance of copyright music without the consent of the copyright owner was unlawful even in a non profit-making members' club where the music was performed only to members and their guests. Lord Justice-Clerk Wheatley ruled (at p. 154) that "the members and their guests are enjoying the fruits of [the copyright owner's] brain and labour just as they would if they went to a public place like a hotel, or restaurant, or a dance hall where the law of copyright would apply."

In *Performing Right Society* v. *Harlequin Records* (1979), it was held to be an infringement of musical copyright to play records via loudspeakers to customers in a record shop.

In practice, of course, it would be impossible for an hotelier or restauranteur to contact individually all those whose music might conceivably be performed on his premises, and it would be equally impossible for every owner of musical copyright to collect royalties in person. This problem is solved by the existence of The Performing Right Society which represents almost all British composers, and many more from other countries. It is the Society's task to collect an annual licence fee from all those who cause music to be performed publicly (*e.g.* dance hall proprietors). This fee is based upon the amount of such music performed during the course of a year, and the Society's receipts are then distributed among the members. Public performance without the cover of the Society's licence is a breach of copyright.

In addition to the copyright in the music itself, there is a separate copyright in all authorised *recordings* of that music. Thus, where an hotel possesses a juke box or record player, not only must they pay royalties in respect of the *music itself*, but also in respect of that particular recording of it.

Copyrights in recordings are protected by an organisation known as Phonographic Performance Ltd., which represents almost all the world's leading recording companies and issues licences similar to those issued by the PRS. Such a licence is just as important as a licence from PRS, and a re-recording requires a licence just as much as an original recording; thus the taping of records does not eliminate the need to pay the licence fee.

However, it is not a breach of recording copyright to cause a public performance of recordings to persons sleeping or residing on the premises. Thus, the "piping" of records to residents in an hotel does not require the authority of a licence from Phonographic Performance Ltd.

A test case in this area was that of *Phonographic Performance Ltd.* v. *Pontins* (1968), which concerned the practice of the defendants, in a holiday camp in Sussex, of transmitting records through tannoys which covered the entire camp. This music could be heard not only by the residents, but also by friends of residents who were allowed into the camp between certain hours of the day. There was no general "day visitor" system in operation. The plaintiffs sought an injunction to prevent the defendants from playing copyright recorded music to the "public" without a copyright licence. It was held that since the music was provided mainly for residents, the defendants did not require a copyright licence in order to provide recorded music in the camp.

There is also an exception in the case of records played to the members of a club or society which exists for "charitable" purposes. In all cases, however, a PRS licence must be obtained.

3. Billiards licences

By virtue of the Billiards (Abolition of Restrictions) Act 1987, the licensing system which used to cover the public playing of billiards, snooker etc. and bagatelle has been abolished. Such facilities may therefore be provided for the public without the need for any licence.

4. Tobacco

It is no longer necessary for a caterer to obtain an excise licence for the sale of tobacco; in licensed premises, it may be sold by virtue of the licence during permitted hours, while elsewhere it may be sold during the normal trading hours as laid down by the local authority under the Shops Act.

By virtue of the Protection of Children (Tobacco) Act 1986 it is an offence for any person to sell tobacco or cigarette papers to any person apparently under the age of 16, whether for his own use or not. It is no longer a defence for the tradesman to show that he was not aware that the person was under 16, and had no reason to suspect it. Where it is apparent that cigarette vending machines are being used frequently by persons under 16, the operator will be ordered to take precautions, or remove the machine altogether. None of these regulations has any application where the person under 16 is an employee of a tobacco company or is employed as a messenger by a messenger company.

The Act applies in both England and Wales and Scotland.

5. Cinematograph licences

By virtue of the Cinematograph Acts of 1909 and 1952 and the Cinematograph (Amendment) Act 1982, no film show of any kind may be given unless the regulations laid down by the Secretary of State are observed. They include matters such as the adequacy of exits, notices, passageways and seating arrangements, the competence and sufficiency of staff, the adequacy of fire appliances, the fire-proofing of fabrics, the storage of inflammable film and the inspection of equipment and fittings. There are special rules for children's shows.

In addition, a *cinematograph licence* must be obtained for any premises upon which film shows (public or otherwise) are given except in the cases of (a) private dwelling-houses used for private shows to which the general public are not admitted; it would seem that not even the regulations need be observed in these cases; (b) premises used for film shows on not more than six days in any one calendar year; the county council the police and the fire authority must be informed of such shows at least seven days in advance, and the regulations must be observed; (c) film exhibitions given either privately or free of charge to the public which are part of the activities of some educational or religious institution; it is customary for the regulations to be observed on such occasions.

Cinematograph licences are obtained from the local authority, which may if it chooses delegate its authority to the local magistrates. Such licences may be granted to whomsoever the licensing authority sees fit, and subject to such conditions as it may see fit to impose. It may, for example, prohibit shows on Sunday, Christmas Day or Good Friday. Cinema licences are granted for one year at a time, being renewable annually, and they may be transferred. Twenty-eight days' notice suffices in either case (with a copy of the notice being sent to the police and the local fire authority).

The actual details concerning applications are the concern of each separate licensing authority, and the clerk should be consulted on all matters. Fines may result from operation without a licence, or for a breach of any of the conditions imposed in the licence. The police, the fire authority, and the local authority have the right to enter any premises upon which there is cause to believe that the Acts or regulations are being ignored; fines may result from a refusal to admit such persons.

It was held in *BACTA* v. *GLC* (1985) that video games in amusement arcades are "exhibitions" of moving pictures, and by virtue of the 1982 Act now require cinema licences.

6. Theatre licences

By virtue of the Theatres Act 1968, no premises may be used for the public performance of any dramatic work unless they possess either "letters patent," or, more commonly, a licence from the local authority. These licences may be granted to any applicant at the discretion of the authority, and there is a right of appeal to the magistrates' court. Restrictions and conditions may be imposed (*e.g.* no sale of liquor on the premises), and provisional licences may be granted. These restrictions may not, however, relate to the *type* of play which is presented, or the manner of its performance. With the abolition of the censorship powers of the Lord Chamberlain under the 1968 Act, this means that such performances are governed only by the normal laws concerning defamation, obscenity and so on.

However, the Act itself contains penalties for the public performance of plays which are obscene, or which stir up racial hatred or cause a breach of the peace. There are also penalties for operating without a licence, or in breach of any conditions imposed in the licence; among the penalties for the latter is loss of the licence.

A justices' licence is not required for the sale of liquor in a licensed theatre, provided that the proprietor notifies the clerk to the licensing justices of his intention to sell. The normal permitted hours apply (see Chap. 5). By virtue of the Sunday Theatre Act 1972, theatres licensed under the 1968 Act may open for public performance on Sundays, as an exception to the Sunday Observance Act 1780, although they must be closed from 2 a.m. to 2 p.m. on Sundays.

7. Late night catering establishments

The Late Night Refreshment Houses Act of 1969 (which does not apply to Scotland), requires that all premises which remain open for public refreshment between the hours of 10 p.m. and 5 a.m., and which are not licensed for the sale of liquor after the normal "closing time" for the area, must be licensed as "late night refreshment houses." These licences are granted by the local authority, and are required whatever the nature of the refreshment served.

However, in *Frank Bucknell and Sons* v. *London Borough of Croydon* (1973), it was held that a late night refreshment house licence was not required in respect of a coffee stall which had once been on wheels, but was now cemented into the ground covered in breeze blocks, and which was used for serving refreshments through a hatch to customers such as lorry drivers. No-one could be served inside the structure, and there were no tables and chairs on the pavement. The patrons simply stood under the canopy while consuming their refreshments, or else took them away with them. (But see now the 1982 Act below.)

Licences may be obtained at any time, and will then be renewable on April 1 of each year. Conditions may be imposed, including one which requires that a tariff of charges be displayed in a convenient place on the premises where members of the public may read it before entering. No one may "tout" for custom outside the premises, and the local authority often imposes a ban on business between the hours of 11 p.m. and 5 a.m. in the interests of local residents.

The police have the right to enter late night refreshment houses at any time, and a refusal to admit them can lead to fines, imprisonment and disqualification. The same general rules of conduct apply as for liquor-licensed premises, and the usual penalty is disqualification. *N.B.* that if the licensee of residential, restaurant or combined liquor-licensed premises is convicted of an offence under the 1964 Act for which he may be disqualified from holding such a liquor licence, he may also be disqualified from holding a late night refreshment house licence.

In order to bring within some sort of official control the sort of premises identified in the *Frank Bucknell* case (which are not subject to the 1969 Act), Parliament took the opportunity of the Local Government (Miscellaneous Provisions) Act 1982 to introduce, under section 4, a system for the early closure of "take-away" food shops (including mobile vans) where they are satisfied that it is desirable to do so in order to prevent unreasonable disturbance to anyone living in the area.

Such orders may be imposed by the district council on individual premises, and may order closure at any time between midnight and 5 a.m. The closure laws may vary from day to day in the week. There is a system of appeal to the magistrates court. It is a fineable offence to contravene a closing order.

Further controls on mobile food businesses are imposed under section 19 of the Act, which allows local authorities, if they wish, to introduce a registration system for such businesses.

In Scotland, provisions for the regulation of "late hours catering" businesses by means of licence are introduced under section 42 of the Civic Government (Scotland) Act 1982, for premises operating between 11p.m. and 5a.m.

CHAPTER NINE

The contract of employment

1. General introduction

THE law relating to the employment of staff comes from a variety of sources. Basically, it is a question of contract, being concerned with a legally binding agreement between the employer and the employee. In addition to this, it is necessary to study various Acts of Parliament which restrict the freedom of the two parties to negotiate just whatever terms they wish. Finally, it is occasionally necessary to take into account the existence of long-established customs, which still have their part to play in the law of employment.

Basically, then, we are concerned with the contract of employment, which is the basis of all employer/employee relationships. It is no different from any other type of contract; both parties must agree to certain clear terms, each must provide something of value to the other, and the purpose of the contract must not be illegal, or contrary to public policy.

One particularly important question is that of the capacity of each of the parties to sign a contract; in particular, the extent to which a person under 18 (now known in law as a "minor" but formerly called an "infant") may make a valid contract for his own employment. Such persons are limited in their contract-making powers, and the legal rule is that no contract of employment will be binding on a minor unless, taken as a whole, it can be seen to be for his own benefit. This is always a question of fact in the circumstances; thus, a young man of 16 could validly sign an agreement whereby he was to train, at a low wage, to be a chef, since the ultimate benefit would, several years later, be his.

It is also important at this stage to distinguish between an employee and other persons who might seem at first glance to be employees. The relationship of employer and employee is a very special one, giving rise to many rights and duties on both sides which are not present in any other relationship. This special relationship used to be known as that of "master and servant," but it is no longer fashionable to speak of them in these terms, and "employer and employee" will suffice.

There are several rough guides which may be followed when attempting to determine whether one man is the employee of another. For example, it is often said that one man is the employee of another where the latter may tell the former not only what job to do, but also how to do it. This test, however, falls down in certain cases where a man is employed for special skills which the employer does not possess; few hoteliers would dream of telling a chef his job, but such a chef will nevertheless be an employee in the eyes of the law.

A second possible test is to say that a man is an employee when he occupies a permanent position in the organisation of the establishment, and his name is permanently on the payroll. These two tests, taken together, are usually enough to distinguish an employee from an independent contractor, who sells his skills on a part-time or short-term basis. Nevertheless there may be borderline cases, as for example where an hotelier keeps a list of "casual" staff whom he calls in for special functions or during busy seasonal periods. In *Wickens* v. *Champion Employment* (1984), for example, it was held that "temps" supplied by an agency are not "employees" of anyone, and in *Daley* v. *Allied Supplies* (1985), the same was held to be true of M.S.C. trainees under the "YOPS" Scheme.

The distinction is important, since certain important legal considerations depend for their very existence on the fact that one man is an employee of another. Many of these will be dealt with in detail later, but some of the more important may be listed as follows:

1. An employer is only required to make National Insurance contributions and deduct PAYE in respect of an *employee*, and no one else.
2. An employer is only under a duty to provide a written statement of the terms of the contract to an employee—see below.
3. An employer owes a higher duty of safety to an *employee* than he does to anyone else.
4. Only an *employee* is entitled to redundancy payment.
5. An employer may in certain circumstances be liable to third parties for the wrongful acts of an *employee*, whereas he will rarely be liable for those of an independent contractor.

2. The written contract

To refer to a "written contract" in the context of employment is a little misleading, since the law will presume the existence of a contract between two parties who behave as employer and employee, whether one is apparent or not, and an English contract of employment does not, with the exception of a contract of apprenticeship, require to be in writing before it is valid. Indeed, many contracts of employment are made verbally, following an interview. In Scotland, contracts of employment for more than a year must be in writing.

However, since 1963 governments have protected the interests of employees by insisting that where an employee does not have a written contract of employment, he must at least be presented with a document which contains certain vital terms of the contract between the parties. The latest Act to continue this requirement is the Employment Protection (Consolidation) Act, 1978, referred to hereafter simply as EPCA, s. 1 of which requires that the employee be presented *either* with a written contract, *or* with a written statement, either of which must specify the following:

> The names of the parties; the date of the commencement of the contract; whether or not any period of employment with a previous employer will count as part of the employee's "continuous period of employment," and if so, the date of commencement of that period; the rate of pay, or the method by which it may be calculated; the intervals at which payment falls due (*i.e.* weekly, monthly, etc.); the hours of work; what arrangements exist (if any) for holidays and holiday pay, sickness and sick pay, pensions and pension schemes; the length of notice required to terminate the contract on either side; the date of termination in the case of a fixed-term contract; the title of the job which the employee is employed to perform; whether or not the employer is contracted out of the State pension scheme.

In addition, these written particulars must also contain a note specifying any disciplinary code to which the employee will be subject, or referring him to a document which contains the code. At the same time, the particulars must specify a person to whom the employee may apply if he is dissatisfied with any disciplinary decision relating to him, and any person to whom the employee may refer if he has any grievance connected with his employment, and the manner in which any such application should be made. This does not apply where the disciplinary code or procedure relates to the health and safety of employees at work.

This notice must be given to the employee not less than 13 weeks after the commencement of his employment, and if no provisions are being made in respect of certain matters (*e.g.* payment during sickness), this fact should be stated. Any changes in the terms and conditions indicated by the notice must be communicated to the employee in writing within four weeks of such change.

It is not necessary for the employer to lay out in full what may in practice be very complicated terms (*e.g.* the method of calculating pay). It is sufficient that in the written notice (or the written contract, if one is given instead), the employer directs the employee's attention to some document made reasonably accessible to him in which he will find the necessary information. Thus, for example, an employee may be directed to the latest Wage Council Order (see Chap. 10) for details of his minimum wage.

The obligation to provide written particulars does not apply in certain cases, the main ones being:

1. Where the employee normally works for less than 16 hours per week. However, the obligation still remains where (a) the employee formerly worked for 16 hours per week or more, but was reduced to between eight and 16 hours per week, in which case the obligation continues for 26 weeks after the reduction; (b) the employee has been employed for a continuous period of five years for eight hours per week or more.
2. Where the employee is the husband or wife of the employer.
3. Where the employee is employed by the Crown.
4. Where the employment will be wholly or mainly outside Great Britain.

Quite apart from those matters which *must* be dealt with in writing under the 1978 Act, an employer would be well advised to ensure that certain other vital matters are recorded in writing. For example, any power of search which he wishes to retain over the employee should be written down in the contract in such a way that the employee cannot later deny that he agreed to it. Similarly, all disciplinary matters which are a little unusual should be specifically stated, rather than left for the employee to discover in a code to which he is referred. Thus, in a catering context, smoking in a food area is often made a ground for "instant dismissal," where it might not be in any other production area, and the employee should be specifically directed to this fact as a term of his employment.

3. The terms of the contract

A. Terms implied at common law

In addition to those terms of the contract of employment which must be expressed in writing, the law will presume or "imply" the existence of certain others, unless the contrary is actually stated in the contract itself. Many of these "implied terms" are little more than rules of common sense, but nevertheless they should be noted with care, since they are just as binding as express terms.

Since 1971, successive Acts of Parliament have taken various of these implied terms, and in effect made them express terms, in the sense that the contract of employment will be taken to contain them, not by virtue of custom, but because a statute says so; such terms may *not* be overridden by express terms in the contract itself, as may implied terms.

Thus, for example, the employer's implied duty to provide an employee with a safe place of work has been superseded by the Health and Safety at Work etc. Act 1974, the Employers' Liability (Compulsory Insurance) Act 1969, and the Employers' Liability (Defective Equipment) Act 1969, while the implied term at common law that an employer will pay wages when they fall due has been overtaken by the concept of "constructive dismissal," introduced in 1974, and now incorporated into the "unfair dismissal" provisions of EPCA.

The result of this rapid legislation in favour of the employee has been to shorten the list of terms of the contract "implied" at common law to the point where most of those which remain are duties owed by the employee to the employer. The most important of these are as follows:

Obedience

At common law, the employee, when taking on a contract of employment, is implied to have undertaken to obey all lawful, reasonable and authorised instructions concerning his employment. An employee is not obliged to commit acts which are criminal, or otherwise unlawful, nor need he take orders from someone who is not authorised to give them. But otherwise, for an employee to refuse to carry out the duties he was employed to carry out will amount to a breach of contract, at least where such conduct is persistent. Thus, to take just one example, in *Pepper* v. *Webb* (1969) a man employed as head gardener to a private householder had been behaving unsatisfactorily for some six weeks. One Saturday morning, he refused to carry out a simple instruction concerning his work, and when tackled about his attitude, replied, "I couldn't care less about your bloody greenhouse and your sodding garden." He was dismissed on the spot, and the Court of Appeal held that the dismissal was lawful. Even the modern tendency to "work to rule" during an industrial dispute has been taken to be a breach of contract where its effect is highly disruptive of the employer's business; *Secretary of State for Employment* v. *ASLEF (No. 2)* (1972).

Fidelity and good faith

It is at the very root of a contract of employment that an employee will act honestly and in good faith towards his employer. Many types of action may be included under this heading, for example taking bribes or accepting secret commissions. By tradition, tips are excluded from this category. Persistent idleness or lateness might constitute a breach of good faith, as would the carrying out of any activity in direct conflict with the employer's business interests (*e.g.* encouraging guests to visit rival establishments).

An interesting case in this context was *Sanders* v. *Parry* (1967). The defendant had worked on the staff of the plaintiff's firm of solicitors as an assistant. He left the job after a few months, taking the plaintiff's secretary with him to work as his own secretary, and after making an arrangement with one of the firm's best clients to the effect that the latter would henceforth take all his business to him. It was held that in both matters the defendent was in breach of his duty of good faith to his ex-employer, and the latter was entitled to damages. It is not difficult to imagine how the decision in this case could be applied, for example, in a case in which an assistant manager in a restaurant leaves to set up a rival establishment, taking with him his ex-employer's regular patrons.

Under this heading of good faith towards the employer may be included the duty of an employee to refrain from disclosure of confidential information imparted to him in the course of his employment. There is an apparent exception to this rule where disclosure would be in the general public interest, as was seen in the case of *Initial Services* v. *Putterill* (1968) in which the defendant had been employed by the plaintiffs as a manager, and in this capacity had come into possession of information which revealed that his employers were involved in an illegal price-fixing agreement with other companies. Upon leaving his job, he revealed this information to the press. It was held that the disclosures were justified, since it was in the public interest that these facts be revealed.

In *Woodward* v. *Hutchins* (1972), this same principle was employed to allow a former public relations officer employed by the singer Tom Jones to write a series of articles in a national newspaper concerning the artist's private life.

The duty of "good faith" also, of course, includes the duty of honesty and integrity, but it goes further than that in situations in which mutual trust is essential. Thus, in *Sinclair* v. *Neighbour* (1967), S was the manager of a betting shop owned by N. One evening, contrary to his instructions, S took £15 out of the till and replaced it with an I.O.U. He used it to place bets with other bookmakers, and replaced it the following day. Upon discovery, he was dismissed on the spot, and he claimed damages for wrongful dismissal. It was held by the Court of Appeal that S's conduct, while not dishonest, was sufficient to justify summary dismissal.

Although there is no general rule that an employee should disclose to the employer the misconduct of his fellow employees, it is generally assumed that such information should be revealed where it is likely to cause injury to the employer's business interests, or loss or injury to third parties. The employee should also disclose any facts about himself which may have a material and fundamental bearing on his duties; thus, the employer is entitled to know whether or not his barman has the "warning signs" of alcoholism, or whether or not one of his drivers is prone to dizzy spells.

Accountability

The employee must account for all money or property received by him either on behalf of his employer, or for use in his employer's business. Thus, an hotel cashier is obliged to account for the "float" which she is given at the start of the day, and also for all the money given to her on behalf of the management by guests. At the same time, the employer may claim the rights to any discovery or invention made by his employee while engaged on his employer's business and using his property or materials; thus, the "chef's special" may well become the property of the management. This legal principle has now been enshrined in the Patents Act 1977, which at the same time allows the employee to retain the patent where the invention or discovery was not to be expected from the nature of the employee's job.

The duty of care

Both employer and employee owe each other a general "duty of care" at common law, but the duty owed by the employer to the employee has in more recent times found its way onto the statute books in Acts such as the Health and Safety at Work etc. Act 1974, as explained elsewhere in this book. It is therefore only the duty owed by the employee to the employer which is still covered by older common law concepts.

In particular, an employee must exercise reasonable care and skill in the performance of his duties, and if he does not, he may be called upon by the employer to indemnify him against damages payable to innocent third parties

Thus, in *Lister* v. *Romford Ice and Cold Storage Co. Ltd.* (1957) a lorry driver who injured a fellow employee by reversing a lorry into him was held liable to reimburse his employers for the damages which they were subsequently ordered to pay to the injured employee.

Similarly, in those circumstances in which an employee is

entrusted with the power to act as agent for his employer, he must conduct his employer's business affairs with the same skill and diligence as he would conduct his own; (see Chapter 2).

B. Terms imported into the contract by statute

As mentioned above, successive Acts of Parliament in recent years have made great inroads into the freedom of the parties to a contract of employment to negotiate their own terms. These terms imported into the contract by statute over-ride and countermand anything to the contrary in the contract itself, and in every case, the effect is to benefit the employee.

The following are the most important rights conferred upon the employee by statute in recent years.

Equal pay

As part of a lengthy process to remove sexual discrimination from the field of employment, the Equal Pay Act 1970, which did not come into full force until 1975, and which was extended in 1983 set out to equalise the remuneration paid to men and women carrying out comparable work. Lack of space precludes any detailed examination of the Act, which has in any case been to some extent overtaken by the provisions of the Sex Discrimination Act 1975, but the following general points may be made.

Under the 1970 Act, any contract of employment of a woman is deemed by law to contain what is referred to as an "equality clause," which is a provision which ensures that where a woman is employed on "like work" with a man in the same employment, or on work which is "rated as equivalent" to his, following a job evaluation exercise, the woman's contract shall be "no less favourable" than the man's and shall include all the benefits granted to a man under his contract. The only exceptions to these rules are permitted where the employer can show that the variation is genuinely due to a "material difference" between the man and the woman other than a purely sexual one.

These somewhat vague terms, which clearly cover more than just rates of pay, have proved difficult to interpret in practice, but the Act assists so far as equal pay is concerned by defining "like work" as being work of a "broadly similar nature" in which any differences between the work done by the man and that done by the woman are "not of any practical importance" in relation to the whole contract, regard being had to the frequency of such differences. In defining work "rated as equivalent," the same section allows the employer to take into account the demands made upon a worker in terms of effort, skill, decision and other factors by means of a job evaluation exercise.

The clear object of the legislation, however verbosely it may have been expressed, was to ensure that men and women doing the same job should be paid exactly the same amount. For that reason, the Act is expressly stated to apply equally to *men*, so as to give them equality with women where necessary. The failure of an employer to comply with equal pay legislation entitles the employee to refer her case to an industrial tribunal.

An example of the legislation in action was the case of *Sorbie* v. *Trust House Forte Hotels* (1976) in which T employed six waitresses and one waiter in the grillroom of one of their hotels. The waiter received higher wages than the waitresses, and when the 1970 Act came into effect on December 29, 1975, the waitresses immediately claimed that they were entitled to the same remuneration as the waiter. The employer retaliated by promoting the waiter to "Banqueting Supervisor." It was held that the waitresses were entitled to at least the rate which the waiter had been receiving prior to his promotion.

Several fairly obvious evasions of the Act were dealt with in *National Coal Board* v. *Sherwin and Spruce* (1978), in which A and B were two canteen workers in a colliery, both female, and both working on alternating shifts from 6 a.m. to 2 p.m. and 2 p.m. to 11 p.m. They claimed parity of wage with T, a man who worked alone on permanent nightshift, but who otherwise performed exactly the same tasks as they did. The NCB claimed (a) that the women were not employed on "like work" with T, or alternatively that (b) there was a material difference between their cases. It was held that the work of A and B *was* "like work" with that of T, and that the fact that the work was performed at different times of the day did not alter that fact. Also, that the disadvantage of working inconvenient hours could be compensated by an additional premium, but that the basic wage rates should remain the same. The fact that T was in sole charge during his shift did not make his job materially different from that of A and B, and it was no justification for paying a higher wage to claim that no man could have been recruited for a lesser wage. All in all, there was no evidence to show that the difference in pay was due to any reason other than that of sex discrimination.

In *Capper Pass* v. *Allan* (1980), on the other hand, sixteen female employees in a canteen were employed to prepare, serve and sell food, clear away the tables and clean generally. All except the supervisors were classed into three grades; all those in Grades One and Two were male, worked shifts and received an hourly rate differential in respect of this shift working. Grade One staff also received an hourly productivity bonus for working unsupervised, for being responsible for stock control, and for taking care of £150 or so of cash generated each shift. A female Grade Three employee claimed parity (on the basis of "like work") with her Grade One colleagues, and applied to a tribunal for a productivity bonus. It was held that if matters such as stock handling and responsibility for money justified the difference between the grades, then the two were not engaged on "like work," and equal pay could not be demanded. Likewise in *Thomas* v. *NCB* (*The Times*, May 20, 1987), it was held that day and night staff in a canteen are not employed in "like work."

In *Commission for the European Communities* v. *UK* (1982), it was held that the 1970 Act did not go far enough in granting equality to women in employment, and the gap was filled with the Equal Pay (Amendment) Regulations 1983, which grant equality of pay etc. whenever it may be said that a woman performs work of "equal value" to that of a man. Under these Regulations, an industrial tribunal may commission a job evaluation study from an expert, and may award arrears of pay to January 1, 1984. In the first successful case under the 1983 Regulations, *Hayward* v. *Cammell Laird Shipbuilders* (1986), a female cook in a shipyard canteen secured parity of pay with skilled shipyard workers.

Non-discrimination

Another area of the law of employment in which Parliament has taken a firm hand in recent years is that of discrimination, of which equal pay, dealt with above, is only one example. It is proposed in this section to outline the legislation which now outlaws the two broad forms of discrimination which have hitherto plagued the employment field, namely sex discrimination and racial discrimination. Again, lack of space precludes lengthy detail.

Sex discrimination

The Sex Discrimination Act 1975, set out to eliminate sex discrimination in many walks of life, of which employment was merely one, if an important one. Part II of the Act deals with discrimination in employment, and reference should be made to the section on equal pay (above) for the central concept of the Act, as expressed in section 8, that an "equality clause" should be imported into all contracts for the employment of women.

Section 6 of the Act goes further than that, and renders it unlawful for an employer to "discriminate" against a woman in his selection and recruitment of employees, and the terms and conditions upon which he offers employment. The section goes on to make discrimination unlawful in the case of women already employed who are denied equal rights to promotion, transfer, training or other benefits, facilities or services normally provided, and concludes by rendering unlawful any form of discrimination in the matter of dismissal or disciplinary procedures. The ban on discrimination in recruitment does not apply where sex is a "genuine occupational qualification," as defined in section 7, which goes on to give as examples matters such as physical strength, stamina, authenticity in entertainment, decency and privacy, the nature and location of the job and the problem of living accommodation, and the nature of the establishment (*e.g.* prisons). A permitted exception of particular relevance to the catering industry is that where the job is one of two to be held by a married couple, in which case the employer may discriminate against single applicants.

"Discrimination" for the purposes of the 1975 Act consists of treating a person less favourably than a person of the opposite sex would be treated, or imposing requirements and conditions which are designed to make the job unnecessarily difficult for a person of the opposite sex. It is also unlawful to discriminate against a person because she is married, although not because she is single (see above).

A recent illustration of the law in practice was *Hurley* v. *Mustoe* (1981), in which H, a married woman with four children, applied for a job as a waitress in a bistro. The manager invited her to work a trial Saturday evening, but while she was doing so, the owner came in and recognised her as having young children. Because he believed that women with young children were unreliable employees, he refused her the job. She claimed that she had been the victim of sex discrimination, and her claim was upheld. The Employment Appeal Tribunal held that the owner's policy concerning employees with children applied *only* to women, and there was no evidence that he applied it to men. Even if that were not the case, it would have been *indirect* discrimination against H on the grounds of her married status. The owner's policy was not justifiable, since there was no evidence that married *men* with children are unreliable even *if* married women *are*, and even if they were, this would not justify such an exclusion policy against *all* of them. Each person must have her case dealt with on its own merits.

It should be carefully noted that although section 6 refers throughout to discrimination against a woman, section 2 of the Act states clearly that all sections of the Act dealing with discrimination in employment shall be taken as applying equally to men. In other words, sex discrimination in employment is unlawful, regardless of the sex of the person discriminated against.

Another important point to note is that there are exceptions to section 6, the most important of which is that discrimination is not unlawful where the employment is in an establishment outside Great Britain. Thus in *Haughton* v. *Olau Line* (1985) it was held that the Act offered no protection to a stewardess on a ship which was normally outside British waters. The employer may also discriminate in the provision of living accommodation for staff; thus, the hotelier may have a "men only" or "women only" staff block. He may also engage in "positive discrimination" in order to redress an imbalance between the sexes in a particular type of job (*e.g.* receptionist).

Any person who feels that he or she has been discriminated against on sexual grounds may bring an action before an industrial tribunal for the fault to be remedied. An attempt may first be made by a conciliation officer to bring the parties together amicably, but if that fails, the action may proceed, and the tribunal has a variety of powers available to it in a proven case. It may, for example, make an order declaring what it considers the rights of the parties to be, or order the employer to make financial reparation to the employee, or order the employer to take certain courses of action such as reinstating the employee, or promoting her. It may take all three steps together if it wishes. The Equal Opportunities Commission may also issue "non-discrimination" notices enforcible in the courts.

The cases so far decided under the 1975 Act indicate only too well the dangers of making fundamentally false assumptions about the jobs which may be offered to women. In *Wylie* v. *Dee and Co. (Menswear) Ltd* (1978), for example, W, an unemployed young lady, was directed by the Glasgow Jobcentre to a men's outfitters where four vacancies for assistants were being advertised. The main items for sale were men's slacks, there were already seven males employed as assistants, and the management had specifically asked the Jobcentre for male applicants. After some hesitation, W, was informed that she was not suitable because part of the job involved taking inside leg measurements from male customers. W, explained that she had done this regularly during the five years in which she had been employed in other menswear shops, but she failed to obtain the post. She complained to a tribunal that she had been discriminated against on the grounds of her sex, and the employer's defence was that being a man was a "genuine occupational qualification" for the post because of the potentially embarrassing physical contact with male customers. It was held that there *had* been unfair discrimination, since there was no evidence that taking inside leg measurements was a vital and frequent requirement of the job. Many men know their own measurements anyway, and there are in any case many other ways of arriving at a correct measurement. In addition, there would be many male colleagues to assist if necessary. W, was awarded compensation of £30, being two week's net wages.

Quite apart from protection against direct discrimination, women are now also protected from indirect discrimination arising from pregnancy, and these maternity rights are dealt with on page 125, below.

Racial discrimination

Under the Race Relations Act 1976, s. 4, it is unlawful for an employer to "discriminate" against any potential employee or job applicant on the grounds of his colour, race, nationality or ethnic or national origins (referred to in the Act collectively as "racial grounds"). Once a person is in employment, section 4 of the Act makes it equally unlawful to discriminate on racial grounds in matters such as the conditions of employment, opportunities for promotion, transfer or training, or the benefits, facilities or services normally made available to such employees. Section 4 of the Act also renders it unlawful to discriminate against a person on racial grounds in the matter of dismissal or other disciplinary action.

"Discrimination" is defined as treating a person less favourably than another person would be treated, and includes the imposition of conditions which because of his racial origins that person is less likely to be able to fulfil, and which cannot be justified on any but racial grounds.

An interesting case in this connection was *Singh* v. *Rowntree Mackintosh Ltd* (1979), in which a Sikh applied for a job in an Edinburgh sweet factory in which there was a strict rule against wearing beards in any process involving contact with the product. He would have got the job had he been prepared to shave off his beard, but he refused on religious grounds, and claimed that there had been "indirect" discrimination under the 1976 Act in that fewer Sikhs than non-Sikhs can comply with that condition. The tribunal held that since the use of a face mask would not have been a reasonable alternative to being clean-shaven, the rule, although discriminatory, was justified on the grounds of hygiene, and not merely racial discrimination.

The provisions of the 1976 Act, it will be noticed, are remarkably similar in style to those of the 1975 Act, outlined above, which deals with discrimination on sexual grounds in the field of employment, and in fact the 1976 Act was modelled on the 1975 Act.

Section 5 of the 1976 Act establishes an exception to section 4 where being a member of a particular racial group is a "genuine occupational qualification." The examples quoted in section 5 as being the *only* permitted cases include authenticity in entertainment, modelling work, racial welfare, and, most significantly for present purposes, working in a place where food and drink is provided for the public in a particular "setting" where the authenticity of staff is important. Obvious examples of the latter are Chinese and Indian restaurants.

Two other points are worthy of note. The first is that section 6 of the Act provides an exception to section 4 where a worker is being trained in Great Britain who is not ordinarily resident in Great Britain, and who will ultimately be employed outside Great Britain; the same is true of staff employed in a private household, except where the discrimination takes the form of "victimisation" because the employee has brought a complaint under the Act. The second point is that the provisions of section 4 are now also applicable to workers not directly employed by the employer, but hired through an agency; it is now just as unlawful for a proprietor to discriminate in terms of working conditions, etc., against staff hired to him by an agency as it would be for the employer to discriminate against his own direct employees. At the same time, an employer may "positively" discriminate in order to improve the racial balance in a particular job.

Complaints under the 1976 Act are normally brought before an industrial tribunal, and, as with sexual discrimination, there may first be an attempt by a conciliation officer to effect an amicable settlement without recourse to a tribunal. If a tribunal is satisfied that a complaint is genuine, it may make exactly the same type of order as it may in the case of sexual discrimination. The Commission for Racial Equality may also issue "non-discrimination" notices which are enforcible by the courts.

An example of the law in practice was the case of *Race Relations Board* v. *Mecca* (1976), brought under the equivalent provisions of the old Race Relations Act 1968, in which a woman, applying for the post of buffet assistant, telephoned the catering manager of the defendant company and asked "if it would make any difference if she were coloured." The manager replied that it would, and rang off. The lady was awarded £73 damages and costs.

Guarantee payments

EPCA, ss. 12–18 grants the right to "guarantee payment" to any employee who suffers a "workless day," that is, a day or part of a day in which that employee would normally be required to work in accordance with his contract of employment, but is not provided with work because of a diminution in the work available from the employer, which in turn is due to a diminution in the amount of business being done by the employer, or is caused by any other occurrence which affects the normal working of the employer's business so far as the type of work undertaken by that employee is concerned.

Guarantee payment is calculated on an hourly basis (*i.e.* one week's pay divided by the number of normal working hours per week). Using this formula, the employee is entitled to one hour's guarantee payment for every "workless" hour, up to a limit of £10.90 per day. An employee can only claim for up to a maximum of five "workless" days in any three-month period. Thus, the maximum claim by any one single worker for any three-month period will be £54.50.

For obvious reasons, the Act states that no guarantee payment may be claimed where the unavailability of work is due to an industrial dispute involving the employer or an associated employer, nor may any claim be made where the employer has offered "suitable" alternative work, and it has been unreasonably refused, nor where the employee does not comply with reasonable requirements imposed by the employer to ensure that his services are available.

In *Meadows* v. *Faithful Overalls* (1977), for example, Mrs. M was employed as a machinist at the company's premises, and arrived for work one morning in February to find that all the central heating was off due to lack of oil, and that the temperature was considerably less than the statutory minimum. M was also the shop steward, and she advised the management at 9 a.m. that the girls were talking about going home. The usual arrangement when this sort of thing happened was that the staff were supplied with hot tea in the canteen, and were paid the basic rate for the time missed (piece rate being the normal rate). On this occasion, the staff were asked to wait until 9.30 a.m., and then 9.45 a.m., and were then advised that the central heating oil was expected at 10 a.m. They were also warned that they might not receive any wages if they left at 9.45 a.m., but they nevertheless left, and were now claiming a guarantee payment for the day in question. It was held that by leaving the factory when they did, the staff had failed to comply with a reasonable requirement of the employer to ensure that their services were available, and were not therefore entitled to guarantee payments.

Certain employees are exempted from the right to guarantee payments. These are employees who have worked for the employer for less than four weeks, employees who are the husbands or wives of their employers, and employees who normally work for less than 16 hours per week. Where the employee has worked for the same employer for a continuous period of five years or more, this is reduced to eight hours per week.

Disputes concerning guarantee payments are heard by an industrial tribunal, which has the power to vary the amount payable, and to order the payment to be made. Payments are, of course, made by the employer.

Right to payment while suspended on medical grounds

By virtue of EPCA, ss. 19–22, an employee who is suspended by his employer on medical grounds in consequence of any requirement imposed under any Act of Parliament or Statutory Instrument, or in consequence of any recommendation in any Code of Practice issued or approved under the Health and Safety at Work etc. Act 1974, is entitled to payment during such suspension for a period not exceeding 26 weeks.

The entitlement is to a "normal" week's pay, being the wage he would normally receive if he worked his "normal" hours. A "suspension" only occurs where the employee in question is not provided either with the work he normally does or with suitable alternative work. The right to payment also only applies to employees who have been continuously employed for at least four weeks, and no payment need be made where the worker is actually incapable of work by reason of physical or mental illness, or does not make himself reasonably available for work. No claim may be made by an employee who is the husband or wife of the employer, nor by any employee who is employed for less than 16 hours per week (eight hours per week after five years).

This section is clearly intended to cover the situation in which the employer is ordered to curtail operations, or close down altogether, in work areas in which employees would otherwise be "at risk" and is an attempt to cushion the employee against any artificial "layoff" which may result.

Maternity rights

In keeping with the general tenor of the Sex Discrimination Act 1975, the provisions of various sections of EPCA and the Employment Act 1980, set out to ensure that a female employee, on becoming pregnant, is not unduly prejudiced so far as her employment prospects are concerned. The Acts in fact deal with four distinct matters; (a) the right to seek ante-natal advice during working hours; (b) the right to maternity payment from the employer; (c) the right not to be dismissed because of pregnancy; (d) the right to reinstatement following confinement.

The right to make ante-natal visits

Under the terms of the Employment Act, 1980, an employee who is pregnant (or suspects that she is) is entitled to "reasonable" time off with pay in order to make ante-natal visits. She may be required by her employer to produce documentary confirmation of the date of the visit, and the fact that she is pregnant. All employees are entitled to this time off, regardless of their length of service, and may complain to an industrial tribunal if they do not receive it.

Maternity payment from the employer

An employee who is absent from work wholly or partly because of pregnancy or confinement is entitled under the Maternity Pay Scheme to statutory maternity payment (SMP) from her employer for a period not exceeding six weeks at the "higher rate" of $\frac{9}{10}$ of a "normal" week's pay and thereafter at the "lower rate" fixed by Regulations for a further twelve weeks. In order to qualify for the higher rate, however, she must have been employed by that employer for a continuous period of two years or more up to and including the "qualifying week" (which is the 15th week before the expected week of her confinement"), she must remain in employment with the employer until that week, and she must inform her employer at least three weeks before her absence, or as soon as reasonably practicable thereafter, that she will be absent through pregnancy. Staff who normally work for between 8 and 16 hours per week can claim after 5 years. An employee who has worked for at least 6 months up to and including the qualifying week is entitled to 18 weeks at the lower rate of SMP. In all cases, in order to qualify for SMP, the employee must earn above the "lower earning's limit" for National Insurance liability, which is £38 per week. Provided that the employee is otherwise qualified as above, she can apparently still claim the maternity payment if she has been legitimately dismissed for the reasons outlined below. In all cases, an appropriate medical certificate is required.

The right to payment is, of course, only for such periods as the employee is actually off work for reasons connected with her pregnancy, and cannot be claimed before the start of the eleventh week before the expected week of confinement. The two years' continuous employment required in order to qualify for maternity payment will not include any week in respect of which the employee worked normally for less than 16 hours (eight hours after five years).

The payment of maternity payment is made initially by the employer, who is then entitled to recover it from his overall liability to the Inland Revenue in respect of National Insurance contributions (see Chap. 10). Where the employee has taken all reasonable steps to acquire maternity pay from her employer, and failed, or if the employer is insolvent, she may secure payment directly from the DHSS who may then seek by legal means to secure reimbursement from the employer.

Dismissal due to pregnancy

It will be regarded as "unfair dismissal" for an employer to dismiss an employee for any reason connected with her pregnancy other than (a) that she is, by virtue of her pregnancy, incapable of doing the job which she was employed to do; or (b) that by remaining at work in her condition, she would be contravening some statute or other enactment.

Even where the grounds for dismissal are as above, she will still be regarded as having been unfairly dismissed if she is not offered a new contract before the termination of her employment, designed to take effect upon the expiry of the old contract, and which entitles her to work which is suitable for her, taking into account her previous employment and her current condition, and which is not substantially less favourable to her than the previous contract in terms of conditions of employment. The obligation on the employer to offer such a new contract is only applicable where there is a suitable vacancy for her, and the employee cannot claim a new contract unless she has worked for the employer for a continuous period of at least 52 weeks at a minimum of 16 hours per week.

Reinstatement following confinement

A female employee with at least two years' continuous service at a minimum of 16 hours per week is entitled, upon leaving for her confinement, to require that her job be held open for her return. She must, in order to qualify for this right, give notice to her employer of her intention to return, this notice being given along with her notice to the employer that she will be leaving for reasons of pregnancy (*i.e.* the notice given at least three weeks before she actually leaves), and again at least three weeks before her intended return, at some time before the end of the 29 week period beginning with the week of her confinement.

Alternatively, the employer has the right to ask her to confirm her intention to return to work by writing to her at any time after the 49th day following the predicted or actual date of the birth. If the employee does not confirm her intention of returning by writing to the employer within 14 days, or as soon as is reasonably practicable thereafter, she will lose the right to return.

She is entitled to return to the same job, on terms and conditions no less favourable than they would have been if she had not been absent—in other words, she apparently does not lose even her seniority. If her job has disappeared in the meantime, for genuine reasons of redundancy or if it is not "reasonably practicable" for the employer to offer her back her exact original job, she is entitled to a suitable alternative job when a vacancy arises. "Suitability" is judged by the same criteria as in (c) above.

When the employer receives the employee's notice of intention to return, he may delay that return by four more weeks for reasons specified in writing, provided that he then gives her a firm starting date. The employee herself may postpone her return from the twenty-ninth to the thirty-third week upon the production of a suitable medical certificate.

If, following her return from pregnancy, the employee is denied reinstatement by the employer, she may claim either redundancy pay or damages for unfair dismissal. If the employer has engaged a replacement for the pregnant employee, and has made it clear to the replacement at the time of her engagement that the post is temporary, then he will not be liable for unfair dismissal if he dismisses the temporary employee upon the return of the original one.

Where, prior to her absence, the employer employed five or less staff, and it is not "reasonably practicable" for him to permit her to return to work, and he has no "appropriate" alternative work to offer her, then the employee has no right to claim for failure to reinstate or re-employ her. This is the effect of the Employment Act, 1980.

Time off for trade union duties

Sections 27 and 28 of EPCA, lay down certain provisions concerning an employee's right to time off from his employment for certain matters connected with trade unions. Those rights may be considered as follows:

Trade union duties

By virtue of section 27 of the Act, any employee who is an official of an independent trade union recognised by the employer must be allowed time off by that employer during his normal working hours, in order to allow him (i) to carry out any union duties concerned with industrial relations between his employer and any associated employer, and their employees, or (ii) to undergo training in aspects of industrial relations relevant to those duties, or approved by the TUC or the union of which he is an official.

The actual hours to be allowed off are left by the Act as a matter to be dealt with in an appropriate Code of Practice, but the current Code, effective as from April 1, 1978, merely states that the time off must be "reasonable" in the circumstances, and makes no effort to give guidance as to how much time off must actually be allowed, which is still therefore a matter for individual negotiation.

The time off must be "with pay."

Trade union activities

Section 28 of the Act permits employees who are ordinary members of a trade union recognised by the employer to take time off from work for trade union activities short of actual industrial action; this right extends to activities in which the employee is acting as a representative of his union. Once again, the matter is governed by the

Code of Practice, which offers no practical guidance on what is "reasonable" in terms of time off.

There is no right to payment for time off under section 28.

Time off for public duties

Where an employee has certain public duties to perform, section 29 of the Act states that the employer shall permit him time off from work in order that he may perform those duties. The main public duties involved are those carried out by magistrates, local councillors, and members of tribunals, health authorities, educational governing bodies and water authorities.

Once again, the time allowed off need only be "reasonable in all the circumstances," and once again, no practical guidance is offered on the matter from any official source. The employer is not obliged to pay the employee during his time off.

Unjustified refusals to permit time off under sections 27–29 are matters which may be taken before an appropriate industrial tribunal.

Statutory Sick Pay

Since 1983, most employees have been entitled to payment of Statutory Sick Pay (SSP) from their employers if they are off work through illness, however caused. Since April 6, 1986, this entitlement has been extended to a total of 28 weeks, and SSP replaces the old sickness benefit formerly payable directly to the DHSS. The main exemptions from the scheme are persons over the State retirement age (65/60), staff who earn less than the national insurance "lower earnings limit" (£38 per week at the time of writing) and staff within the "qualifying period" for claiming Statutory Maternity Payment see p. 126 above).

Such payments are at one of three rates (Standard, Middle and Lower rates), which are fixed by reference to the employee's normal average earnings, and the rates for 1987/8 were £46.75 standard (earnings of £74.50 per week or more), £39.20 middle (£55.50 to £74.49) and £31.60 lower (£38 to £55.49).

The "daily rate" of SSP to be paid in respect of each day of sickness is then calculated by dividing the appropriate weekly rate by the number of days in respect of which SSP is being paid (the "qualifying days"). Before an employee is entitled to SSP, he or she must suffer a minimum of four consecutive days of sickness, but this period may include Sundays and holidays. The first three of these days ("waiting days") do not qualify for payment of SSP, and payment therefore begins on, and in respect of, the fourth day. It is for the employer to satisfy himself as to whether or not the employee qualifies as having been off sick.

"Periods of incapacity for work" (PIWs) may be linked together if they are separated by periods of work of eight weeks or less, so that, in respect of the second period, the waiting days do not have to be observed, but payment of SSP can commence immediately. The employer having paid SSP to an employee, may reimburse himself by withholding from the Inland Revenue an appropriate amount from the money due by him in respect of national insurance contributions.

4. The duties of an employer at common law

Much has been written in this chapter about the duties which have been imposed upon the employer by statute, much of it recent. However, we must not lose sight of the fact that an employer owes considerable duties at common law, not only to the employee, but also to third parties.

Duties owed to the employee

At common law, the employer owes his employees an important duty in respect of safety. The employer may well be legally liable for any illness or injury sustained by the employee during the course of his carrying out his duties, if it is held that the illness or injury was due to a failure on the part of the employer to fulfil the "duty of care" which he owes to the employee at common law.

First of all, he must provide a safe place of work; this entails ensuring not only that the structure is safe and healthy, that the electrical wiring is properly maintained and so forth, but also that the floors are kept dry and free from obstruction, that emergency exits are kept clear, and that guards and stair rails are secure. Although such safety precautions need only be reasonable in the circumstances, it follows that the greater the risk, the greater must be the efforts to prevent accidents.

In addition to providing a safe place of work, the employer must also supply safe machinery and equipment by which to do such work; to this may be linked the duty of providing a safe system by which to do the work. One serious problem so far as the employee is concerned has been removed. Very often, when an employee claimed damages for injuries caused through defective equipment the employer was able to claim the defence that the defect arose from manufacture rather than from inadequate maintenance. In many cases, therefore, the employee was left with a choice between giving up any claim to compensation, or attempting to sue the manufacturer, often a formidable task.

The effect of the Employer's Liability (Defective Equipment) Act

1969, is to place initial liability for defective equipment, whatever the defect, firmly on the employer, who must pay damages to the employee regardless. It is then up to the employer to sue the manufacturer, if he feels that he has a claim.

Finally, the employer owes a duty to his employee to provide him with competent colleagues. If one employee through his negligence in the course of his duties injures another employee, the injured party may sue the employer for damages. The employer is said to be "vicariously" liable for the negligence of his employee, although, as noted above, he may claim an indemnity from him—see *Lister* v. *Romford Ice and Cold Storage Co. Ltd.* on page 116, above. However, the employer will not be liable where the act is not committed in the course of the man's employment, or where the act is deliberate (as distinct from negligent), unless it may be argued that the employer was negligent in employing such a man.

It should be noted in conclusion that the employer is only expected to take reasonable precautions for the employee's safety, and that the injury in respect of which the employee claims must be one which is a direct and foreseeable result of the employer's failure to take care. If the employee is himself partly to blame for what happened to him (that is, if he was "contributorily negligent"), then the amount of damages will be reduced accordingly. But the courts are very loath to hold that an employee "volunteered" to undertake the risk of injury, and some damages are nearly always paid.

In the course of this book, reference is made to Acts of Parliament such as the Health and Safety at Work etc. Act 1974, and the Offices, Shops and Railway Premises Act 1963, which have placed statutory duties on the employer in connection with the safety of his employees. Two points should, however, be kept carefully in mind when referring to these statutes. The first is that, on the whole, their effect is to render the employer liable to *criminal* sanctions (*e.g.* a fine) if he fails to comply with their provisions, whereas a breach of the common law duties outlined above will normally expose the employer to an action for damages by the employee. The second point is that even if an action or omission by an employer is not unlawful by virtue of any of these Acts, it may still, at common law, constitute a failure on the part of the employer to fulfil his duty of safety to the employee.

To complicate matters, however, there is always the possibility that an employee may claim damages at common law for a failure on the part of his employer to carry out some duty owed to him under statute. A recent example of this process in practice was *Black* v. *Carricks (Caterers) Ltd* (1980), in which the manageress of a bakery shop arrived at work one day to find all her staff off due to illness. She telephoned Head Office, and was told to do "as best she could"; in particular, if she needed to move anything heavy, she was to ask a customer to help her. In attempting to move a tray full of bread by herself, she slipped a disc, and she claimed damages from her employers on the ground that they had been in breach of that provision of the Offices, Shops and Railway Premises Act 1963, which states that no employee shall be "required" to lift any weight which is too heavy for him. It was held that she could not claim, since she had not been "required" to lift the tray (in the sense of "left with no adequate alternative"). Nor could she claim for simple negligence at common law because, in view of the instructions which she had been given, it was not "reasonably foreseeable" that she would be injured in the way she had.

Duties owed to third parties

An employer is "vicariously" liable for all acts of negligence committed by his employees in the course of their duties which cause loss or injury to third parties. The injured third party may, of course, choose to sue the employee himself, but there are obvious advantages in suing the employer, who may then claim an indemnity from the employee.

Negligence

Before the employer may be sued, however, the acts complained of must have been committed in the course of the employee's duties. Thus, the employer will normally be liable for loss or injury to guests in the dining room where a careless waiter causes a fire through his misuse of a spirit lamp; he will not, however, be liable in the case of a fire started by a hall porter in the kitchen, since the latter has no reason to be there working during the normal course of his duties, and no right to be using any equipment. However, he may find himself directly liable if he has been personally negligent in allowing the hall porter to go into the kitchen or to use the equipment.

Once an employee *is* acting within the scope of his normal employment, the employer will still be liable for his actions even if he is disobeying strict instructions; thus, in *Stone* v. *Taffe* (1974), a licensee, an employee of a brewery, allowed drinking after hours, contrary to his employer's normal policy, and a man was injured as he descended the stairs, which were unlit, at one a.m. His widow successfully sued the brewery for damages for negligence arising from the unlit stair, even though at that time in the morning, the licensee was disobeying orders by allowing drinking to continue.

The employer will not be liable for deliberate acts of the employee, unless they were carried out at his express instruction, or unless it may be argued that the employer himself was negligent in allowing a man with such tendencies to remain on the staff. The fact that the employer did not know of the man's nature will be of no defence to him if the court decides that he should have known.

Contract

Whenever an employee is given the authority to act as his employer's agent, then the employer will be liable in contract to any third party with whom that employee negotiates in the exercise of that authority. Whether or not an employee may be said to be the agent of his employer is a question of fact to be answered in each individual case. Clearly he will be where that authority is expressly given, or where he may be implied to be (as where a barman is left to order new stock for the bar). An employee may also be regarded as the agent of his employer where the latter has allowed third parties to form that opinion. The law is concerned solely with protecting the interests of the third party in such a case; thus, where the employer has allowed one man to act as his agent for years, he cannot expect to change that situation without giving regular suppliers some warning. Further information on this point may be found in the section on agency in Chapter 2.

Crime

As a general rule, an employer cannot be made liable for the criminal acts of his employees, unless he is a party to them, or unless he fails to prevent them when he possesses the opportunity. There are, however, certain exceptions to this rule. Thus, the employer will be liable when his employee commits a public nuisance, such as allowing large quantities of smoke or strong cooking smells to be emitted from the building. In addition, certain Acts of Parliament have rendered the employer liable for certain crimes, even though they were actually committed by an employee. Several good examples of this practice may be found in the chapter on the conduct of licensed premises.

Also, of course, the employer may be liable for negligence where he employs a man who later commits a crime in the course of his duties. Thus, if a floor waiter steals valuables from a guest, that guest may be able to sue the hotelier, if he can prove that the latter was negligent in employing a man with such dishonest leanings.

An interesting case in this context was *Daniels* v. *Whetstone Entertainments Ltd.* (1962), in which a "bouncer" in a dance hall assaulted D because he thought, wrongly, that he had assaulted him. He was told by the management to leave him alone, but followed him outside and assaulted him again. It was held that the employer was liable to pay damages in respect of the first assault, since the steward was authorised to use force if necessary to keep order, but not the second, since the steward had then been pursuing a personal grievance.

CHAPTER TEN

Wages

WAGES fall due for payment at the time and the place stipulated in the contract of employment, and this is often the last day of the wage period. The contract may, however, stipulate that payment be made after the end of the wage period, and this is perfectly lawful. The period between the end of the wage period and the date of payment is known as "lying time," and it allows the employer time in which to calculate the employee's wages in full (*e.g.* taking into account overtime).

It depends upon the terms of the contract whether or not payment will be made for odd days worked during the wage period, and whether the employee is required to work for the whole of that period (unless absent through illness or excused) before he is entitled to any payment at all. The general principle in the absence of any such contractual term is that payment should be made for every day worked.

Successive governments have, over the years, passed many statutes dealing with the payment of wages, the size of wages and deductions from wages. It is the purpose of this chapter to examine the more important of these in detail.

1. The Wages Act 1986

The Wages Councils Act 1979 was passed in order to consolidate certain previous statutes concerning the control of minimum wage rates in certain industries; among them was the Catering Wages Act 1943, which until 1959 dealt with wage rates in the catering industry. The 1979 Act is a clear example of a statute which restricts the freedom of the parties to a contract of employment to negotiate their own terms.

Under the Act, power was given to the Secretary of State to establish a wages council for the benefit of employees within a given trade or industry in three circumstances: (i) where there was no adequate machinery for the effective negotiation of minimum wage rates; (ii) where a commission of inquiry had recommended to the Secretary of State that a wages council be established for a particular industry; (iii) where it was believed that existing negotiating machinery would soon become inadequate. Today, there are various wages councils in existence for many employees in the hotel and catering industry with the exception of those who work in unlicensed hotels, boarding-houses and holiday camps; schools, hospitals and universities; and industrial and staff canteens. However the effect of the Wages Act 1986 is that no new wages councils may be established, the procedure for the abolition of wages councils has been simplified and the matters covered by a Wages Council Order have been reduced, leaving the way clear for more open collective bargaining, and in particular the setting up of Joint Industrial Councils to replace Wage Councils.

Wages councils are made up as follows; (i) not more than three persons chosen by the Secretary of State as independent experts, two of whom assume the roles of chairman and deputy chairman; (ii) such number as the Secretary of State shall see fit of persons representing the workers covered by the wages council; (iii) such number as the Secretary of State shall see fit of persons representing the employers covered by the wages council.

The wages councils submit proposals to the Secretary of State on the question of wage rates, hours of work and overtime rates. They are no longer empowered to determine rest days and holidays for the workers in their industry, but such holidays as workers enjoyed prior to the 1986 Act are preserved by Regulations and by the normal laws of contract. The Secretary of State then circulates these proposals throughout the industry, for comments and suggestions from both employers and employees. The proposals, plus any amendments, then become law in the form of a *Wages Council Order* published by the Secretary of State as a statutory instrument, coming into force on the date set by him. It may not be backdated. After 1986, no wage order may cover staff under 21 who are therefore not protected by wages councils at all.

All employers in that area of an industry covered by a new Wages Order are legally obliged to observe it; the new wage rates, operate as a compulsory change in the terms of the contract of employment, and all employees covered by the Order are entitled to receive the new minimum figures as from the commencement date of the Order. In the case of those who, even after the change, are receiving more than the minimum, there is no legal obligation on the part of the employer to pay more. Any employer who fails to comply with the new minimum requirements at once may be punished with a fine of £400, and can be ordered to pay arrears of wages for up to two years. Alternatively, the employee may sue for these arrears.

The minimum wage figure laid down for a particular employee under a Wages Order represents the *minimum gross wage* which the employer is legally obliged to pay personally to the employee *in cash*. Only certain deductions may be made from this gross wage, namely (i) income tax; (ii) national insurance; (iii) deductions authorised by the Wages Act 1986; (iv) deductions requested by the employee in writing. These are all dealt with later in the chapter.

One question which arises is that of staff gratuities from guests and customers. The position would appear to be that any "tips" received directly by the employee from the guest are his property, and cannot be counted towards the basic wage. Equally, the service charge levied by the employer is the property of the employer, and may be used as part of the minimum wage. The problem of the service charge in lieu of gratuities has yet to be resolved.

Inspectors have been appointed in order to ensure that the provisions of the 1986 Act, and those of the Wage Orders made under the Act, are complied with. Every inspector carries a certificate bearing his authority, and can be called upon to produce it. His powers are considerable; he may (i) enter any premises covered by a Wages Order, at any reasonable time, and interview the employees on relevant matters; (ii) question employers concerning matters dealt with by the Wages Order; (iii) inspect those books and records which the employer is required by the Act to keep. Failure to comply with any such requests by an inspector, or the making of any false statement to an inspector, is punishable with a fine, which may be as high as £2000. In addition, under a new system introduced under the Employment Protection Act 1975, employers may be required to complete questionnaires on matters covered by the Inspectorate.

As stated above, employers who have staff who are covered by a Wages Order must keep adequate records to show that they have complied with the Order, and such records must be kept for a period of three years. In addition, employers must display all notices issued by the Secretary of State or the wages council. Failure to comply with any of these requirements may result in a fine of £400, or imprisonment.

An employer who has on his staff an employee who is covered by a Wages Order but who, by reason of some infirmity, is unable to work in such a way as to earn the statutory minimum, may apply to the wages council for a certificate which entitles him to pay a specified lower minimum wage to that person.

We may now examine in more detail those wages councils which legislate for the hotel and catering industry.

The Unlicensed Place of Refreshment Wages Council (UPR)

The UPR Wages Council regulates the minimum rates of pay of those who are employed in the preparation or service of food and drink, or any work incidental to such preparation or service, in unlicensed restaurants, cafés, coffee bars, etc. It includes those who are employed to provide food, drink or sleeping accommodation for the staff of such premises, and it includes those who are employed by catering firms which specialise in contract work. It does not, however, cover those who are employed by the Crown or by a local authority, or those who work in hostels, holiday camps, hotels, boarding-houses, hospitals, nursing homes, schools, universities, colleges, railway refreshment units, places of public entertainment (except where it is part of the employer's contract business), and industrial and staff canteens.

The latest Wages Order to be produced by the UPR Wages Council came into force on June 13, 1987. Its main provisions are a basic working week of 39 hours and a basic wage of £2.10 per hour. After 39 hours have been worked in any one week an overtime rate of £3.15 per hour is payable for all subsequent hours.

These figures are *reduced* by a set amount where the worker is supplied with acccommodation, and further deductions may be made for the provision of food and drink. These are not fixed under the Order.

The Licensed Non-Residential Establishment Wages Council (LNR)

The LNR Wages Council regulates the minimum rates of pay, holidays, etc., of those who are employed in the preparation or service of food and drink, any work incidental to such preparation or service, any work connected with the provision of living accommodation, or any work connected with the retail sale of goods, in any establishment which is licensed for the sale of liquor, but which is not residential (*i.e.* it has less than four bedrooms normally available for guests). It thus covers staff employed in public-houses and clubs, but not hotels and holiday camps. It also excludes staff employed by the Crown, and staff in industrial and staff canteens, theatres, music halls and railway refreshment units.

The latest Order came into force on January 15, 1988.

The basic working week is 39 hours and the basic rates for this period are £2.16 per hour, with £3.24 payable for every hour worked over 39 in any one week. Staff who receive free living accommodation may have a maximum of £1.32 per day deducted from the last wage paid to them, with additional deductions in respect of the provision of free food and drink. These are not fixed under the Order.

The Licensed Residential Establishment and Licensed Restaurant Wages Council (LR)

The LR Wages Council regulates the minimum rates of pay, holidays, etc., of those who are employed in the service or preparation of food and drink, any work incidental to such preparation or service, the provision of living accommodation, the retail sale of goods, office-work, or any work reasonably connected with any other service or amenity, on any premises which are licensed for the sale of liquor, and which are either *residential* (*i.e.* four or more bedrooms normally available for guests) or used as a *restaurant*.

The Council thus covers licensed holiday camps, licensed hostels, and licensed railway refreshment buffets. It excludes hospitals, schools, etc., staff employed on railway trains, in theatres or music halls, and staff employed by catering contractors.

The latest wages Order to be produced by the LR Wages Council came into force on November 1, 1987. Its main provision is a basic wage of £2.00 per hour for a 39 hour week, and an hourly rate of £3 for every hour worked thereafter.

£2.15 per day may be deducted in respect of the provision of free living accommodation and additional amounts in respect of food and drink supplied; these are not fixed under the Order.

2. Deductions from wages

When introducing the Wages Act 1986, above, reference was made to the fact that the minimum rates specified in a Wages Council Order could only be reduced by way of certain authorised deductions. These are dealt with under the 1986 Act. Under this Act, all workers are protected from unfair or unlawful deductions from their wages, the only exceptions being merchant seamen and persons ordinarily working outside Great Britain. The provisions which used to apply under the Truck Acts, by means of which restrictions were placed on the method by which wages could be paid (cash, kind, cheque etc.) are not replaced under the 1986 Act (which itself replaces the Truck Acts) and the the method of payment is therefore a matter for agreement between employer and employee.

The main effect of the 1986 Act is that henceforth no worker may suffer deductions from the gross wage payable to him, either under contract or by virtue of a Wages Council Order, unless it is either authorised by statute, or covered by a contractual provision or a written agreement between employer and employee. Into the first category (authorised by statute) come items such as income tax, national insurance and attachment of earnings orders, the first two of which are considered later in this chapter.

So far as concerns written agreements between employer and employee, this will cover the situation in which the employer deducts sums to be paid to third parties at the request of the worker (*e.g.* subscriptions to a social club organised by the employees of the company). In *Hewlett* v. *Allen* (1894), these were held by the House of Lords to be perfectly lawful, and in the more recent case of *Williams* v. *Butlers* (1975) it was held that it is not illegal to deduct subscriptions to a trade union.

The most contentious area, however, concerns those situations in which an employer may, as a term of the contract of employment, deduct money from wages by way of "fines" for incidents such as stock losses and breakages. Before such an arrangement will be valid the employer must have given the employee notice of its terms in writing (*e.g.* in a disciplinary code to which he is referred), and in cases in which the employee is employed in "retail employment" (*i.e.* the sale or supply of goods or services to the public, to fellow workers or to "other individuals in their personal capacities") there are additional restrictions on deductions by way of fines. These are obviously of considerable importance to staff in the catering industry, and the effect of the special provisions is that

1. In the case of fines in respect of stock shortages and/or stock deficiencies, the deductions must be made within twelve months of the date when the shortage or deficiency was discovered, or ought reasonably to have been;
2. No fine or deduction may exceed 10 per cent. of the gross wage on any one pay day. This does not prevent the employer from reclaiming the whole loss eventually—it simply prevents him from doing so all at once.
3. The employer must give the employee prior written notice of his total liability to him in respect of the shortage or deficiency and must follow that up with a written demand for payment on a pay day on or before the first deduction.

In non-retail cases, there appears to be no limit on the amount of wages which may be deducted.

Where the employee leaves his employment, for whatever reason, without the full amount outstanding having been deducted from wages, the 10 per cent. limit is lifted, to allow the employer to recover as much as possible or necessary from the money still due to him by the employee.

Enforcement of the provisions of the 1986 Act is initially carried out by Wages Inspectors, with the possibility of an action being taken before an industrial tribunal for any necessary repayment or compensation to an aggrieved worker. It remains to be seen to what extent industrial tribunals will follow rulings under the old pre-1986 Truck Acts, in which certain types of fine were held to be unlawful. Thus in *Bristow* v. *City Petroleum* (1987), a case which arose before the 1986 Act became law, it was held to be unlawful to fine a petrol forecourt attendant for losses occurring on his shift regardless of whether or not they were his fault, even though he had signed an agreement to that effect, while in *Riley* v. *Joseph Frisby* (1982) it was held, on similar facts, to be unlawful to "charge" a shop manageress the full retail value of stock lost, quite apart from the question of whether or not the loss was her fault.

3. Income Tax

Everyone who is employed under a contract of service, and who earns more than a certain fixed amount, must pay income tax. Today, this payment is made by means of the PAYE system, which means that the amount of tax owing to the Inland Revenue by the employee is deducted at source from gross wages. It is the employer's duty to organise this deduction, so that he is in effect a tax collector for the government. Such a duty involves considerable paperwork, and depends upon efficiency in the wages office. The basic outlines of an employer's duty under PAYE are given below; further information may be obtained from the Government publication *Employer's Guide to Pay as You Earn*.

Before April 6 every year, the employer will be sent annual deduction cards or code lists for every one of his employees who is known to be taxable on his income. At the same time, the employer will receive tax tables for the year, and form P24, which gives him formal notice of his duties under the PAYE system. The employer's first task is then to enter the employee's national insurance number on the appropriate deduction card.

The actual weekly or monthly deduction of tax is calculated as follows. The employer begins by calculating gross wages paid so far during the tax year beginning on April 6 last. This gross wage figure should include all bonuses, commissions, overtime, holiday pay and gratuities, but not (in most cases) expense reimbursements, board and lodging or rent-free accommodation (when it is essential for the carrying out of the employee's job), meal vouchers, payment in lieu of notice and redundancy payments (up to a certain amount which changes periodically with the Budget).

To this gross wage figure, the employer applies the worker's own code number (supplied by the Inland Revenue), in order to ascertain how much of the worker's gross wage to date is tax free. By deducting this sum from the gross wage figure, the employer arrives at the net taxable income so far during the tax year. From this figure is deducted the amount of tax already paid during previous wage periods, and the amount remaining (tax payable) is the amount to be deducted from gross wages for this wage period. If the figure arrived at is a negative one, then a tax refund is payable.

These figures must be carefully recorded in the appropriate columns of the deduction card, unless the employer has arranged with the Inland Revenue to use his own wage records for the purpose, in which case the deduction cards need only be used for annual totals. The worker, of course, receives a copy of these figures in his normal wage slip (see below).

Before April 19 of each year, the employer is obliged to fill in form P35 (the annual declaration and certificate), and send it, along with the deduction cards, to the Inland Revenue. At the same time, the employee should be sent form P60, which, like the completed deduction cards, shows the annual totals for gross salary, tax payable, tax deducted, National Insurance paid, and any additional items. At the end of his employment, the employee should also receive form P45, which gives the same information for the whole period of his employment.

The total amount of tax deducted, less any refunds, should be sent for payment to the Inland Revenue within 14 days of the end of the tax month; this payment should be accompanied by a special payslip issued by the Inland Revenue. Payment for National Insurance contributions (see below) should also be made.

4. National Insurance

In addition to his duty to deduct Income Tax at source from the employee's wages, the employer must also ensure that on behalf of each of his employees (with very few exceptions), a deduction is made in respect of National Insurance. Since National Insurance contributions are the main method by which the Government finances areas of the Welfare State such as unemployment benefit, redundancy payments and maternity benefit, the latter is of the greatest practical importance, and the modern system entails a contribution by both the employer and the employee, the employer thereafter deducting the employee's share from his wages.

National insurance contributions are now collected by a single comprehensive percentage method. The contribution is a fixed percentage of the worker's "gross pay" (*i.e.* before the deduction of tax), eventually reaching a "ceiling" at a gross wage level which changes from time to time, but which at August 1, 1987, stood at £285 per week.

The deduction is actually made by the employer, and it is now simply one more deduction to be made when completing the weekly tax and wage forms. Contribution Tables advise the employer how much to deduct for the *whole* payment (to be remitted to the Inland Revenue along with the income tax remittance in the normal way), and how much of that total to reclaim from the employee via his wage packet; the balance is, of course, the amount payable by the employer.

The only exceptions, other than those for staff earning a gross wage below the "threshold," are in the case of staff under 16 years old (for whom no payments are made at all), persons "treated as retired" although still in employment (for whom the employer *alone* makes a contribution) and married women and widows paying a "reduced rate" contribution. Certificates of "non-liability" or "reduced liability" are required from the DHSS before any of these exceptions may be operated, and the Contribution Tables make the necessary allowances.

5. Itemised payment statement

Before leaving the topic of deductions from wages, it should be noted that the Employment Protection (Consolidation) Act, 1978, s. 8, states that every employee has the right to demand from his employer, at the time of the payment of his wages or salary, an "itemised pay statement" in writing, specifying

1. The amount of the gross wage or salary
2. The amounts of any variable and fixed deductions from that gross amount, and the reason(s) for which they are made
3. The net amount of wages or salary payable
4. Where different parts of the net amount are paid in different ways, the amount and method of payment of each part-payment.

In the case of fixed deductions, the employer may discharge his duty to itemise by providing the employee at least every 12 months with a separate written "standing statement" of the nature and amount of that deduction, and the intervals at which it will be deducted.

In *Cofone* v. *Spaghetti House Ltd.* (1980), C was a waiter who, in addition to wages, was entitled to keep tips from customers provided that he gave a weekly sum to the manager, which was not shown as part of his gross wage on his itemised pay statement. He applied to a tribunal for a ruling on what *should* be shown on his itemised pay statement, claiming that the payments to the manager ought to be shown as part of his gross wage. It was held that tips are not "wage payments" which have to be shown in the itemised pay statement, since the precise amount will not be known to the employer; nor, for the purposes of the Truck Acts (now the Wages Act 1986), was the payment to the manager a deduction from "wages." It was a deduction from tips, and as such not covered by the legislation. It was also held in *Coales* v. *Wood* (1986) that an employee is entitled to an itemised pay statement whether he/she asks for one or not.

CHAPTER ELEVEN

Dismissal and redundancy

1. Dismissal

UNDER the old common law rules, an employee could be dismissed for almost any reason, and provided that he was given *either* a reasonable period of notice, *or* payment in lieu of such notice, he had very little right of redress if that dismissal was unjust. The employer was not even legally obliged to give a reason for the dismissal.

That is most certainly no longer the case, following a series of statutes, and the modern employer must give a written reason for dismissal if called upon to do so, must defend his actions before an industrial tribunal if it is alleged that he dismissed an employee for an "unfair" reason, or by an unfair method, and must run the risk of the employee resigning and claiming "constructive dismissal" where he considers that the actions of the employer justify such a course.

This area of the law of employment is therefore, like so many others, a mixture of the old and the new, the common law and the statutory. One can only arrive at a reasonable understanding of the present law by commencing with the common law, and assessing to what extent it has been superseded by statute. Basically, one may state as the general rule that the common law principles concerning the termination of a contract of employment are still effective, subject to an overall statutory protection against "unfairness" by the employer. The rest of this section is based on that underlying proposition.

Once again, lack of space precludes more than an outline examination of what has become a very complex subject.

The position at common law

At common law, there are four basic ways in which a contract of employment may come to an end, namely (1) on the expiry of a fixed term; (2) by the giving of notice; (3) by summary dismissal; (4) automatically, upon the occurrence of some event.

1. The expiry of a fixed term

Where staff are hired on a seasonal or fixed-term basis, their contracts will normally expire at the end of that given period. In the case of staff employed for more than 13 weeks with a normal working week in excess of 16 hours, the closing date for such a fixed-term period should be stated in writing as required by EPCA, s. 1; see page 112, above. In fact, by virtue of s. 142 of EPCA, as amended by the Employment Act, 1980, where the fixed-term period is for one year or more, and the employee has, before the expiry of that period, agreed in writing to exclude any claim for unfair dismissal under that contract, then the mere ending of the contract on the expiry of that term cannot be made the subject of any claim for "unfair dismissal."

But all other fixed-term contracts (*i.e.* those for less than one year and those for longer than one year where the employee has not signed away his rights) are as much subject to the "unfair dismissal" provisions of the 1978 Act (for which see p. 151, below) as are normal permanent contracts. The result is that an industrial tribunal may step in and stigmatise as "unfair" any termination by the employer of a contract of employment which was only ever intended to operate for a fixed period.

Whether or not it will be regarded as "unfair" for an employer to terminate employment at the *end* of the period, in accordance with the agreement, is uncertain, but it is quite likely that an abrupt termination by the employer *before* the fixed expiry date, without substantial reason (see p. 148, below) *will* be deemed unfair.

A case in which an employer *successfully* terminated a contract *within* the fixed period was *Cohen* v. *London Borough of Barking*, (1976) in which C was employed for "one year only" as an educational psychologist, on condition that she enrolled on a professional course during that period. The contract was terminable on two months' notice, and when C failed to secure admission to such a course, she was dismissed. It was held that the dismissal was "fair," since it was for a "substantial reason." The same principle might apply, *e.g.* to trainee management in the catering industry who are required to obtain professional qualifications within a given period. And see "qualifications" as a ground for dismissal, at page 155, below.

2. Notice

Perhaps the most obvious way in which a contract of employment may come to an end is where one of the parties gives notice to the other. An alternative, in both cases, is to give payment in lieu of notice, provided that the other party agrees to this. Even if he does not, he may find it very difficult to seek damages merely because of the lack of notice (as distinct from the "unfairness" of the dismissal itself), where he has been offered financial compensation already.

Reference to page 112 above will recall that the length of notice required from either party to the contract of employment is one of those matters which should be recorded in writing under EPCA, s. 1. Parliament, however, has taken no chances, and section 49 of the same Act provides for certain minimum periods of notice, which cancel out any shorter periods (but not longer periods) which may have been written into the contract, and which apply even if there is nothing in writing.

After only four weeks continuous employment, the *employee* is entitled to certain minimum periods of notice according to the length of continuous service which he has given to the employer. They are; from four weeks to two years—one week; from two years to 12 years—one week's notice for each year of continuous employment; for 12 years or more—not less than twelve weeks' notice. "Continuous" employment consists of working for at least sixteen hours per week (eight hours after five years). This continuous service is not broken when the business is taken over as a going concern by a new employer, nor where the employee is absent through sickness or pregnancy, unless this operates so as to bring the contract to an end (see p. 149, below).

The *employer* is only entitled to a minimum period of one week's notice, regardless of the length of service of the employee giving notice. It is, of course, always open to the parties to negotiate for longer periods of notice on either side, and the employer would be well advised to ensure that the employee agrees in writing to give the same amount of notice *to* the employer as he is entitled to receive from him.

At common law (*i.e.* apart altogether from the provisions of the 1978 Act), both parties to the contract of employment are entitled to notice which is "reasonable" in the circumstances, and it may well be that this "reasonable" notice is *longer* than the minimum period laid down by the 1978 Act, in which case the aggrieved party may sue in the normal courts, by-passing the 1978 Act and the industrial tribunal system. Thus, the employer may well feel that the minimum of one week's notice to which he is entitled from his employee, as mentioned above, is grossly inadequate, and may sue if a long-serving and key employee attempts to leave with only one week's notice, *even if* a longer period was not fixed under the contract.

In *Hill* v. *Parsons*, (1972) following the introduction of minimum periods of notice under the Contracts of Employment Act 1963, it was held that a chartered engineer of 35 years' service was entitled to at lease six months' notice at common law, and in *Richardson* v. *Koefod*, (1969) it was held that one month's notice was reasonable at common law for a café manageress on a monthly salary who was dismissed after only seven weeks.

For the first four weeks of his employment, the "reasonable" notice due to an employee would almost certainly be regarded as one week for a weekly-paid employee.

The employee who is dismissed without the minimum notice required under statute, *and without good cause* (see section (B) below) would appear to have a choice between bringing an action before an industrial tribunal for unfair dismissal, and suing in the ordinary courts for wrongful dismissal at common law. Damages at common law would be limited to the sum actually *lost* by the employee by not being allowed to work out his notice (*e.g.* wages, tips, board and lodging), and would be *reduced* by the ease with which the employee could have, or did, find another job during that period. On the whole, therefore, the employee is likely to do better financially from an industrial tribunal hearing.

The winding-up of a company operates as the giving of notice to all its employees, who will from that date begin to work out their notice. The bankruptcy of the employer is also best regarded as having the same effect, although the exact position is unclear.

3. Summary dismissal

At common law, either party may bring the contract to an end summarily (*i.e.* without notice) because of the behaviour of the other party. Where it is the *employee* who takes this action, the situation is now covered by the 1978 Act in those cases in which a tribunal feels that the employee's behaviour was justified—such a situation is referred to as a "constructive dismissal" by the employer, and is dealt with separately on page 158, below.

We are concerned in this section solely with summary dismissal of the employee by the employer, a right which exists at common law, and is acknowledged by both section 49 of the 1978 Act and the ACAS Code of Practice on Disciplinary Practice and Procedures, 1977 as still valid in circumstances in which it is merited. In other words, notwithstanding the unfair dismissal provisions of the 1978 Act, an employer may still dismiss an employee without notice, and without payment in lieu of notice, where his behaviour justifies it.

Since this right exists under common law, it is the common law which defines the situation in which it is lawful, *i.e.* in which it will not be deemed "unfair dismissal" under the 1978 Act. There is no closed list of categories of behaviour which will merit summary dismissal, and one must look to the decided cases for guidance. Basically, summary dismissal is justified whenever the behaviour of the employee is inconsistent with the delicate relationship between employer and employee.

A classic example was the behaviour of the employee in the case of *Pepper* v. *Webb* (1969), which was examined on page 114, above. A single act of disobedience may be sufficient where the result is to shatter the trust which must exist between the two parties, as was seen in *Sinclair* v. *Neighbour* (1967), on page 115.

Other examples of behaviour sufficient to warrant summary dismissal might be a physical assault on a guest or fellow employee, an act of arson in the hotel, gross dishonesty (but not necessarily dishonesty outside work—see below), and open defiance of management authority. Whether or not an act is sufficiently serious depends upon the position of the employee in the organisation, and the nature of the work which he is employed to do; thus, in *Alidair* v. *Taylor* (1976), it was held that an airline pilot was justifiably dismissed after an incident while landing an aircraft full of passengers, since the consequences of even one failure on the part of such a man could be disastrous.

In *Dalton* v. *Burtons Gold Medal Biscuits Ltd.* (1974), it was held to be enough to justify "instant" dismissal for an employee to be caught falsifying a fellow employee's time-clock card.

4. Automatic termination

Where some event occurs which is the fault of neither party, but which has the effect of rendering the contract impossible to perform in anything like its originally intended form, the contract is said to be "frustrated," and the legal consequences are that the contract comes to an end there and then, from the time of the occurrence of the event. Obvious examples are the death of the employee, and the burning down of the place of employment.

This common law position has not changed despite the emergence of statutory provision, but any dismissal which results from such a "frustrating event" will be subject to the normal rules against unfair dismissal. We will deal here with just two of the "problem" situations, where a dismissal may be either justified on the grounds of "frustration," or condemned as "unfair," depending upon the circumstances.

First of all, there is the common problem of the employee who is absent through serious illness, mental or physical. For how long is the employer required to hold the post open? Is it "fair" to dismiss the employee when it is obvious that, even if he returns, he cannot perform the contract in the manner originally envisaged?

There must come a point at which the illness of the employee "frustrates" the contract, and this was held to be the case in *Condor* v. *The Barron Knights* (1966), where the drummer of a pop group which relied for its success on the group being together seven days a week was so ill that he was declared fit only to play on four nights a week. It was held that the rest of the group were entitled to regard the contract as "frustrated." On the other hand, the ACAS Code of Practice 1972, states that the employer should afford stability of employment and reasonable job security for employees absent through sickness, and this requirement will cetainly be taken into account when assessing whether or not an employee has been unfairly dismissed.

In any case, following the case of *Harman* v. *Flexible Lamps Ltd.* (1980), in which the Employment Appeal Tribunal ruled that illness could not be cited as a "frustrating event" where the situation might just as easily be remedied by a dismissal, it seems that all future dismissals on the grounds of ill-health will be at least challengeable on the grounds that they are unfair.

Another problem arises where the employee is in prison. The ACAS Code of Practice 1977, states than an employee should not be regarded as automatically dismissed solely because a charge is pending against him, or because he is remanded in custody, and that a criminal conviction should not be regarded as an automatic ground for dismissal. But tribunals are bound to observe rules of commonsense, particularly when an employee's prison sentence means that he is no longer available for work, and in *Hare* v. *Murphy Bros* (1974), it was held that a contract of employment automatically came to an end where an employee was given 12 months' imprisonment for an offence which had no connection with his work, since he was thereby "incapable" of working for the employer. He was therefore not entitled to either a redundancy payment or compensation for unfair dismissal.

Where the conviction arises from an incident at work, of course, it is almost certain to be held that the employee's conduct has merited "summary dismissal," without the need to consider the possibility of the contract having been "frustrated." Thus, a conviction and prison sentence for theft from the place of employment, resulting in dismissal, is hardly likely to place the employee in a strong position to claim that he has been unfairly dismissed.

Unfair dismissal

Notwithstanding the common law rules outlined above, the employee has, since 1971, possessed a statutory right to challenge his dismissal on the grounds that it was "unfair." Such a claim may be brought before an industrial tribunal, and it must then be shown that the dismissal was indeed fair.

A dismissal may be "unfair" in either or both of two ways;

1. For unfair reasons
2. By unfair methods

Proof of either will entitle the employee to a legal remedy, but they may be studied separately.

Dismissal for unfair reasons

Section 54 of EPCA gives most employees the right not to be dismissed "unfairly." At this stage, however, one must note carefully those employees who are *not* covered by the paragraph, namely

1. Employees under a fixed term contract for one year or more whose terms have expired, and who have "signed away" their rights to continued employment (see p. 146, above).
2. Employees with less than 2 years' continuous service at the date of termination, unless the dismissal was on the grounds of trade union involvement. Such grounds are regarded as dismissal for an "inadmissible reason," and result in an almost automatic finding in favour of the employee who has been so dismissed.
3. Employees who have reached the retirement age (65 for men, 60 for women) on or before the date of dismissal.
4. Employees who normally work for less than 16 hours per week (eight hours per week after five years' service).
5. Employees who, under the terms of their contracts, normally work outside Great Britain.
6. Employees who are married to their employers.

It should also be kept in mind that an employee does not require any period of continuous employment to bring an action alleging racial or sexual discrimination under the 1976 or 1975 Acts.

Apart from these exceptions, every employee is covered by section 54, and has the right not to be unfairly dismissed. Where the employee feels that he *has* been unfairly dismissed, he may bring an action before an industrial tribunal, who will then consider the reason for the dismissal and assess whether or not this reason was a justifiable one.

To facilitate the lodging of such an action by the employee, section 53 of the 1978 Act provides that any employee who is dismissed, and who at the time of his dismissal had completed at least 26 weeks' continuous service (*i.e.* at 16 hours per week or more) may demand a written statement giving the reasons for his dismissal, to be provided by the employer within 14 days of the dismissal. Such a statement will be admissible in evidence in any subsequent proceedings. In *Hotson* v. *Wisbech Conservative Club* (1984) it was held that an employer who had informed an employee that he was being dismissed for gross inefficiency could not, at the subsequent tribunal hearing, claim that the real reason for the dismissal was dishonesty.

An unreasonable failure on the part of the employer to provide such a statement, or the issuing of a statement which the employee feels to be inadequate or untrue, can itself be made the basis of an action before an industrial tribunal. If the tribunal finds in favour of the employee, it may make an award of financial compensation to the employee of a sum not exceeding two weeks' pay (no more than £316 in all).

Any subsequent action for unfair dismissal will obviously centre upon the reasons for dismissal specified in the statement given to the employee. Section 57 of the 1978 Act in fact lays down six main reasons which will be regarded as "fair" reasons for dismissal. These may now be examined individually, bearing in mind that before the employer may win his case, it must be shown that the reason for the dismissal falls within one of these six categories.

The conduct of the employee

The Act does not specify what sort of conduct will enable the employer to dispense with the services of an employee, and one therefore has to fall back on common law principles. There can be little doubt that the sort of conduct which at common law will justify summary dismissal (see p. 148, above) will be taken to be sufficient to show that the dismissal was "fair," but the question then remains of whether or not conduct resulting in dismissal *with* notice will also be regarded as "fair." Clearly, an employer cannot escape the consequences of an "unfair" dismissal merely because he gave the employee adequate notice at common law.

The sort of conduct which might successfully be quoted as sufficient to justify "fair" dismissal includes bad timekeeping, lack of care and attention to duties, drunkenness on duty, and dishonest behaviour short of actual conviction in the courts. It always creates a difficult situation where an employee is *suspected* of theft or other criminal behaviour which cannot actually be proved, but recent cases have suggested that dismissal in such a case might still be "fair."

Thus, in *Conway* v. *Matthew Wright and Nephew Ltd.* (1977), a nightwatchman was strongly suspected of malicious damage to company property, and the police reported the case to the Procurator Fiscal, who in Scotland is charged with the duty of deciding whether or not to prosecute. He decided not to, but the employers still dismissed the nightwatchman. It was held, on appeal, that the dismissal was justified, since the employers had enough evidence to satisfy themselves on a balance of probabilities that the employee was guilty, whereas the Procurator Fiscal required evidence beyond reasonable doubt. A similar decision was given in *Harris* v. *Courage (Eastern)* (1982).

But in such cases, the method of investigation chosen by the employer can be all-important, as was illustrated by *Tesco* v. *Hill* (1977), in which a supermarket cashier was dismissed for failing to record £7 on her till. During the company investigations, the cashier was asked to account for her actions, but claimed that she felt too ill to talk, and was sent home. A letter of dismissal was sent to her that day, and the police were called in. It was held that the company had not given their employee the chance to explain her actions at a time when she was fit enough to do so, and the ex-employee was awarded damages, reduced by 30 per cent. on the grounds of her contributory fault.

In cases in which an employee is dismissed on the grounds merely of *suspected* theft, the employer must show, not only that suitable enquiries were made *before* the dismissal, but also that the employer *genuinely* entertained a *reasonable* belief in that employee's guilt.

The conduct of the employee *outside* his place of work may also give grounds for dismissal where it conflicts with the nature of the job which the employee was employed to do, as in *Singh* v. *London CBS* (1976), in which it was held that a bus company was entitled to dismiss the driver of a one-man bus after his conviction for a fraud on a building society, and *Gardiner* v. *Newport County Borough Council* (1974), in which a local authority was allowed to dismiss a college lecturer mixing with young students following his conviction for an offence of gross indecency with another man.

In *Secretary of State for Employment* v. *ASLEF* (1972), it was held to be sufficient grounds for instant dismissal (and therefore presumably a "fair" dismissal under the 1978 Act) that a group of employees "worked to rule" in such a way as to disrupt the workings of the national rail network, while EPCA, s. 62, gives the employer a statutory right to dismiss employees who are on strike.

An important case in this context is *Trust House Forte* v. *Murphy* (1977), in which a hotel night porter failed to account for some £8 of his liquor stock, and admitted to having stolen some of it. It was held that such behaviour, while not being sufficiently serious to have amounted to a "breach of confidence" with his employer, was nevertheless bad enough to justify dismissal, and that such dismissal was "fair."

The capabilities of the employee

It is obvious that any reasonably workable system of rules for the dismissal of employees must allow for the employer to dismiss a worker who is truly incompetent, and this suggestion has never seriously been challenged, even under recent legislation. The heading of capabilities will, of course, also include matters such as the employee's absence through illness (if sufficiently lengthy) and imprisonment, which are both also covered under common law by the "doctrine of frustration" (see above). The same is *not* true of absence through pregnancy, as has already been seen at page 126, above.

However, certain important principles have emerged during the course of cases involving the capabilities of the employee, and chief among these is that the employer must make all reasonable effort to indicate to the employee how he is progressing, and not merely dismiss him without warning. It has been suggested, for example, that alternative employment should be sought for an employee whose declining faculties after years of faithful service make his performance less satisfactory, and that employers should avoid promoting people to posts which they are not capable of filling. Adequate and sympathetic training schemes should be devised, with frequent assessments, the results of which are communicated to the employee concerned.

In short, an employer stands a far greater chance of proving fair dismissal on the grounds of "capabilities" if he can show that the worker received every chance and encouragement, and adequate warning. Those cases in which the employer has lost have almost all fallen down on this point.

Legality

An employer will succeed in proving that the dismissal of a particular employee was fair if he can show that to have continued to employ that employee would have been an illegal act. Obvious examples are the continued employment of a pregnant woman in a "high radiation" area, the continued employment of a driver who has been disqualified from driving, and the continued employment of a kitchen assistant who is suffering from an infectious disease.

Once again, the employer will be required to at least consider the possibility of either suspending the worker on medical grounds, or finding suitable alternative employment.

Qualifications
An obvious ground for dismissal occurs where the employee is not qualified for the job he or she was appointed to do, and this is a permitted ground for "fair" dismissal under the 1978 Act. The most obvious examples will arise where an apprentice fails to qualify after a reasonable period, or where an already qualified professional man is struck off; in such cases, the circumstances of dismissal must still be just and equitable.

Thus, in *Blackman* v. *Post Office* (1974), a postal officer was dismissed from a recruitment scheme after he had failed an aptitude test on the maximum number of occasions. It was held that this dismissal was fair in the circumstances.

Redundancy
If an employee is dismissed for *genuine* reasons of redundancy, then that dismissal will not be deemed "unfair." But redundancy is an obvious excuse to put forward to hide what is really an unfair dismissal, and so tribunals tend to be very cautious when dealing with cases under this heading.

The specific laws on redundancy are dealt with below, in the next main section, but the point must be made at this stage that before any dismissal for redundancy will be regarded as "fair," the employer must show clearly and unequivocally that the ground of redundancy was a *genuine* one. Not only that, he must also show that the particular employee in question was not unfairly singled out for redundancy (*e.g.* because he was a union official). Thus, the *choice* of a particular employee for redundancy may in itself give rise to "unfair" dismissal.

The ACAS Code of Practice 1972, in fact recommends that the management liaise with the unions on all matters concerning redundancy, and the persons selected for it. Alternative methods of reducing the workforce (*e.g.* less recruitment, voluntary redundancy schemes, early retirement) should be considered, and in all, the employer must be seen to be acting reasonably.

Under the Employment Protection Act 1975, s. 99, as amended in 1979, any employer who is considering the redundancy of any worker who is a member of a union recognised by him must consult the appropriate trade union representative at the earliest opportunity. Where the redundancy will affect 100 or more employees at the same establishment within 90 days, the union must be consulted at least 90 days before any dismissal takes effect, and where the proposal will affect 10 or more employees within 30 days, the union must be consulted at least 30 days before any dismissal takes effect. The employer must, in consulting with the union, give specific details, and must consider any union representations, giving reasons in writing for refusing any of them.

Failure to give such warning, or to consult with the unions, gives each employee concerned the right to a "protective award" of compensation by an industrial tribunal, being one day's pay for every day of the notice period which the employer failed to give.

Some other substantial reason

This category is obviously an attempt by Parliament to ensure that where an employer has a strong and valid reason for dismissal, that dismissal should not be stigmatised as "unfair" merely because it does not come within one of the five categories above.

Several decided cases will serve to illustrate the sort of matter which may come under this heading. Thus, in *Hendry* v. *Scottish Liberal Club* (1977), a husband and wife were employed as joint managers of a club. Mr. Hendry was "unfairly dismissed," but the club argued that since they were jointly employed, they were obliged to dismiss Mrs. Hendry once they had dismissed Mr. Hendry. It was held that, had Mr. Hendry been fairly dismissed, then Mrs. Hendry might have been fairly dismissed, not for any fault on her part, but because the break in the joint employment might have been a substantial reason for that dismissal. But since Mr. Hendry had been unfairly dismissed in the first place, it followed that Mrs. Hendry's dismissal was also unfair. However, the principle, if fairly used, can be a very important one for the catering trade.

In *Skyrail* v. *Coleman* (1980), Mrs. C was a booking clerk in S's travel agency, married to an employee of a rival operator. Prior to her marriage, she had assured her employers that she would do and say nothing to prejudice their interests, but the two employers met and agreed that after the marriage, Mrs. C would be the one to be dismissed, since her husband was "the breadwinner." Two days after her marriage, she was dismissed with two weeks' pay in lieu of notice. It was held that there had been sex discrimination, since she had been treated less favourably than a man would have been treated in the circumstances. There was no justification for assuming that the man was "the breadwinner." All in all, the dismissal was unfair despite the confidential nature of the information she handled in her job, as was the method of dismissal, with little warning to enable her to find another job, particularly in view of the undertaking she had given, and the fact that there was no evidence that she had ever "leaked" information.

A rather more disturbing decision was that in *Bouchaala* v. *THF Hotels Ltd.* (1980), in which B, a Tunisian, joined a management training scheme in the U.K. prior to his employment as a manager in Tunisia. THF applied for a visa extension from September 1978 to allow his training to continue, but were informed by the Department of Employment that it could not be renewed because his entitlement to a work permit would have expired. The position was explained to him when he was dismissed in July, 1978, but shortly afterwards, the Department of Employment wrote to the employers informing them that their original advice had been inaccurate.

It was held that the employer could not justify the dismissal on the grounds that it would have been illegal to continue employing that person, since it would not have been, despite the incorrect advice given. But the genuine belief of the employer in this case *did* constitute a "substantial reason" for the dismissal, which was therefore a fair one.

One final point should be noted before leaving the subject of dismissal for unfair reasons. That is that the behaviour of the employee himself, if it is shown to have contributed to his dismissal, will result in the damages awarded to him being reduced by the tribunal, even though the dismissal was basically unfair. Such behaviour may also lessen the chances of a tribunal ordering the employer to re-engage or reinstate the employee. An example of this process in practice has already been seen in the case of *Tesco* v. *Hill*, above.

Dismissal by unfair methods

As indicated above, an employer cannot escape legal action by an ex-employee merely by showing that he was dismissed for a fair *reason*; he must also be able to show that, in all the circumstances of the case, the *method* used to dismiss the employee was *also* fair.

In recent years, the emphasis in this context has been on the duty of the employer to make the employee aware from the very start of his contract of employment of the disciplinary rules which apply to him. It is one of those matters which must be recorded in writing from the outset (see p. 112), and once a disciplinary system has been established, it must be adhered to. The employer must also comply with what are known as "the rules of natural justice," *i.e.* the employee must know what he is accused of, he must be allowed to state his own case, and he must be fairly and impartially judged.

All these matters are dealt with in ACAS Codes of Practice, the latest of which came into force on June 20, 1977. Like its predecessors, it does not have the force of law, being merely a "yardstick" against which the actions of the employer may be judged, but frequent references to it in tribunal hearings necessitate it being given more than a passing glance. Lack of space prohibits any detailed reference to the Code, but the following are its main provisions.

1. All employees should be given a copy of the disciplinary code, which should be specific in its terms and facilitate the speedy disposal of disciplinary matters.
2. Employees should be fully informed of complaints against them, and given ample opportunity to "state their case." They should be allowed to be accompanied by a trade union representative or a colleague of their choice.
3. Every case should be fully investigated before any disciplinary action is taken. Immediate superiors should not have the power to dismiss employees without reference to senior management.
4. Except in the case of "gross misconduct," no employee should be dismissed for a first breach of discipline.
5. Every employee should be given a reason for any disciplinary penalty imposed, and should have a right of appeal, following specified procedures.
6. Disciplinary action other than dismissal should be accompanied by a formal oral warning for a minor offence, and a written warning for a more serious offence.
7. Special provisions should be considered for night shift workers, or workers in isolated locations for whom the full procedure is not immediately available.
8. No action beyond an oral warning should be taken against a trade union official without consultation with a senior trade union official.
9. Criminal offences outside the place of employment should not be treated as automatic reasons for dismissal.

Constructive dismissal

As mentioned elsewhere, it is now possible for an employee to resign, following some serious behaviour on the part of the employer, and claim damages, etc., for "constructive dismissal," *i.e.* to claim that, in effect, he was forced to leave because of the employer's behaviour. In such circumstances, the employee need give no notice to the employer.

It is then for an industrial tribunal to decide whether or not the behaviour of the employer was such as to justify this precipitate action by the employee. Among the more obvious grounds upon which an employee could base such a claim would be a failure on the part of the employer to pay wages when they fall due, a reduction in the wage rate without consultation, a substantial change for the worse in working conditions, harrassment by colleagues or superiors which the employer failed to check, harsh discipline, and discrimination on sexual or racial grounds. In certain circumstances, it might be sufficient merely that the employer failed to provide work, even though he continued to pay wages, as for example where an apprentice requires such work in order to learn his trade, or where a chef requires to keep up an international reputation.

In all these cases, an employee might resign and then bring an action for unfair dismissal. It is, however, now well settled that before an employee may claim in respect of constructive dismissal, the behaviour on the part of the employer which is complained of must constitute a breach of a term of the contract of employment, express or implied. In *B.A.C.* v. *Austin* (1978), for example, the employee was held to have been constructively dismissed when the employer failed to provide him with adequate safety goggles after frequent complaints and requests by the workforce.

In *Associated Tyre Specialists (Eastern) Ltd.* v. *Waterhouse* (1977), W began work as a clerk, and the office manager praised her work, causing resentment by fellow employees. She was persuaded not to resign, and in fact promoted to supervisor. She was then told by her superiors that the other staff under her found her too strict, and was ordered to change her style of supervision. Further complaints were received, but never communicated to her, then finally her staff walked out. She resigned, and claimed unfair dismissal. It was held that the failure of the employers to support her in her duties was unfair dismissal, but the damages were halved because of her contributory fault in being over-sensitive.

Finally, it should be emphasised that the mere fact that the employee has been "constructively" dismissed does not mean that he is automatically entitled to compensation; before this may happen, the "dismissal" must be shown to have been *unfair*. In *Burdett-Coutts* v. *Herts County Council* (1984) for example, it was held that school meals ladies need not accept a lower rate of pay in order to protect their jobs, but might resign in protest. Whether or not such behaviour by the employer would be regarded as "unfair," however, was another matter.

Industrial tribunal powers

As has already been indicated, actions for unfair dismissal are brought before an industrial tribunal. Lack of space prevents any explanation of tribunal procedure, although general reference to the position of tribunals in the legal system may be found in Chapter One. If a tribunal finds in favour of a dismissed employee, it may take one or more of the following courses of action.

1. It may award financial compensation. The actual amount will depend upon length of service, age, weekly wage before dismissal, expenses incurred as the result of the dismissal, loss of benefits, and the degree to which the employee was guilty of "contributory fault." The theoretical maximum for an award is approximately £23,000.
2. It may order the employer to "reinstate" the employee, *i.e.* replace him in his former position as if nothing had happened, and give him arrears of pay as well as arrears of benefit, seniority, etc.
3. It may order the employer to "re-engage" the employee, in such capacity and on such terms as the tribunal shall see fit.

In the case of both (2) and (3), the tribunal will take into account the views of the ex-employee, and the feasibility of such a course in the circumstances. Failure on the part of the employer to comply with the terms of a reinstatement or re-engagement order may result in severe financial penalties, but it does seem that, if the employer is prepared to suffer enough financially, he can avoid actually having to take the ex-employee back onto his staff.

2. Redundancy payments

The Redundancy Payments Act 1965 was an attempt by Parliament to protect employees in all industries against the consequences of future trade recessions, or a reduction in staff by employers. The 1965 Act was absorbed into the redundancy provisions of EPCA, whose basic purpose is to require employers to make compensatory payments to those of their workers who become genuinely redundant. There is a central Redundancy Fund from which employers may recover *part* of this payment.

Redundancy

An employee's right to redundancy payment arises only where he becomes genuinely redundant, so that it is vital from the very start to define closely what is meant by the term "redundancy." An employee is dismissed for reasons of redundancy where the whole or main reason for his dismissal is that his employer's needs for employees to do work of a particular kind have diminished or ceased. The reasons why this has happened are of no relevance; the question is essentially one of whether or not the employee was replaced after his dismissal.

We can draw up a list of the circumstances in which a redundancy can be said to have occurred; these are:

1. *Straight dismissal*—where the contract of employment is terminated by the employer in the normal way because he can no longer supply work of a particular kind to that employee, in that particular place.
2. *Lay-off*—where the employee is laid off completely for either four consecutive weeks or six weeks out of any 13, in that he receives no payment of any kind from the employer because, although he is available for work, there is no work for him to do. Weeks during which there are stoppages due to industrial disputes are not counted.
3. *Short-time*—where the employee is unable, by virtue of the fact that work is less available than usual, to earn at least half his week's pay for the normal working week for either four consecutive weeks, or any six weeks out of 13. Once again, weeks involving industrial disputes do not count.

In the case of (1), the redundancy will be immediately apparent, and the employee may proceed with his redundancy claim without further ado. In the case of (2) and (3), however, the employee must give official notice to the employer of his intention to claim redundancy compensation. He must also give the required amount of notice in order to terminate the contract of employment.

If the reason for the lay-off or short-time is merely that the employer's business is going through a temporary lean spell, and the employer considers that there is a reasonable chance of a resumption of normal working within the next four weeks, for a period of at least 13 weeks, he may issue a "counter-notice" to the employee within seven days of receiving his notice of intention to claim. The matter then rests with an industrial tribunal to decide whether or not a redundancy has occurred.

In fact, the prevalence of guarantee payments, minimum earnings agreements between management and unions, and the possibility of claiming for constructive dismissal in such circumstances have all combined in recent years to make this procedure less common, particularly since the onus is now on the employer to notify the workforce (via the union) of pending redundancies—see above. In practice, the most common problem now is that of distinguishing between a borderline redundancy and an "unfair" dismissal; this distinction has been dealt with earlier. It should also be kept firmly in mind that a person fairly dismissed for misconduct, etc., receives no compensation (not even for redundancy), even if he is never replaced.

Persons excluded from the Act

The Act covers all persons who work under a contract of employment in any industry, except the following:

1. employees of less than 104 weeks' "continuous service" (see below) with the employer in question;
2. employees who work for less than 16 hours per week (eight hours after five years);
3. employees who are under 18 or over 65 (60 for women);
4. employees who are husbands or wives of their employers; also close relatives generally in the case of "domestic servants."
5. employees under a fixed-term contract of two years or more who have "signed away" their rights;
6. crown servants, or employees who normally work outside Great Britain;
7. employees covered under a separate redundancy scheme approved by the Department of Employment and Productivity; *N.B.* the employer must still pay contributions to the main scheme.

There are others not covered by the Act, but the above are the only ones of any relevance to the catering industry.

Continuous service

It will already have been noted (and the same point becomes apparent again below) that entitlement to redundancy payment is based, at least partly, on the length of continuous service with the employer in question. It is necessary to examine more closely what exactly this means.

The period of continuous service is measured basically in weeks, and any week which does not qualify will break the continuity of service (assuming that the contract of employment does not cover that week automatically) unless:

1. the employee is absent for all or part of the week through sickness or injury (limit 26 weeks);
2. there is a temporary cessation of work (for strikes, see below);
3. where by arrangement or by custom, the employment is regarded as continuing;
4. the employee is absent from work due to pregnancy or confinement.
5. the employee used to be employed under a contract which normally required him to work a 16 hour week, but he has

now been transferred to a contract which requires him to work between 8 and 16 hours per week (limit 26 weeks).

A week ends on a Saturday, and to qualify as a service week, it must be one in which the employee is employed for more than 16 hours (eight hours after five years), unless it is a week which is included in a contract which normally involves employment for 16 hours or more per week; thus, temporary lay-offs and holidays do not break the continuity of service. As indicated above, if the contract of employment *does* require the employee to work for 16 hours or more per week, and it continues in force even though the employee is not at work and not receiving wages, continuity of employment will not be broken anyway.

An interesting case in this context was *Ingram* v. *Foxon* (1984), in which a chef, originally employed in 1979, was dismissed from an hotel in 1981 and then reinstated after legal advice to the employer. He received a letter from the employer confirming continuity of employment, but shortly after the hotel changed hands in 1982, he was dismissed. The new employer maintained that he did not have the necessary two years' service to claim in respect of dismissal, but it was held that the letter he had received from the former employer had ensured continuity of employment back to 1979, and was also binding on the new employer.

Change of employer

The concept of continuous service is of great significance in any case involving the "takeover" of one business concern by another. If employer A sells his business to employer B, and the latter decides to conduct some totally different business on the premises, and to dispense with the existing staff, such staff have a valid claim for redundancy payment against employer A. If, on the other hand, employer B buys the business as a going concern, and continues as before, employing the same staff in the same capacities (or substantially similar—see below), such staff have no claim for redundancy payment against employer A, but must continue to serve employer B.

In a situation such as this, there is deemed to be no break in employment; if, at a later stage, an employee decides to make a claim for redundancy payment for some other reason, the years of service with employer A are linked with those with employer B in order to make one complete period. In other words, when taking over a business as a going concern, employer B also takes over the accrued periods of continuous service of all the employees. This fact should be written into the new contract of employment—see page 112, above.

Similarly, if an employer dies, and the business dies with him, the employees will be able to claim redundancy compensation from the deceased's estate. If, on the other hand, the personal representatives of the deceased decide to carry on the business, and they offer to re-engage the employees on the same terms as before within eight weeks of the employer's death, there is no break in the continuity of employment, and no claim to redundancy payment arises. In all cases, an employee who unreasonably refuses an offer of re-employment in the same job, or some "suitable alternative" one, loses all claim to redundancy payment.

Cases can arise in which it is difficult to determine whether the new employer has taken over the business as a going concern, or merely bought out the assets, and put them to other uses (in which case he acquires no existing redundancy liabilities, and there is no "continuity of employment" between employers). Thus, in *Melon* v. *Hector Powe* (1980), a clothing manufacturer sold off an "annexe" in Scotland which had previously specialised in a particular type of garment. The workforce was retained, but within six months they were all engaged in the manufacture of a totally different product. It was held that the takeover had been a mere "disposal of assets," and that there was no continuity of employment from one employer to another.

In *Ubsdell* v. *Paterson* (1973), U was employed by P as head waiter in an hotel, at a salary of £10 per week, plus a share in the "tronc." The business was sold to M, and for the first two weeks following the change, U continued to work for the new employer on the same basis as he had worked for P. He then accepted an offer from M to continue working in his old job for a total cash wage of £20 per week, and no more; a few weeks later he was dismissed, and he claimed redundancy payment from P, alleging that he had not received an offer from M to re-engage him on terms which did not differ from those of the previous contract. It was held that the mere fact U had for a short while worked for M and accepted wages for that work was not necessarily conclusive evidence that he had accepted a suitable offer of re-engagement on all the terms and conditions of the previous contract. The burden lay upon P to prove that U *had* accepted such an offer; this might be implied from the conduct of the parties, but in the circumstances, this burden had not been discharged, and U was entitled to a redundancy payment from P.

All these cases must now be read in the light of the Transfer of Undertakings (Protection of Employment) Regulations 1981, under which a transfer or merger of a business will no longer automatically terminate the contracts of employment of the employees, who will instead continue in employment with the new employer with all their rights intact. Any employee whose services *are* disposed of after the transfer will be entitled to claim against the transferee unless there is an "economic, technical or organisational reason entailing changes in the workforce." The "recognised" unions will have the right to be consulted on behalf of the workers they represent *before* the transfer, *and* by the proposed transferee concerning his plans for the workforce, and all existing collective and recognition agreements will transfer with the business if it maintains a separate identity.

There have been some interesting cases under the 1981 Regulations. For example, it was held in *Kestongate* v. *Miller* (1986) that an employee who was dismissed between the exchange of contracts for the sale of a business and the date of the transfer could claim against the seller, while in *Secretary of State for Employment* v. *Anchor Hotel* (*Kippford*) (1985) it was held that an employee made redundant on the day of the transfer of a business could claim redundancy pay against the purchaser of the business.

In *Secretary of State for Employment* v. *Spence* (1986), however, it was held that there was no continuity of employment, and no prospect of a claim against anyone, when a business went into receivership and was then bought by a new employer who re-engaged the staff on the same terms as before. There was held to be no "transfer of a business" in such a case.

An example of a transfer of business in which "economic reasons" justified the dismissal of staff, and in which, therefore, there was no prospect of a claim under the 1981 Regulations, was *Meikle* v. *McPhail* (1983), in which a man who took over a public house business realised that severe economies were required, and sacked all but one of the existing staff within four days of taking over. It was held that the dismissed staff had no claim against the new owner because, although the reason for the dismissal was the transfer of the business to the new owner, he was justified in taking the action for "economic reasons," and his recklessness in taking over the business without making more investigation did not render the dismissal unfair.

Change in employment

The concept of continuous service also assumes importance in the case in which an employee is offered alternative employment by the same employer, because he can no longer offer him his old job. If the alternative job is one which in the eyes of the tribunal can be regarded as a reasonably suitable one in relation to the old job, then no claim to redundancy payment arises, and the employee has no claim to anything if he "unreasonably" refuses it. If he accepts it, there will be no break in the continuity of employment, and if, at a later date, a claim for redundancy payment arises, both periods may be taken into account when calculating the amount due.

If the offer is *not* deemed suitable, the employee may regard himself as being redundant, and claim redundancy payment in the normal way. To be suitable, the offer must take effect within four weeks of the termination of the old job. In practice, many factors go into deciding whether or not an offer of alternative employment is suitable, including the nature of the work, the remuneration, the location of the work, and any fringe benefits.

An offer of work with another employer is not a suitable offer, although of course, a transfer from one hotel to another within the same company, if it is suitable in other respects, will not constitute employment with another employer. However, it *will* be "suitable" if the work is with an "associated employer." The following cases illustrate the type of problem dealt with by the Tribunal under this heading.

In *Cooper* v. *Fiat* (1966) the plaintiff was employed by the defendant motor company as a bodywork inspector, although only about a third of his time was spent in doing this, and the rest in driving and body finishing. The company asked him to work full time as a body finisher, at the same rate of pay, and with the same benefits, but he refused. He was then given notice, and was never replaced. He claimed redundancy payment. It was held that he had unreasonably refused a suitable alternative offer of employment, and that he was therefore not entitled to compensation.

In *O'Brien* v. *Associated Fire Alarms* (1968), the plaintiff was an electrician employed by the defendants in and around the Liverpool area. Work diminished in that area, and his employers offered him a job in Barrow-in-Furness, which he refused in view of the disruption this would cause to his domestic life. The Court of Appeal held that, since there was nothing in his contract which required him to make such a move, he was entitled to refuse such a change, and was entitled to redundancy payment. If the contract specifies travel around the country, or the nature of the job implies it, then of course the answer may be different. In *Johnson* v. *Notts Combined Police Authority* (1974), it was held that a mere change in the hours of work without a change in duties will not be sufficient to constitute redundancy, since it does not constitute a change in the "kind of work" performed by the employee.

Strikes

The position of strikes in relation to redundancy payments is as follows; in calculating the period of continuous service, any participation in a strike does not break the continuity of employment, although the period of the strike is not counted in the computation of the total period of employment. Thus, if a man has 250 weeks of service with his employer, but weeks 100 and 101 were strike weeks, the worker will be credited with 248 weeks of continuous service.

An employee may, however, lose his right to redundancy payment if, while working out a period of notice, he goes on strike before this period has expired. It is for the tribunal to decide, since all cases are referred to it.

Calculation of redundancy payments

The amount to which any given employee is entitled by way of redundancy payment depends upon three factors: (a) the length of continuous service (which for this purpose is calculated first in weeks, and then in years); (b) the age of the employee during this period; (c) his weekly wage at the time of redundancy. Using these factors, payment is calculated as follows:

1. for every year of continuous service between the ages of 18 and 22—half a weeks' pay;
2. for every year of continuous service between the ages of 22 and 41—one week's pay;
3. for every year of continuous service between the ages of 41 and 64 (59)—one and a half week's pay.

Once a man has reached 64, or a woman 59, these payments are reduced by one-twelfth for every month over 64 or 59, so as to phase out completely by 65 or 60.

Reference has already been made to the Schedule by means of which a "week's pay" is calculated; this sum will include any regular bonus, but not payments for overtime unless this is normally earned under the contract of employment. Allowance is not made for payments in respect of board and lodging, unless they form part of the minimum wages paid in accordance with the Wages Council Order currently in force. Nor will redundancy payment take any account of travel allowances paid during the employment. No wage in excess of £158 per week will be counted, and the maximum number of years which may count towards continuous service is 20. There is thus a maximum payment of £4,740 to any one worker, but all payments are currently tax free.

The amount thus calculated is all paid initially by the employer, who must supply the employee with a written statement explaining how it has been calculated; this will in practice be done on a standard form obtainable from the local Jobcentre. Payment cannot be claimed more than six months after the date of the termination of employment, unless the case has already been referred to the tribunal. Receipt of redundancy payment does not in any way affect the employee's right to unemployment benefit, and he is still entitled to redundancy payment however quickly he obtains another job. Payment may be affected by any sum which the employee receives from the employer by way of superannuation, although payment in lieu of notice, holiday pay, etc., do not count. It may be claimed by the employee's estate should he die before payment has been made.

Redundancy Payments Fund and Tribunal

Throughout the duration of the contract of employment, the employer will have been paying a weekly contribution for redundancy payments on behalf of every one of his employees for whom he pays a National Insurance contribution. The amount in question is in fact part of the composite sum which the employer pays monthly to the Inland Revenue in respect of National Insurance—see page 142, above. The money thus collected is paid into a central Redundancy Fund.

The employer is then able to claim a rebate from the Fund in respect of the amounts (if any) which he has paid out to his ex-employees in redundancy payments. He does not receive a full rebate; the amount he receives is the subject of a somewhat complicated calculation, the general effect of which is to give him approximately 35 per cent. of what he has paid in the form of a rebate.

In cases in which the employer either cannot or will not pay, payment of the whole sum may be made directly out of the Fund to the employee; it is then the duty of those in charge of the Fund to take appropriate action where possible. Since redundancies often occur in the bankruptcy of the employer, this is far from being a rare occurrence, and the government's prime concern is for the employee.

3. References

No employer is legally obliged to provide a reference for one of his employees unless he has agreed to do so as one of the terms of the contract. In most cases, then, he will have a choice. However, as has been seen above, he may be required to give a written statement of the grounds upon which the employee was dismissed. He may, in any case, agree to give a reference. In either case, there are several important points which he must bear in mind. This section refers hereafter to "references," but should also be taken to refer to statements given upon dismissal, where relevant.

Perhaps the most obvious is the existence of the laws against defamation of character and the simplest definition of defamation is "an untrue statement of fact which tends to lower a person in the eyes of right-thinking people." It takes two forms; *libel*, which is defamation in some permanent form (*e.g.* writing or films), and *slander*, which is defamation in some transient form such as speech, unless it is recorded, in which case it becomes libel. For present purposes, the distinction is not too important.

It will already have been noted that it is not defamation to make a statement which is true. Thus, the employer who has incontrovertible proof that his ex-employee stole money from the till need have no fear of stating so in any reference, since he will be able to claim the defence of justification if ever that employee attempts to sue him.

But few employers are in such a clear-cut position. In most cases, the most they have are suspicions, and they have decided to give the employee notice rather than dismiss him summarily for theft. If they decide to give a reference, the problem is twofold. On the one hand, there is the fear of being sued for defamation if their suspicions later than turn out to be unfounded. In *Lawton* v. *B.O.C. Transhield* (1987) it was also held that an employer giving a reference owes a "duty of care," to the person about whom he is writing, and may be sued for negligence if what he writes is untrue. On the other hand, as will be seen below, employers owe a certain duty to any future employer to give the most accurate picture of the employee that they can.

Fortunately, the law has recognised this difficulty, and has provided a remedy to defamation actions (but not to actions for negligence) in the defence of *qualified privilege*. The effect of this is that whenever one person is under a duty, moral or otherwise, to state what he honestly believes to be the truth about someone, and the person to whom the statement is being addressed has some vital interest to protect in receiving and assessing this information, then provided that the statement is made with an honest belief in its truth, the maker cannot later be sued for any untruth contained in it.

This state of affairs is ideal for the employer with genuine suspicions but no solid proof. He may state what he honestly believes, and need later only prove that he had reasonable grounds for that belief. Any suggestion of malice, or lack of honest belief, will rob the employer of his defence. The main thing which an employer must remember, therefore, is to state nothing which he cannot later show reasonable cause for believing at the time. It is obviously a very appropriate procedure for an employer who has dismissed his employee on suspicion of dishonesty.

Mention was made above of the fact than an employer giving a reference owes a duty not only to the employee about whom he is writing, but also to the employer who is considering the possibility of hiring that person. If such a statement is wilfully false in that it paints far too complimentary a picture of the employee, and the second employer employs the man on the strength of it, he may sue the maker of the statement for deceit if he later suffers any loss or damage as a result.

Alternatively, if the statement is negligently made, in that the employer has carelessly allowed the employee to appear better than he is, then again the new employer (at least, in England) may sue for any loss or damage he sustains as a result of relying on that statement. In both cases, therefore, any employer who omitted to mention in a reference that the employee in question had been responsible for stock losses during his employment, could be sued by a future employer who had relied on the reference, and suffered stock losses himself.

If, therefore, an employer decides to give a reference, he has nothing to lose, and everything to gain, by stating clearly what he honestly believes to be the truth about his ex-employee. His troubles begin when he leaves vital matters unsaid, or begins inventing a few of his own.

CHAPTER TWELVE

Working conditions

THERE are three major Acts of Parliament which impose certain basic working conditions for the benefit of staff employed in the hotel and catering industry; they are the Shops Act 1950, the Health and Safety at Work Act 1974 and the Offices, Shops and Railway Premises Act 1963.

The Shops Act 1950

A series of Acts known as the Shops Acts, the most important of which is now the Shops Act 1950, was passed in order to regulate the hours of work of all those who could be classed as "shop assistants." A shop assistant is "Any person wholly or mainly employed in a *shop* in connection with the serving of customers, the receipt of orders, or the despatch of goods."

At first glance, this definition would not appear to cover anyone employed in the hotel and catering industry, but in fact a "shop" is defined as "Any premises where any retail trade or business is carried on," and it includes any premises used for the sale by retail of refreshments and/or intoxicating liquor. The term "shop" in fact includes all those catering premises in which there is the sale of food and/or drink to the *general public, i.e.* cafés, restaurants, public houses and hotels with a public area (*e.g.* public bar or dining room).

Where such premises (or part of the premises) may be classed as a shop, then those members of staff employed within them as kitchen staff, waiters, cashiers and managers, will be classed as shop assistants, and will therefore be covered by the provisions of the Shops Acts. Within an hotel which is mainly residential, but which has certain public areas, the staff employed in these public areas will be classed as shop assistants, while the others will not. The term shop does not, in fact, cover a fully residential hotel, an industrial canteen, or a registered club.

The Shops Acts were primarily designed to cover staff employed in the more conventional retail establishments such as department stores, and the inclusion of catering establishments has led to certain difficulties. The problems have in fact been dealt with in two ways; (i) by ensuring that certain provisions in the Acts (*e.g.* early closing on one weekday, and full closure on a Sunday) do not apply to catering premises; and (ii) by the provision of separate schemes for catering employers who find the general scheme inconvenient. This latter system requires a much more detailed explanation, and a distinction must be made at this stage between shop assistants who are over 18 and those who are not.

Shop assistants who are over 18

An employer within the catering industry who has staff over 18 who may be classed as shop assistants has a choice of one of two schemes which he may apply to his staff. The first may be called the *General Scheme* (referred to below as GS), or the 1912 Scheme, since it originated in the Shops Act 1912. This Scheme is the one primarily intended for those employed in more conventional retail establishments. The second is the *Catering Trade Scheme* (referred to below as CTS), sometimes called the 1913 Scheme, since it first appeared in the Shops Act 1913. This Scheme may be used in respect of those shop assistants who are employed in the service of liquor and/or refreshments for consumption on the premises.

An employer may change from one scheme to the other annually, and he indicates his choice by displaying a notice in the prescribed form in a prominent part of the premises where it may be seen by the staff to whom it relates. This notice, standard copies of which may be obtained from H.M.S.O. lays out in detail the various terms of the scheme which has been chosen. The employer is in fact presumed to have chosen the General Scheme, unless he specifically announces his choice of the Catering Trade Scheme in the above manner.

Lack of space prohibits a fully detailed examination of all the details of the two schemes, but the main distinctions between the two are as follows.

(1) The GS covers those members of staff concerned with the serving of customers, the receipt of orders or the dispatch of goods. The CTS covers *all* staff employed in any capacity wholly or mainly in connection with the sale of liquor or refreshment for consump-

tion on the premises. The CTS is therefore somewhat wider in its application.

(2) The GS requires that each member of staff covered by the Scheme be given a half-holiday, beginning not later than 1.30 p.m., on one weekday, except in the week prior to a Bank Holiday. The week begins at midnight on Saturday for the purposes of the Shops Acts. The CTS, mindful of the staffing needs of the catering trade, carries no direct provision concerning half-holidays (but see (4) below).

(3) The GS carries no restriction on the maximum weekly hours of work, but the CTS requires that no member of staff covered by the Scheme shall be called upon to work for more than 65 hours in any one week, exclusive of mealtimes.

(4) The GS makes provision for a one-hour lunch break (45 minutes if the meal is to be taken on the premises), to be taken between 11.30 a.m. and 2.30 p.m. (or 10.30 a.m. and 3.30 p.m. where the establishment is one which sells refreshment or liquor). The GS also provides for a half-hour tea break where the employee is being called upon to work from 4 p.m. to 7 p.m. The CTS merely provides for a total of two hours by way of mealbreaks, with no stipulation as to when these shall be taken. This period is only 45 minutes on days upon which the hours of work end before 3 p.m., and the total number of hours worked does not exceed six (such a day is referred to as a "half-holiday").

(5) The GS requires that the above mealbreaks be so arranged that every worker has a 20-minute break at least every six hours. The CTS provides for 30 minutes at least every six hours.

(6) The GS lay down strict rules concerning Sunday working. For every four hours which an employee is required to work on a Sunday, he must receive a full day in lieu either the week before or the week following. This day must not be the one normally allowed as a half-holiday, and there may be no more than three such Sundays in any month. For every period under four hours worked on a Sunday, a half-holiday must be given in lieu either the week before or the week following, on a day other than that upon which the half-holiday is normally allowed. These rules do not apply to staff employed wholly or mainly for the sale of liquor, but they do include those under the GS who are employed upon the sale of refreshments. Nor are these rules applicable to Scotland.

The CTS requires that every worker be given 26 Sundays per year completely free; there must be one such free Sunday in every three. These provisions apply to *all* staff covered by the CTS, including those employed for the sale of liquor.

(7) The GS makes no provision for annual holidays. The CTS, on the other hand, requires that every worker be given 32 weekdays per year as holidays, six of which must be consecutive so as to form an annual holiday, and the rest spread so as to give two per month. Two half-holidays given in the same week will count as one full weekday.

These holiday periods do not, as might be supposed, clash with those laid down under the Wages Council Orders, since the Shops Act and the Wages Councils Act deal with different things. The former deals with the minimum holiday periods which may be granted to a worker, while the latter states how much of this holiday period shall be given with pay. In any case, the two systems fit together in many ways; thus, the rest day given under the Wages Order will in most cases be the Sunday required under the Shops Act, while the "days off" required by the Shops Act will be partly used up in the "customary holidays" required under a Wages Order.

Shop assistants who are under 18

An employer in a residential hotel or a place of public entertainment, who has staff under 18 has a choice of three different schemes. The *General Scheme* (1912) and the *Catering Trade Scheme* (1913) each have their own set of provisions which deal with persons under 18 who may be classed as shop assistants, but in addition to these, there is another scheme laid down under the Young Persons (Employment) Act 1938, as amended by the 1964 act of the same name.

The employer may, if he wishes, choose either the 1938 Scheme or the General Scheme by giving notice to the local authority of his intention to do so. If he takes no steps towards choosing either of these schemes, then he will be presumed to have chosen the Catering Trade Scheme for those of his staff who are under 18. In all cases, the employer must exhibit a notice on his premises, in a place where the staff concerned may read it, stating the main provisions of the scheme chosen. Standard notices are available from H.M.S.O.

Once again, lack of space prohibits full detail, but the outline of the three schemes is given below.

The General Scheme

The General Scheme covers all persons under 18 who are wholly or mainly employed in connection with any retail trade or business, but excluding staff in residential hotels who are not shop assistants. In other words, it covers the under-18 equivalents of those dealt with under the General Scheme above.

The maximum weekly hours of work for persons aged 16 to 18 is 48, while for those under 16 it is 44, in both cases exclusive of mealbreaks. Those aged 16 may, in periods of seasonal or exceptional pressure, work a maximum of 50 hours a year overtime. These hours must be worked so that no person covered by the Scheme is called upon to work more than 12 hours overtime in any one week, and the employer may only take advantage of these overtime provisions for six weeks in any year. *Persons under 16 are not permitted any overtime at all.*

All young persons covered by the General Scheme are entitled to the same mealbreaks as adults (see above), and they must be arranged so that there is a break of 20 minutes at least every five hours (five and a half hours on the half-holiday). In addition, the hours of work must be so arranged that no person is called upon to work between the hours of 10 p.m. and 6 a.m., and so that every person has a break of at least 11 consecutive hours between midday and mid-day. In the case of persons aged 16 to 18 whose employment is wholly or mainly in connection with the service of meals for consumption on the premises, the eleven hours need *not* include the hours between 10 p.m. and midnight if the employee in question is carrying out such duties.

Every young person covered by the Scheme is entitled to a half-holiday on a weekday, beginning no later than 1.30 p.m., for every week during which he works for more than 25 hours, except during a week prior to a bank-holiday. The same provisions concerning Sunday working apply here as apply under the Scheme for persons over 18 (see above).

The Catering Trade Scheme

The Catering Trade Scheme covers all persons under 18 who are wholly or mainly employed in connection with the business of serving meals, liquor or refreshment to customers for consumption on the premises, but excluding staff in residential hotels who are not shop assistants. In other words, it covers the under-18 equivalents of those dealt with under the Catering Trade Scheme above.

The maximum weekly hours of work for persons aged 16 to 18 are normally 48, but the employer may, by displaying the appropriate notice, arrange matters so that during a maximum of 12 specified fortnightly periods, the maximum hours of work shall be 96 for the fortnight, of which a maximum of 60 may be worked in either of the two weeks. There may be no overtime worked during such periods.

The maximum weekly hours of work for persons under 16 are normally 44, but during the fortnightly period which includes Christmas Day, persons covered by the Scheme who are under 16 may work a maximum of 88 hours, of which no more than 48 may be worked in one of the two weeks.

As with the General Scheme, persons aged between 16 and 18 may, in periods of seasonal or exceptional pressure, work a maximum of 50 hours a year overtime. But no more than eight of these hours may be worked in any period of two consecutive weeks, and although there is no limit on the number of weeks over which this overtime may be spread, no person may work overtime during one of the specified fortnightly periods mentioned above. *Persons under 16 are not permitted any overtime at all.*

All young persons covered by the Catering Trade Scheme are entitled to the same mealbreaks as adults (see above), and they must be so arranged that there is a break of 30 minutes at least every six hours. Those provisions of the General Scheme which relate to nightwork and breaks between periods of duty apply here also.

The Catering Trade Scheme does not provide for a half-holiday during the week (as has been seen above, it does not for adults either), but the rules concerning Sunday working are the same as those for adults under the Scheme.

The 1938 Scheme

The 1938 Scheme introduced by the Young Persons (Employment) Act 1938 covers all persons under 18 who are employed (i) in a residential hotel or club, in carrying messages, running errands or receiving guests; or (ii) in licensed premises, in any capacity, where such premises are licensed to sell liquor after 11 p.m., or in a registered club where liquor may lawfully be supplied after 11 p.m. Employment in residential hotels which are so qualified is not included in this second category. By virtue of the Licensing Act 1964, of course, persons under 18 may not be employed in the bar of such premises during permitted hours, although they may work as restaurant waiters.

A residential hotel, in the context of both the Shops Act and the 1938 Act is one "used for the reception of guests and travellers desirous of dwelling or sleeping therein." Where an employer has on his staff shop assistants who are not covered by the 1938 Scheme, he must apply one of the Shops Act schemes to them; he may, at the same time, apply the 1938 Scheme to those covered by it.

The maximum weekly hours of work for persons aged 16 to 18 are 48, and there is no provision for a fortnightly system of hours. The figure for persons under 16 is 44, and both periods are exclusive of mealbreaks. Those aged 16 to 18 may, in periods of seasonal or exceptional presssure, work a maximum of 50 hours a year overtime. These hours must be worked so that no person covered by the

Scheme is called upon to work more than six hours' overtime in any one week, and the employer may only take advantage of these overtime provisions for 12 weeks in any year. *Persons under 16 are not permitted any overtime at all.*

All young persons covered by the 1938 Scheme are entitled to a mealbreak of at least 45 minutes between 11.30 a.m. and 2.30 p.m., and rest periods must be so arranged that there is a break of 30 minutes at least every five hours. The rules concerning nightwork and breaks between periods of duty are the same as for persons under 18 covered by the General Scheme (see above), except that they do not allow waiting staff to work beyond 10 p.m.

Every young person covered by the Scheme is entitled to a half-holiday on a weekday, beginning no later than 1 p.m. In addition, there may be no Sunday work unless a whole day's holiday is given in lieu either the week before or the week following, on a day other than upon that which the half-holiday is normally allowed.

An employer who has persons under 18, covered by one of the above Schemes working for him must keep a complete record of their hours of work, mealbreaks, rest intervals and overtime. It is an offence to fail to comply with any of these requirements.

The enforcement of the Shops Act and the 1938 Act is the responsibility of the local authority, whose task it is to appoint inspectors, who have all the powers of factory inspectors. They may enter premises covered by the Acts, demand records or other documents relating to matters dealt with by the Acts, interview staff, and instigate criminal proceedings against employers who contravene the Acts in any way (*e.g.* by failing to keep records, by employing young persons for longer than the maximum permitted hours, by obstructing an inspector, by making false statements and so on).

It should be noted carefully that since the raising of the school-leaving age to 16, the employment of young people under 16 has been severely limited, both by statute and under local authority byelaws. Lack of space prohibits further detail, but all hoteliers, restaurateurs, etc., should take further legal advice before taking on any person under 16 in *any* capacity, even if their employment would comply with the provisions of the Shops Acts.

The Health and Safety at Work etc. Act 1974

The passing of the Health and Safety at Work Etc. Act 1974, heralded a new approach to the law concerning the health and safety of employees at work. Hitherto, protection had been on a piecemeal basis, each industry being governed by its own set of regulations or, in some cases, hardly governed at all. The catering industry was, and still is, governed to a large extent by the Offices, Shops and Railway Premises Act 1963, which is dealt with in more detail in the following section, and this position has not altered despite the passing of the 1974 Act.

However, the 1974 Act affects all industry, including the catering trade, in two major ways; (1) by laying down *general* rules of policy covering employee safety at work; (2) by establishing a national Health and Safety Executive with inspectorate powers, to gradually replace the individual inspectorates under various Acts. The enforcement of the Offices, Shops and Railway Premises Act 1963, however, remains largely in the hands of the Environmental Health Officers employed by each district council.

The general tone of the Act is set by section 2, which makes it the legal duty of every employer to ensure, so far as is reasonably practicable, the health, safety and welfare of all employees while they are at work. This duty extends not only to the active protection of staff from dangerous or defective equipment, but also the provision of safe systems of work, and for suitable training and instruction of staff. Every employer is also required by section 2 to produce and keep up to date "a written statement of his general policy with respect to the health and safety at work of his employees," and this statement must be brought to the notice of all employees; employers with less than five employees are exempted from this requirement. The Act does not indicate exactly what such a notice or statement is supposed to contain.

Section 6 of the Act renders the employer liable for defects in any equipment supplied to employees for their use at work. To be precise, the employer must ensure "so far as is reasonably practicable" that the equipment is designed and constructed in such a way as to be safe when properly used, arrange regular testing of such equipment, and ensure that workers are sufficiently educated in the uses to which the equipment may be put. The correct installation of such equipment is also the responsibility of the employer.

Other provisions of the 1974 Act render each individual employee liable (under pain of prosecution) to ensure, not only his own health and safety, but also that of his colleagues. In addition, the employer must ensure the health, safety and welfare of not just his employees, but all those who are likely to be affected by his activities (*e.g.* in the case of an hotel, the guests and people such as delivery drivers entering loading areas).

The Act established the Health and Safety Commission and the Health and Safety Executive, whose primary functions are to publicise the need for safety at work, and to instigate prosecutions for breaches of the Act. The position is that whenever an accident occurs to an employee in the course of his employment, the Executive may investigate with a view to prosecution; many prosecutions have already been brought under the Act, and various other acts now covered by the Executive.

Regulations and Codes of Conduct may be issued under the Act, and while failure to comply with any such Code will not in itself be an offence, it will carry great weight in any subsequent criminal or civil action. The Executive have all the usual powers of entry, inspection, sample and interview. In Scotland, offences are reported to the Procurator Fiscal, who has the final decision on whether or not a prosecution is to be brought.

If an employer is found to be infringing the Act, even though no one has been injured as a result, he may be served with an "improvement notice," setting a time limit for improvement. In serious cases, the employer may even receive a "prohibition notice" which may forbid certain activities on the premises until all dangers have been removed. There is a right of appeal against either type of notice. In the very worst cases, Inspectors may seize and remove items which in their opinion constitute an "imminent danger" of serious personal injury.

One particular effect of the Act was referred to in Chapter 3 above, namely that all places of work are, by virtue of the 1974 Act, brought within the network of the Fire Precautions Act 1971, and every employer may now be required to comply with regulations concerning lighting, heating, means of escape, fire precautions, and so on. Regulation and enforcement is by the Executive in conjunction with the local fire authority.

This opportunity may also be taken of noting the effects of the Notification of Accidents and Dangerous Occurrences Regulations, 1980, which require every employer to notify the local Environmental Health Officer when an accident occurs at the workplace which causes death or a "major injury" to himself, an employee or a member of the public (*e.g.* a hotel guest). A "major injury" includes most fractures of the bone, amputation of a hand or foot, the loss of the sight in one eye, and any other injury which requires the victim to be admitted to hospital for at least 24 hours, other than merely for "observation."

Initially, the employer must notify the Environmental Health Officer as quickly as possible (presumably, by telephone), and he then has seven days from the accident to submit a full written report. In addition, certain "notifiable" dangerous occurrences must be reported whether anyone is injured or not; a full list of these is available from the local Environmental Health Office. Even where an employee, although not seriously injured, is unable to work for three or more days, a record must be kept. Since *all* accidents occurring to employees at work should, by law, be recorded anyway, it is recommended that the employer make use of the standard-form Accident Book available from HMSO.

The Offices, Shops and Railway Premises Act 1963

Over 25,000 catering premises in Great Britain are subject to the Offices, Shops and Railway Premises Act 1963 which was passed in order to lay down certain minimum working conditions for those workers who come within its provisions.

So far as the catering industry is concerned, those who are covered by the Act are: (a) shop assistants as defined under the Shops Act 1950 (*i.e.* staff employed in kitchens, restaurants and bars which serve the general public and staff employed in retail units within larger hotels such as hairdressing salons, florist's shops and bookstalls), and thus excluding staff employed in purely residential hotels or registered clubs; (b) office workers such as receptionists, typists, cashiers, general office staff, telephonists and staff employed in ticket agencies within catering establishments; (c) canteen staff working in canteens which exist for the benefit of those employed in offices and shops, even if such canteens are run by independent contractors.

All such persons are entitled to certain basic working conditions laid down in the 1963 Act, or those Regulations made under the Act by the Secretary of State. Eventually, the Act will be absorbed by new Regulations issued under the 1974 Act, but at present the main provisions of the Act may be summarised as follows.

Health and welfare

Cleanliness

The cleanliness of working premises is obviously a prime consideration with regard to the health and welfare of staff, and the Act requires that premises, furniture, fittings and staircases be kept in a clean state, free from dirt and accumulated refuse. It is the Food and Drugs legislation which legislates for the cleanliness of the *product* of catering premises; the 1963 Act legislates for the cleanliness of the *premises* themselves, on the basis that many accidents (particularly falls) occur as the result of premises being unclean, with greasy floors and obstructed stairways.

Lighting

Adequate and sufficient light, either natural or artificial, is obviously of great importance to the health of staff, not least because many accidents occur through inadequate lighting on working premises. Windows and skylights must be kept clean both inside and out, and the illumination levels for working premises must be adequate with regard to the work carried on there. The D.E.P. booklet *Lighting in Offices, Shops and Railway Premises* is of great assistance in assessing the amount of light required.

Temperature

No one can work efficiently or comfortably unless room temperature is kept within reasonable limits, and the Act requires that this be done without the use of equipment which is likely in itself to cause discomfort or danger through fumes. A temperature of 16 degrees centigrade must be the minimum in rooms in which work is mainly sedentary, and into which the public does not normally come. Thermometers must be kept in a conspicuous place on all working floors of the building covered by the Act. All rooms covered by the Act must be adequately ventilated, either by natural means or by air-conditioning units.

Sanitation and Water

Employers must provide sufficient and suitable sanitary facilities for both sexes, and these must be maintained and kept clean. Washing facilities must be made available, with hot and cold water, soap and drying facilities. An adequate supply of drinking water must also be provided, along with drinking vessels, either disposable or washable. Alternatively, a drinking "fountain" system may be employed.

Seating and Working Space

Adequate seating must be provided for those members of staff who have a reasonable opportunity of doing their work while seated, and each member of staff is entitled to 40 square feet of room space, and 400 cubic feet of breathing space, except in rooms frequented by the public. The number and type of items of furniture and equipment must not be such as to constitute conditions of overcrowding. Staff must be provided with somewhere in which to dispose of outdoor clothing not required during working hours and, wherever possible, drying facilities for such clothing.

Safety

Premises

Many of the provisions of the 1963 Act which deal with the safety of working premises have already been touched upon above, and it is sufficient to add here that all passages, gangways and staircases must be secure, free from obstruction and adequately maintained. Suitable handrails must be installed on all staircases.

Machinery

Although accidents due to machinery do not form as great a proportion of industrial accidents in the catering trade as is sometimes supposed, the 1963 Act contains many regulations on the subject of machinery and working equipment in general. All dangerous parts of machinery (*e.g.* blades, belts, cutters and screws) must be securely fixed and adequately guarded against all foreseeable injuries, even to careless or disobedient staff. Warning notices are not enough, and machines must be virtually foolproof.

No young persons may be allowed to clean machinery without adequate supervision if there is any conceivable risk involved, and all persons using certain types of machinery which are classed as "dangerous" must be instructed in both their use and their dangers. In addition there is an absolute ban on the cleaning of "dangerous" machines by young persons. Dangerous machines include food mixers, mincers, slicers and chippers.

Hoists and Lifts

Regulations provide a special set of rules for the installation, maintenance and inspection every six months, of hoists and lifts. These Regulations are obtainable from HMSO No person may be called upon to lift by hand any load heavy enough to cause him injury.

Fire

As explained in Chapter 3 and elsewhere in this Chapter, those provisions of the 1963 Act which used to deal with fire precautions are repealed, and the employer's obligations are as laid down under the Fire Precautions Act 1971.

First Aid

All premises covered by the Act must be equipped with an adequate first aid box, which must be in an accessible place, and regularly checked. A separate box must be provided for every 150 employees, and where more than 150 staff are employed on the premises, one member of staff must be competent in first aid, and placed in charge of the first aid facilities.

All accidents which either cause death, or result in a person being unable to work for three days or more, must be reported to the local authority; see page 179 above. The Health and Safety (First Aid) Regulations 1981 also apply.

The enforcement of the 1963 Act is in the hands of local Environmental Health Officers. They have all the usual powers of entry, search, inspection and interview, and an adverse report may lead to prosecution. Fines are heavy, particularly where a breach of the Act has led to death or serious injury, or is likely to if left unremedied.

CHAPTER THIRTEEN

Inns and private hotels

1. Introduction and definitions

INNS have been in existence for many centuries, and the profession of innkeeper is one of the oldest in the country. It is therefore not surprising that a certain amount of case law and several statutes exist which deal with the rights and duties of the innkeeper. As these rights and duties attach *only* to inns and innkeepers, these two terms must be defined very closely.

When we speak of an *inn* under the modern law, what is really meant is "an hotel within the meaning of the Hotel Proprietors Act 1956." But for convenience, and to save possible confusion, we continue to refer to such establishments as inns and all those which do not qualify as inns we call private hotels. By virtue of the 1956 Act, hotels within the meaning of the Act have inherited all the old rights and duties which belonged to inns under the old law, so we are in effect talking about the same thing anyway.

An inn may therefore be defined, in the language of section 1 of the 1956 Act, as "An establishment held out by the proprietor as offering food, drink, and, if so required, sleeping accommodation, without special contract, to any traveller presenting himself who appears able and willing to pay a reasonable sum for the services and facilities provided, and who is in a fit state to be received." The vital element in all this is the "holding out" of the establishment as being ready and willing to take all travellers without picking and choosing between them. The person who does the holding out (*i.e.* the proprietor) is the innkeeper (in many cases it will be a company), and it is upon him that all the rights and duties explained below fall.

It is in practice very difficult to decide in advance whether any given establishment is, or is not, an inn. It is a question which is perhaps best left for the courts to answer, although there are few modern cases dealing with this subject. The fact that the proprietor describes his establishment as an inn, or hotel, or even private hotel is not in itself a guarantee that this is the description which the law will apply; to confuse the matter even further, there appears to be nothing to prevent a proprietor changing from an inn to a private hotel, or vice versa, whenever he wishes. Not even the display of the statutory notice under section 2 of the 1956 Act (see below) is a foolproof guide, since the notice itself contains a clause stating that the mere display of the notice cannot be regarded as evidence that the establishment is an inn.

It is, in fact, simpler to approach the problem from the other side, and to attempt to identify establishments which are *not* inns. This list will include establishments in which the proprietor in some way exercises the right to pick and choose between guests, or bars access to certain types of traveller (*e.g.* "no coaches," or "no children," or "booking by prior contract only"). Clearly outside the category of inns are those establishments which do not offer sleeping accommodation, such as restaurants, public-houses and cafés. Boarding-houses and holiday camps are also normally outside the definition of an inn, and all these establishments will, for convenience, be referred to below as private hotels.

We may now begin to examine the legal rights and duties of an innkeeper in more detail; those of the private hotelier are dealt with later.

2. The duties of the innkeeper

The legal duties of an innkeeper are owed by him to all "travellers." At one time, no doubt the term "traveller" had some special legal meaning, but today it has a very wide application.

The case which may be taken as having extended the definition to the point at which it has become almost meaningless is that of *Williams* v. *Linnit* (1951), in which a farmer on his way home from a business meeting in Nuneaton actually drove past his own front door in order to go to a local hotel a few miles further on. He had no intention of staying there overnight, but was merely meeting friends for a drink, a regular arrangement he had. While he was inside, his car was stolen, and the question arose as to whether or not the hotel proprietor was liable as an "innkeeper." This question in turn hinged upon whether or not the farmer could be regarded as a "traveller," and the court had little difficulty in ruling that he *was*.

Clearly, then, a person may be classed as a traveller even though he is not seeking accommodation, and once he *is* a traveller, the innkeeper owes him a considerable duty. The various elements of that duty may now be examined.

The provision of food and drink

Every innkeeper, at common law, owes a duty to every traveller to provide him with "reasonable refreshment" at any hour of day or night; a failure to fulfil this duty, without lawful excuse, renders the innkeeper liable to a fine. The refreshment, however, need only be reasonable in the circumstances. Thus, the traveller may only demand a set meal during the normal mealtimes of the inn, and he can expect little more than sandwiches and coffee in the early hours of the morning. Similarly, a non-resident may obtain intoxicating drinks during the normal permitted hours, and at no other time.

The innkeeper need only supply such food and drink as he has available; when this is gone, he is under no further obligation to anyone. He is also entitled to put his existing guests first, and to give priority to those who have reserved a room or a table in advance, and who are expected to arrive later. Thus, in *R.* v. *Higgins* (1948), a traveller arrived at the defendant's inn at 12.30 p.m. on a Sunday, and demanded food and drink. The defendant, although he had tables free in the dining room, refused on the grounds that he only had a certain amount of food left, and that this was required for the evening meal and breakfast of existing guests. It was held that this was a sufficient excuse for the refusal, and the defendant was acquitted.

In addition to this defence, the innkeeper may also make use of those provided in section 1 of the 1956 Act (see above), and claim that the traveller in question was not in a fit state to be received, or appeared unable or unwilling to pay. There is nothing to prevent the innkeeper from demanding payment in advance, where this is possible, and where the innkeeper is genuinely doubtful of the traveller's creditworthiness.

R. v. *Rymer* (1877) was a case in which a traveller demanded entry to the refreshment bar of the defendant's inn accompanied by a large dog. The innkeeper refused to serve him unless the dog was left outside, which the traveller refused to do. There had been previous complaints from customers, and loss of business, due to the presence of R's dog in the bar, and it was held that the innkeeper was perfectly within his rights in refusing admission in the circumstances.

The provision of accommodation

Every innkeeper also owes a duty to every traveller to provide him with accommodation; in addition to the possibility of a fine, he may be sued for damages by the traveller if he refuses without lawful excuse.

Once again, the innkeeper's obligation is only to supply what he has available; once this has been accounted for (whether by prior bookings or not), he owes no further duty to the travelling public. And this duty also only extends to public bedrooms; the traveller has no right to demand, for example, a camp bed in the lounge, or a vacant room in the staff block. Thus, in *Browne* v. *Brandt* (1902) a traveller arrived at an inn at 2 a.m. after his transport had broken down, demanding food, drink and accommodation. He was provided with food and drink, but since all bedrooms were full, he was refused accommodation. He demanded to be allowed to sleep on a bench in the coffee room, but was refused. It was held that the innkeeper had done everything required of him, and was under no obligation to provide such accommodation.

The innkeeper may also, of course, make use of the the two defences laid down in section 1 of the Act (*i.e.* that the traveller appears to be unable or unwilling to pay, or that he is unfit to be received). In addition, he has the right to refuse accommodation where he has reasonable grounds for believing that the presence of the traveller would cause annoyance to other guests. Care must obviously be exercised when making use of this defence, but a good example was afforded by the case of *Rothfield* v. *North British Rail Company* (1920), where the plaintiff was a money-lender who was asked to vacate a room in the defendant's hotel, because on an earlier occasion he had stayed in the hotel, and had annoyed other guests by his attempts to do business there. It was held that although the defendants were innkeepers in the eyes of the law, they were within their rights in refusing accommodation in the circumstances. It would therefore seem perfectly in order for any establishment to keep a "black list."

But with these exceptions apart, the innkeeper's duty to provide any traveller with accommodation is absolute. It is no defence to point out that the traveller succeeded easily in obtaining accommodation elsewhere, not even if it was an hotel belonging to the same group or company; thus, in *Constantine* v. *Imperial London Hotels Ltd.* (1944), the plaintiff, the famous West Indian cricketer, was refused admission to the defendant's inn, although there were rooms vacant, on the grounds of his colour. He later obtained accommodation in another hotel owned by the same company, and the defendants argued that this was sufficient to discharge their duty as an innkeeper. It was held that they owed separate duties in respect of each hotel, and that a duty owed in respect of one hotel could not be discharged in another. This case must now also be read in the light of the Race Relations Act, dealt with below.

The innkeeper still has certain rights, however. Thus, he may demand payment in advance (on the same grounds as mentioned above), and he has complete control over which room the traveller occupies, unless of course there is a prior contract in respect of a *particular* room. The traveller may be called upon to occupy a different room every night, and the only requirement is that each room be habitable, and fairly priced in the circumstances.

The guest may be required to leave when his length of stay has been such that he no longer qualifies as a traveller. There can be no hard and fast rules here, since it is always a question of fact in the circumstances. Thus, in *Lamond* v. *Richard* (1897), Mrs. L arrived at a Brighton hotel in November, 1895, and was still there in August, 1896, having paid her bill regularly. She was given verbal notice to quit, which she ignored, and so, while she was out for a walk, her luggage was removed from her room, and she was refused re-entry. It was held that the action of the management was lawful, since she had ceased to be a traveller.

Care of guest's luggage

When a traveller becomes a *guest*, in that he books into the inn for at least one night, the law requires the innkeeper to undertake responsibility for the reception and safe-keeping of all reasonable items of luggage brought in by the guest. This liability extends from the midnight prior to the guest's arrival to the midnight following his departure; if the traveller never becomes a guest, of course, then this special duty never arises (although the innkeeper may be liable on other grounds to take care of the property—see below). However, it does mean, for example, that an innkeeper will be undertaking liability for luggage sent in advance (once the day of arrival has begun), and for luggage left for collection because the guest has been required to vacate his room (*e.g.* by noon on the day of departure).

Such items of luggage must be reasonable in the circumstances, and this will obviously depend upon the facts of the case; thus, for example, in *Robins* v. *Gray* (see below), it included sewing machines brought in by a commercial traveller. The 1956 Act states that the innkeeper is no longer liable for the safety of cars, property left in cars, horses and their harness, or any other type of animal. This does not mean that the innkeeper need not receive such items, if they are reasonable in the circumstances, and he may in any case assume responsibility for their safety on some ground other than his duty as an innkeeper—see below. In all cases, no duty arises until the property in question is actually brought onto the premises.

The most important point to note is the *extent* of the innkeeper's liability for the safety of his guest's luggage. This may best be summarised as follows:

1. Where the loss of, or damage to, the guest's property is caused by (a) act of God; (b) action of the Queen's enemies; (c) total negligence on the part of the guests *then the innkeeper incurs no liability whatsoever.*
2. Where the loss of, or damage to, the guest's property is caused solely by the negligence or wilful act of the innkeeper or his staff, or where the goods had been entrusted to the innkeeper for safe-keeping, or offered for safe-keeping but refused by the management, *then the innkeeper will be fully liable to the full extent of the loss or damage.* The proprietor may insist that the property be placed in a sealed or fastened container.
3. Where the loss of, or damage to, the guest's property is caused by some factor which does not fit exactly into either of the above categories, *and* the innkeeper has displayed the statutory notice (see below) in a conspicuous part of the premises near the main entrance or reception area, *then the innkeeper will be liable for a limited amount.* These limits are £50 per article, or £100 maximum per person, regardless of the number of articles. If the statutory notice is not adequately displayed at or near the reception desk or main entrance, the innkeeper will be liable to the full value of the property. In either case, the innkeeper is clearly regarded in law as *insuring* the safety of the guest's property.

The statutory notice (which is available in printed noticeboard form from several professional organisations) reads as follows:

NOTICE

LOSS OF OR DAMAGE TO GUEST'S PROPERTY

UNDER the Hotel Proprietors Act 1956, an hotel proprietor may in certain circumstances be liable to make good any loss of or damage to a guest's property even though it was not due to any fault of the proprietor or staff of the hotel.

This liability however—

(a) extends only to the property of guests who have engaged sleeping accommodation at the hotel;

(b) is limited to £50 for any one article and a total of £100 in the case of any one guest, except in the case of property which has been deposited, or offered for deposit, for safe custody;
(c) does not cover motor-cars or other vehicles of any kind or any property left in them, or horses or other live animals.

This notice does not constitute an admission either that the Act applies to this hotel or that liability thereunder attaches to the proprietor of this hotel in any particular case.

It is impossible beyond this to lay down any hard and fast rules, since it is always a question of fact in the circumstances, but the above are the official legal guidelines which must be followed. For example, where property is stolen from the premises, it depends upon why, when, where and by whom, whether or not the innkeeper will be fully liable, partly liable, or not liable for the loss. Two cases will serve as illustrations of the complexity of the law in this area. Both concerned the operation of the Innkeepers Liability Act, 1863 (the forerunner of the 1956 Act, under which the limit on the innkeeper's liability was £30).

In *Shacklock* v. *Ethorpe Ltd.* (1939), S stayed overnight in an hotel in Buckinghamshire. She intended to stay the following night, and during the day went up to London, leaving jewellery and money amounting to some £600 in a locked jewelbox in her room. The jewelbox was itself locked up in a heavily secured dressing bag, and then this was placed on her dressing room baggage stand along with other items of luggage. She did not lock her door or hand her key in at reception. On her return, she discovered that her case had been broken into, and the jewelbox removed. The culprit was in fact a professional thief who had taken an adjoining room. The management had not adequately displayed the statutory noticc, and the case therefore fell to be decided on common law principles, the management arguing that S had been negligent in not locking her room, and that she had only herself to blame.

It was held that the management had been negligent in that it had never been their practice to request guests to lock their rooms, and there were in any case no spare or master keys, and room staff relied on rooms being unlocked in order to get their work done. S had stayed at the same hotel on previous occasions, and knew this to be the system, and so had not been negligent in not locking her room. Nor had she been negligent in not depositing the goods for safe-keeping with the management, since she had been led to believe (wrongly) that there was no safe in the hotel. S recovered damages of £550 and costs.

In *Medawar* v. *Grand Hotel Company* (1891), M brought an

action against G as an innkeeper for the loss of his goods whilst a guest at the hotel. The facts were that M, on leaving his room, had negligently left valuables valued at £140 on a stand in the bedroom. The hotel cleaning staff had then negligently left the stand out in the corridor, and the valuables were stolen during that time. It was held by the Court of Appeal that it was for M to prove that G had been negligent if he wishes to claim £140, but that it was for G to prove that M had been solely to blame for the loss. On the facts, neither party had sufficiently discharged the burden of proof he bore, and G was therefore liable to compensate M to the value of £30. A more recent case to the same effect was *Knott* v. *Gordon Hotels* (1968).

Where the guest leaves valuables with the innkeeper for safe-keeping, he must make it clear that he is doing so; merely leaving them at reception in a sealed packet without any word of explanation is not necessarily enough. The property in question must also be left with either the innkeeper in person, or some authorised agent of his; handing it to the chambermaid is hardly enough to justify making the innkeeper fully liable for its safety.

The duty which the innkeeper owes to his guests in connection with their luggage cannot be evaded by means of a suitable exemption clause in his contract with the guest. This is a state of affairs referred to by lawyers as "strict liability."

3. The innkeeper's right of lien

So far, mention has only been made of the duties owed by an innkeeper to the traveller. The innkeeper also has one very important right over the traveller which no other hotelier possesses. This is the *right of lien* over guest's property; that is, the right to detain such property until the bill for food and accommodation is paid in full.

This covers all items of property which appear to belong to the guest, and which are of the type one would normally expect such a guest to bring with him. Thus, in *Robins* v. *Gray*, the right of lien was held to extend to sewing machines brought in by a guest who was a commercial traveller, on the ground that one would normally expect such a person to travel with his employer's product.

This case also illustrates the point that the property in question does not necessarily have to belong to the guest before the right of lien will cover it. Thus, goods on hire will be covered by the lien, and in *Berman and Nathans* v. *Weibye* (1983), the Court of Session held that an hotelier might have had a right of lien over a consignment of theatrical costumes delivered to a television film crew while they were staying in the hotel, and that he might have enforced this right even against the true owner of the costumes, (who had simply hired them out to the television company, which had left the country without paying the full hotel bill), were it not for the fact that the costumes had never been in the personal possession of the guests, but had been stored in outbuildings in the hotel grounds.

It would even seem that stolen goods may be claimed by the innkeeper under his right of lien, as in *Marsh* v. *Commissioner for Police* (1945), where a guest arrived at the Ritz Hotel, and during his stay stole a diamond ring from a local jeweller. When he found himself unable to meet the hotel bill, he handed over the ring as security. He was later convicted of the larceny of the ring, and the jeweller sued for its return. The proprietors of the Ritz refused, claiming a right of lien over it. It was held that the ring, even though acquired *after* the resident's arrival, must be regarded as the property of the guest, since the innkeeper thought it so in all good faith, and that therefore a right of lien covered it.

Several points, however, must be made in relation to this case. The first is that the police have the right to take away any goods which they believe may constitute evidence in a future case; the innkeeper should insist upon a receipt, and claim for the return of the goods as soon as possible. The second is that under section 28 of the Theft Act 1968, a court may, upon the conviction of any thief, order the return of the stolen property to its rightful owner; this may not necessarily be the innkeeper. Difficult questions of law are raised here which are beyond the scope of this book.

The final point to be made on the above case is that it appears to be the only substantial English authority for the statement that the right of lien covers property other than that brought in by the guest at the time of arrival; other sources take the opposite view, and the matter must therefore be regarded as unsettled.

By virtue of the 1956 Act, there is no longer any right of lien on cars, property left in cars, horses and their harness, and other animals. Also, the innkeeper may not attempt to exercise a lien over the clothes which the guest is actually wearing; nor may he detain the guest himself, unless it is pending the arrival of the police, who may be called in where fraud is suspected. The right of lien does not arise until there is a debt in existence, although it is not lost where the guest gives security for the bill, unless such security is expressly understood to be in lieu of lien.

It should be noted that the right of lien extends to any traveller who incurs a debt to the innkeeper, and not just someone who is staying on the premises. Thus, the innkeeper could exercise his right of lien over the property of someone who is merely taking a meal on the premises, even though he could not be made automatically liable for the *safety* of such property (see above). The right of lien therefore covers more property than the innkeeper's duty of care.

The innkeeper will lose his right of lien if at any time he voluntarily and knowingly gives up possession of the property in question; this does not include parting with it temporarily, in order to have it valued, or prepared for sale (see below). Nor would the innkeeper be deemed to give up possession if called upon by the police to hand it over temporarily in order that it may be used as evidence. While it is in his possession, the innkeeper must take as much care of the property as if it were his own, and any damage to it will have to be made good if and when the bill is paid. He may not charge for storage.

The right of lien in itself is of little value to the innkeeper if the guest has no intention of paying his bill, so under the Innkeepers Act 1878, he is given a *right of sale* over lien goods where the bill has not been paid. There are of course certain conditions which must be satisfied first, and these are that:

1. the property must have been in the innkeeper's possession for at least six weeks without the bill having been fully satisfied;
2. at least four weeks before the sale, the innkeeper must place an advertisement in a London newspaper, and in a newspaper circulating locally. These must state the innkeeper's intention to sell the property, give full details of the intended sale, carry a description of the goods, and give the name (if known) of the guest to whom they originally belonged;
3. the sale must be by public auction.

The innkeeper may then deduct from the proceeds of sale the cost of his bill, plus any expenses incurred in the organisation of the sale, and the placing of the advertisements. Any surplus must be handed over to the guest upon demand. The right of lien exists *in addition to* any other right which the innkeeper may have in connection with the payment of his bill (*e.g.* the right to sue for breach of contract).

4. Establishments other than inns

We are now in a position to contrast the legal position of an inn with that of all establishments which are classed as private hotels. It will be remembered that this is the title which for convenience is given to all catering premises which for one reason or another cannot be classed as inns. The following comparisons may be made.

(1) The innkeeper must, with the exceptions noted above, receive

and accommodate all travellers; the private hotelier, on the other hand, is completely free to pick and choose.

(2) The innkeeper incurs *some* liability for loss of or damage to the property of guests in all cases except act of God, action of the Queen's enemies and the total negligence of the guest himself; the fact that the innkeeper himself may not be negligent will affect only the amount he will have to pay. A private hotelier, on the other hand, is never liable for any amount unless either he or his staff are at least negligent, or unless he has accepted liability under the terms of a contract with the guest; even then, there may be an exemption clause in the contract which frees the hotelier of all liability. Where a traveller enters an inn, but is not staying overnight, then the innkeeper's liability in respect of that person's property is the same as that of a private hotelier in respect of all his guests.

The private hotelier (and his staff) cannot be deemed to have been negligent until it can be shown that he or they have failed to take reasonable care for the property of the guest. Such care need only be reasonable in the circumstances, and it will always be a question of fact for the court to determine whether or not such care has been exercised.

As was mentioned above, a private hotelier may also become liable where he has undertaken responsibility for the guest's property under the terms of a contract. Such contracts often taken the form of a "contract of bailment," whereby one party (*i.e.* the hotelier) undertakes to look after certain property belonging to another party (*i.e.* the guest). For example, the proprietor of a dance-hall will normally provide a cloakroom as part of the service he provides in return for the entrance fee to the dance. This is an example of a valid contract of bailment; it is not in fact necessary for any charge to be made.

The property must be handed over by the guest to the hotelier for safe-keeping before such a contract will come into operation; alternatively, the hotelier or one of his staff may take it from the guest for this purpose; thus, in *Ultzen* v. *Nicols* (1894), a waiter in a restaurant took the plaintiff's overcoat from him without being asked to do so, and hung it on a hook behind his chair. The coat was later stolen, and it was held that the proprietor must make good the loss, since by his action the waiter had brought a contract of bailment into existence between his employer and the plaintiff. But, on the other hand, in *Tinsley* v. *Dudley* (1951) it was held that a publican was not liable to the owner of a motor cycle who left it in his public-house yard without informing the licensee, since the licensee was not an "innkeeper," and there was no evidence of a "contract of bailment."

Sometimes, a contract of bailment may be entered into by *implication*, as in *Samuel* v. *Westminster Wine Co.* (1959), in which it was held that the proprietors of an hotel were liable to a non-resident diner who had left her coat in an unattended ante-room from which it had been stolen. The court held that the simple provision of an ante-room for coats was sufficient to indicate that the management accepted liability for coats.

In practice, many proprietors insert an exemption clause into the contract which seeks to rid them of all liability; the nature and affect of exemption clauses are dealt with in the next chapter. All that need be noted at this stage is that such a clause, if it is ever to be effective must be a reasonable one, and must become a term of the contract *at the time when the contract is made.*

(3) An innkeeper has a right of lien over the property of a guest who fails to pay the bill, whereas a private hotelier has no such right, and his only remedy will be to sue for the debt in court. He may choose to detain the guest pending the arrival of the police (where a charge is to be laid), but this will get him no nearer the payment of the bill. However, since the passing of the Torts (Interference with Goods) Act 1977, a bailee (see above) has been authorised to sell goods bailed with him in order to secure payment of his bill.

5. Discrimination

In dealing with the freedom (such as it is) of the innkeeper and the private hotelier to pick and choose between potential guests, no mention has yet been made of the legislation against discrimination. This has an important effect on catering establishments, and what follows concerns public-houses, cafés, boarding-houses and restaurants just as much as it does large hotels.

The Race Relations Act

Section 20(1) of the Race Relations Act 1976 states:

"It is unlawful for any person concerned with the provision (for payment or not) of goods, facilities, or services to the public or a section of the public to discriminate against a person who seeks to obtain or use those goods, facilities or services—

1. by refusing or deliberately omitting to provide him with any of them; or

2. by refusing or deliberately omitting to provide him with goods, facilities or services of the like quality, in the like manner and on the like terms as are normal in the first-mentioned person's case in relation to other members of the public or (where

the person so seeking belongs to a section of the public) to other members of that section."

"Discriminate" is defined as treating a person less favourably than others on the grounds of colour, nationality, race or ethnic or national origins, or imposing conditions which such a person is less likely to fulfil than others, and which cannot be justified on non-racial grounds; and among the examples given of the type of establishments covered by section 20 are "hotel, boarding house or other similar establishment" and "any place which members of the public are permitted to enter." It therefore seems that every establishment within the normal catering field is covered by section 20 (catering in hospitals, schools and industrial canteens will be covered, since section 20 includes "a section of the public"). The one substantial exception arises in the case of premises on which the occupier or a "close relative" of his reside, and which offer accommodation to no more than six people in addition to the occupier and his household; in such a case, the proprietor (presumably, the occupier) *may* lawfully discriminate on racial grounds.

Section 20 therefore provides another legal answer to the problem raised in *Constantine's* case dealt with above; even a caterer who normally has the right to pick and choose (*i.e.* a private hotelier) may not pick and choose on racial grounds.

Any breach of section 20 may result in the matter being brought before the Commission for Racial Equality, which has the power to conduct investigations. Actions may also be brought directly by an aggrieved party before special county courts (in Scotland, sheriff courts), and the damages which may be claimed are not limited by the normal financial limits of those courts. The C.R.E. also has the power to issue "non-discrimination notices" against offenders, and if this fails, may bring an action for an injunction (in Scotland, interdict) against the offender to prevent any further abuses.

Even obscure forms of discrimination can be struck at by using the Act, as may be seen from *Zarczynska* v. *Levy* (1979), in which a white barmaid was sacked by a publican for refusing to implement a colour bar ordered by him. It was held that she could challenge her dismissal before an industrial tribunal on the basis that she had been treated "less favourably" on "racial grounds." A similar ruling in a case involving the manager of an entertainment centre was *Showboat Entertainment Centre* v. *Owens* (1984).

It should also be noted that section 5A of the Public Order Act 1936 provides for a *criminal prosecution* against anyone using, in a public place, threatening, abusive or insulting words which would be likely to stir up hatred against any racial group. To publish or distribute any such material in written form is also a criminal offence.

Sex Discrimination

Section 29 of the Sex Discrimination Act 1975, states:

"It is unlawful for any person concerned with the provision (for payment or not) of goods, facilities or services to the public or a section of the public to discriminate against a woman who seeks to obtain or use those goods, facilities or services—

1. by refusing or deliberately omitting to provide her with any of them, or

2. by refusing or deliberately omitting to provide her with goods, facilities or services of the like quality, in the like manner and on the like terms as are normal in his case in relation to male members of the public or (where she belongs to a section of the public) to male members of that section."

"Discrimination" is defined in the same way as it is for racial discrimination.

Although section 29 of the Act appears to state that sex discrimination in the provision of goods, etc., is only unlawful when it is practised against women, it is provided in section 2 of the Act that this section of the Act shall also render unlawful any discrimination against men. In short, a proprietor whose establishment is covered by section 29 is not permitted to practice *any* form of sex discrimination, against either men or women.

Section 29 of the Act gives examples of the type of "facilities and services" which are covered, and among these are "accommodation in an hotel, boarding house or other similar establishment," and "facilities for entertainment, recreation or refreshment." This clearly is sufficient to cover most of the catering industry and in *Gill* v. *El Vino Co* (1983) it was held to be wrongful discrimination to refuse to allow women to drink at the bar of the famous Fleet Street pub when men were allowed to do so.

Complaints under section 29 are dealt with as civil claims in the county court (in Scotland, sheriff court) and the damages awardable are not limited to those normally awardable in those courts. Damages may be awarded for injured feelings.

CHAPTER FOURTEEN

The guest

HAVING distinguished between inns and private hotels, and noted their separate duties to the travelling public, we may now turn our attention to those laws which govern the relationship between the guest and proprietor. What follows, unless otherwise indicated, applies to both the inn and the private hotel.

1. Contracts of booking

The contract itself

When a guest books a room in any residential establishment, he is making a contract with the proprietor; this contract may be defined simply as "a legally binding agreement between two parties." From the moment that a valid contract is made, the parties to the contract, with certain exceptions such as minors, (for whom see below), are bound together in a legal relationship which neither may break with impunity unless the other party agrees. Such a contract may be either verbal or written, but it is obviously preferable for it to be in writing, in order that its terms may be proved later, should the need arise.

The visible manifestations of a contract are the "offer" and the "acceptance." The offer may be made by either party, who must state clearly the exact terms upon which the contract is being offered; the other party, if he finds the terms to his liking, will make the acceptance. All the terms of the proposed contract must have been dealt with at this stage.

The contract officially comes into existence at the time when the acceptance is communicated to the party making the offer (the "offeror"). In the case of verbal contracts, made face to face or over the telephone, there are no problems, since the acceptance, and its communication, occur almost simultaneously. Problems may arise with written contracts, however, since the rule here is that the acceptance is regarded as having been communicated to the offeror as soon as the letter is placed in the post, whether the offeror ever receives it or not. Thus, the offeror may be bound by a contract even though he is not aware that his offer has been accepted.

An offer must be distinguished from statements which fall short of offers, such as requests for information, or preliminary inquiries. An offer is a definite statement, containing all the terms which it is hoped will form the basis of the contract. In practice, of course, it is never easy to make narrow distinctions, and the proprietor must take great care to ensure that he is not rendering himself liable under a contract without realising the fact. Thus, to take an all too common situation:

1. G writes to P requesting a brochure; this is a request for information;
2. P sends G a brochure, plus current tariff, which together provide all the information required; if nothing else is said, this is capable of constituting an offer in the eyes of the law;
3. G replies by booking a double room with private bath at £50 per night, bed and breakfast, for the nights of August 1 and 2 next. This is an acceptance, and P and G are now engaged in a contract.

This is all very well provided that P receives this acceptance, and provided that he still has such a room available when he receives it. As was pointed out above, P may still be liable even if he never receives it, and the predicament of a proprietor who finds himself double booked is too common to require further mention. All this may be avoided by careful wording: thus—

1. G writes to P requesting a brochure—as above;
2. P sends G a brochure, plus current tariff, *plus a covering letter* stating that all communications are subject to the availability of rooms upon receipt of reply. The same effect may be produced by a statement in the brochure itself. This is not now an offer, but an invitation to G to make an offer;
3. G replies by booking a double room with private bath at £50 per night, bed and breakfast, for the nights of August 1 and 2 next. This is now the offer;
4. P replies, confirming the booking. This is the acceptance, and the contract is complete.

Thus, by the introduction of a simple additional stage in the negotiations, the proprietor has ensured that he will not be bound by a contract which he cannot fulfil. It should be noted in passing that offers remain open only for a reasonable length of time, after which they may not be validly accepted. What will be deemed reasonable will obviously be a question of fact which can only be answered in the circumstances of each case. In the case of most hotel bookings, 10 days or a fortnight may be taken as the general guide.

Any communication may be withdrawn, provided that this is done in time. Thus, any offer may be withdrawn before the moment at which acceptance is made, and any acceptance may be withdrawn before the communication of acceptance reaches the offeror. Thus, any acceptance which has just been placed in the post may be revoked by means of a telegram to the offeror, which will reach him first. The payment of a deposit is some evidence of the existence of a contract, but it is more commonly regarded as a mere sign of good faith.

The terms of the contract

It is obvious from what has already been written that all the terms of the contract must be agreed upon by the two parties before the contract is finalised. It follows from that fact that neither of the parties may seek to add to or vary the terms of the contract at some later date, unless both parties agree to do so as part of a new agreement.

Thus, where the communications are by letter (*i.e.* advance bookings), all the necessary terms must be laid down by the proprietor either in the letters themselves, or in an accompanying brochure. Where communications are by telephone, care must be taken to inform the prospective guest of these terms; it is preferable, of course, to make the telephone conversation merely an initial negotiation, and to finalise the whole matter in writing, in the manner outlined above.

Where the proprietor takes a chance guest, the contract is normally made verbally at the reception desk, and the guest must be informed of all the terms there and then; thus, in *Olley* v. *Marlborough Court Ltd.* (1949), the plaintiff booked a room in the defendant's hotel and having booked in, she went to her room, on the wall of which was a notice stating that the management would not accept any liability for articles lost or stolen unless they were deposited with the receptionist for safe-keeping. She did not deposit her valuables, and they were later lost. She claimed against the management, who sought to rely on the notice in the bedroom. It was held that since a chance contract of booking is made at the time when the guest books in at the reception desk, the proprietor, if he wishes to include extra terms in the contract, must do so there and then, either by informing the guest verbally, or by the display of a notice at the reception desk. Since the so-called exemption clause had, in this case, only been communicated to the guest *after* the contract had been finalised, the management could not rely on it, and must therefore compensate the guest.

On the other hand, the law recognises the proprietor's right to fix certain rules relating to the conduct of his premises, such as mealtimes, no smoking areas, payment in cash only, and so on, and it is unlikely that any court would require that these be made terms of the contract in any formal sense, unless they interfere unduly with the comfort or freedom of movement of the guest.

In addition, there are certain hotel charges which are customary throughout the trade, and which may be *implied* into the normal contract of booking without anything being said or written; examples would be charges for room service, early morning tea and newspapers. At the present moment, it is unlikely that a general service charge would come into this category, although it may not be long before it does. In all cases, of course, the charges must be reasonable in relation to the establishment and its standards.

In an attempt to ensure that guests in British hotels are given as much information as possible concerning prices *before* they enter into a contract, new laws were introduced under the Tourism (Sleeping Accommodation Price Display) Order 1977, which requires the display of overnight accommodation prices in residential establishments with four or more rooms. These prices must be displayed in a notice at reception or in the hotel entrance, and the maximum and minimum prices must be given.

The Order is not applicable to bona fide members' clubs, youth hostels, rooms which are normally in the same occupation for at least 21 consecutive nights, or establishments which provide facilities other than those of a normal hotel as part of the price (*e.g.* holiday camps). Apart from these exceptions, all other residential establishments which qualify as above are covered by the Order.

The information which must be provided in the notice is as follows; (a) the price of a single room; (b) the price of a room for two; (c) the price of any other type of bedroom. If prices are not standard for such rooms, then only the maximum and minimum prices need be given. All prices quoted must be inclusive of service charge, and must clearly show that fact. VAT may be shown separately if desired, but the VAT element in the price must be shown in some form or other. The notice must also make it clear when the room price is inclusive of meals.

The Order is enforced by the local authority, whose inspectors have the usual powers of entry and inspection. There are penalties for failing to comply with the Order or for obstructing an inspector. See also p. 221 for the implications of s.20 of the Consumer Protection Act 1987, which applies to "services" such as hotel facilities just as much as it does to "goods" such as food and drink.

Where the guest in question is one who has stayed in the hotel on frequent previous occasions, and must therefore have been familiar with the normal terms, it may be possible to imply that he was aware of certain terms (*e.g.* 10 per cent. general service charge), where other guests would need to have any such term clearly communicated to them before they would be bound by it.

One very common implied term in a contract of booking which goes almost without saying is that the room which is allocated to the guest must be one which is fit for habitation. Finally, it should be noted that there are now certain important limits on an hotelier's ability to restrict his liability by contract—see below, p. 206.

Minors and agents

Not everyone who goes through the motions of making a contract has the legal capacity to make one, and an hotelier can find, if he is not careful, that he has made a contract with someone against whom his agreement cannot be enforced. The two most important examples of this occur in cases involving minority and agency.

A minor, so far as the law of contract is concerned, is someone who is under 18 years of age, and such a person may only make an enforceable contract for "necessaries" (*N.B.* the question of contracts of employment is a separate one). Necessaries may be defined as "goods and services suitable to the minor's needs, and to his station in life." The rule would seem to be, therefore, that the more wealthy the origins of the minor in question, the more likely the hotelier is to be able to sue under a valid contract for this money. It is, in other words, always a question of fact to be answered in the circumstances, and it is always advisable, where possible, to make the contract directly with the parent or guardian.

Care must also be exercised when negotiating a contract of booking through an agent; many tourist hotels deal with travel agents, and so the matter is of considerable importance to the catering trade. An agent is someone who is employed to conduct business with third parties for the benefit of his client. To be more specific, an agent A is a person employed by his principal P to negotiate a contract between P and some third party X. The actual contract is between X (*e.g.* an hotelier) and P (*e.g.* a tourist), and in many cases, the agent incurs no direct liability to X, and cannot be sued by him.

If, for example, a party of tourists booked into an hotel by a travel agent fails to arrive, the proprietor's only legal redress may be against the guests themselves, about whom he knows next to nothing. Where in fact the identity of the guest or guests has not been revealed by the agent, the courts will very often allow the hotelier to sue the agent himself, on the grounds that the contract is really one between the hotel and the agent. Where, on the other hand, the agent has merely acted as a go-between, and has handed on various items of information, the courts will only allow the hotelier to proceed against the guests themselves. It is clearly in the hotelier's interests for him to arrange the question of the liability for payment in writing with the agent.

Finally, mention must be made of the legal position of married women. They are, of course, perfectly entitled to make contracts in their own right, but they are also, in some cases, entitled to act as agents for their husbands. Thus a married woman may in some cases occupy a room in an hotel, and give instructions for the bill to be sent to her husband. Since the liability of the husband to pay depends upon a variety of factors (*e.g.* the financial circumstances of the husband and wife, their matrimonial relations, etc.) is not automatic and is beyond the power of the hotelier to investigate, it is advisable at all times to insist upon personal payment by the wife or at the very least to obtain certain confirmation from the husband that he will pay.

Breach of contract

Once a contract of booking has been finalised, any cancellation on either side is technically a breach of contract, regardless of the length of notice given. However, the amount awarded by way of damages will vary considerably according to the circumstances, and this matter is best approached as follows.

Cancellation by the guest

When a guest has booked a room in an hotel, he commits a technical breach of contract if he either cancels his booking in advance, or fails to arrive on the appointed day. The hotelier may welcome the cancellation, in which case the contract may be regarded as cancelled by mutual agreement. He may, on the other hand, feel aggrieved, in which case he is a liberty to sue for damages.

He may only recover damages *based upon what he has actually lost.* He owes the guest a duty to minimise (mitigate) his loss, so that the amount which he will actually recover from the guest, should he choose to sue him, will depend entirely on the facts of the individual case.

Thus, if a guest has booked a room during a busy holiday period, but cancels the booking a month in advance, and the hotelier is able to relet the room for the whole period, then he will recover nothing. He will still recover nothing if he makes no effort to relet the room, since the court will almost certainly decide that he has failed in this duty to mitigate the loss. If, on the other hand, the booking is out of season, and the guest fails to turn up without any prior warning, thus leaving the hotelier no chance of reletting, the hotelier will be able to recover the full amount of his actual loss.

These losses are normally computed on the basis of the full flat rate value of the booking, less the amount of the deposit (if any), and the value of the food, lighting and heating not consumed. The proprietor may not charge for such items as service percentage and money which the guest might have spent in the bar, since these are not actual losses.

The two situations cited above are extreme cases, in practice, most of the cases which do arise fall somewhere between these two.

Cancellation by the hotel

Where it is the proprietor who fails to provide the accommodation which has been agreed upon, then it is the guest who has the right to sue for breach of contract, unless he agrees to abandon the contract. The most common situation in this category, of course, is the one in which the guest arrives at the hotel only to discover that the proprietor has double booked his room, and that no other is available. We have already seen that this gives rise to certain other legal implications where the proprietor in question is also an innkeeper, but we are concerned here solely with the question of the breach of contract.

Like the proprietor, the guest may only sue for his actual losses occurring as a direct and inevitable result of the breach of contract. Such losses might include taxi fares to another hotel, or an increase in expense through being obliged to take accommodation in another, more expensive hotel. But also, like the proprietor, the guest is expected to "mitigate" his loss, and make a reasonable effort to keep the increase in cost down to a minimum. Where the proprietor is able to find the guest a similar room in another hotel, of course, the actual loss will be minimal.

In some cases, problems occur where the guest fails to arrive to claim his room at the appointed time, but arrives half-way through the intended period of stay, expecting a room to be available. There comes a point, of course, at which the proprietor is entitled to assume that the guest is not going to arrive at all, and to relet the room; as was pointed out above, the law requires him to mitigate his loss. Such matters should ideally be dealt with as one of the terms of the contract; for example, the hotel brochure may contain a statement that all rooms not claimed by 7 p.m. on the day of expected arrival will be relet. Such a statement will become a term of the contract if the correct procedure (outlined above) is followed.

Misrepresentation and frustration

There are certain situations in which the refusal of one of the parties to fulfil the terms of the contract will not constitute a breach of contract. The two most important of these involve misrepresentation and frustration of contract.

Misrepresentation is a state of affairs in which one of the parties to the contract is induced to enter into the contract by certain statements of fact made by the other party which turn out to be untrue. An obvious example of this would be an hotel brochure which falsely described the services and facilities of the hotel, although not every mere overstatement will have this effect. It is natural for the proprietor to wish to make his establishment sound as attractive as possible, and the trouble only begins where false statements are made which are likely to affect the comfort or convenience of the guest.

Examples of the kind of statement likely to be regarded in law as a misrepresentation might be ones involving cleanliness, quality and quantity of food, and distance of the hotel from attractions such as the beach, the shops or the theatre. In all these cases, the guest would be entitled to repudiate (*i.e.* refuse to continue with) the contract, and claim an indemnity against the proprietor for expenses already incurred. Alternatively he would be entitled to continue with the contract, and claim for damages. In this context, recent cases have illustrated that a guest may obtain damages in respect of his own feelings of disappointment, and for the disappointment experienced by his family.

Thus, in *Jarvis* v. *Swans Tours* (1972), S issued a brochure for a winter sports holiday which included a "houseparty" atmosphere, afternoon tea, a bar, a "yodeller" evening, hire of ski equipment and an English-speaking hotel proprietor. Mr. J booked a holiday on the strength of the brochure, but for the second week he turned out to be the only person there, the afternoon tea consisted of crisps and dry nutcake, the ski equipment was not always available, the yodeller was a man dressed in working clothes who sang a few songs, then hurriedly departed, the bar was only open on one evening, and the proprietor spoke no English. Having received only £31 damages in the County Court (half the cost of the holiday), J appealed to the Court of Appeal, who increased the damages to £125 to take account of the frustration and disappointment of not getting the holiday which he had been looking forward to for a considerable time.

In *Jackson* v. *Horizon Holidays* (1975), J arranged with a travel agency to spend four weeks in Ceylon with his wife and children. In particular, he asked for a communicating door between the room occupied by his wife and himself, and that occupied by the children. In addition, the hotel was described as having facilities such as mini-golf, a swimming pool, hairdressing salon, and rooms with private bath, shower and w.c. In reality, there was no communicating door with the children's room, which was in any case so mildewed as to be unusable, there was no private bath and the shower and w.c. were dirty. The food was unpleasant, and there was no mini-golf, swimming pool or hairdressing salon. After two weeks, the family moved into another hotel which was better even though building work was being carried out. When J sued for damages, he was awarded back £1100 of the £1200 which he had originally paid for the holiday, to take account not only of his own discomfort and disappointment, but also that suffered by each member of his family.

Frustration of contract occurs where some event takes place which was totally unforeseeable, which is beyond the control of either of the parties, and which renders the contract incapable of performance in its originally intended form. Situations such as these are not common, but one example might be if an hotel burned down accidentally, in such a case, all future bookings would be incapable of performance, at least in the near future, both parties would be relieved of their duties under the contract, and all deposits, advanced payments, etc., would be returnable. The death of the intended guest is obviously also a good example of a frustrating event, as also, in most cases, would be serious illness.

It has also been suggested that the air traffic controllers' strike in France in 1980, which resulted in a large proportion of some holidays being spent in airport lounges, could have been regarded as frustrating many holiday contracts.

Exemption clauses

In theory, it is possible for either party to any contract to minimise or even eliminate his liability for breach of contract by inserting into the contract itself a clause which has that effect, and which is binding upon both parties like any other contractual term. The same effect can often be achieved by displaying a notice in some place (*e.g.* reception) where the court will assume it must have been read and agreed by the other party *before* the contract was finalised (see above).

Because of the potential for abuse and injustice where one of the parties is a "consumer" (*i.e.* he is not making the contract as part of some business), and he is dealing with a businessman who insists on recording their agreement in a standard-form contract drawn up by him, the Unfair Contract Terms Act 1977, states that whenever *either* one of the parties is a "consumer" and the other is not, *or* one of the parties insists on doing business on his own written standard terms, then no exemption clause which seeks to protect the businessman or the person insisting on the use of that contract from liability for breach of it will be enforcible unless in the circumstances it may be said to be "reasonable." This test brings in a whole host of factors, including the price charged and the bargaining strengths of the parties, but it does mean that the hotelier cannot expect to automatically apply his own standard terms of business as quoted in some brochure, or displayed in a notice in reception, and always be protected from the consequences of a breach of contract.

The Trade Descriptions Act 1968

It has already been noted that a false and misleading statement concerning the standard or quantity of services or facilities at an hotel may give rise to a *civil* action by the guest on the grounds of misrepresentation. Such statements may also give rise to *criminal prosecutions* under the Trade Descriptions Act 1968.

Section 14 of the Act makes it a criminal offence knowingly or recklessly to make any statement in the course of any trade or business which falsely describes any services or facilities offered. This includes any false descriptions as to quality, quantity, availability, price or location of goods, services and accommodation.

Section 24 of the Act provides a defence to anyone charged under section 14 who can show one of the following; (a) that it was a pure mistake on his part; (b) that he placed reliance on information supplied to him; (c) that the offence was the result of the act or default of some other person. In *all* cases, the defendant must show that he took all reasonable care, and exercised all due diligence to avoid the commission of the offence.

It can thus be seen that every hotelier faces not only a civil action by the guest, but also criminal prosecution, if he makes wild claims for his establishment which he cannot later substantiate. Any travel agent who passes on such claims to a client will also face the risk of prosecution, unless he can bring himself within the provisions of section 24. In addition, he may be ordered to compensate the "victim."

One obvious weakness in the Act has already become apparent. It would seem that provided that the statement in question is true at the time of its making, it makes no difference if the circumstances change later. This point emerged clearly in the case of *Sunair Holidays* v. *Dodd* (1970), in which S a travel agent, made a contract with X, an hotelier in Majorca, whereby all X's twin-bedded rooms with bath, shower and terrace were to be made available for S's clients. S then advertised in a holiday brochure an hotel in Majorca with "twin beds, bath, shower and terrace." Acting upon this statement, two families of holidaymakers booked holidays at the hotel through S. When they arrived, they found that neither of the rooms had terraces. It was held that although S had been negligent in not making a last-minute check on the rooms allocated to his clients, the statement in the brochure had, at the time of its making, been true, since S had contracted with X for rooms of that description. There could not, therefore, be any conviction under section 14 of the 1968 Act. Against this, however, must now be set the ruling in *Wings* v. *Ellis* (1984) to the effect that once a false statement appears in a brochure, the author (*i.e.* the travel company) will be liable to everyone who relies upon it, even though instructions have been given to correct it. It is no defence that the statement was not *known* to be false at the time of making.

An hotelier or travel agent will not apparently be liable if the statements in question may be said to be mere "promises for the future." This emerged in *R.* v. *Sunair Holidays* (1973), in which, in 1969, S published a travel brochure for the 1970 season which referred to an hotel in Spain which had a swimming pool, and in which push-chairs for children were stated to be for hire, as well as special dishes available for children. B, on the strength of this brochure, booked a holiday for himself and his family to begin in May, 1970, but on arrival at the hotel they found that the swimming pool was not completed, and was unusable, while no pushchairs or special dishes were available for children. It was proved as a fact that when S had booked their accommodation with the owners of the hotel, all these facilities had been planned. It was held by the Court of Appeal that section 14 of the Act related to statements which were either true or false at the time at which they were made. The statements in S's brochure were in fact promises for the future, and could not be brought under section 14 unless they contained by implication a statement of present fact. S. could not, therefore, be convicted under section 14.

But if an entrepreneur *is* found liable under the Act, he commits a separate criminal offence in respect of each and every client who is misled by his statement. So far as overbooking by hotels is concerned, the position will in future no doubt be governed by *British Airways Board* v. *Tyler* (1976), in which it was held that a flight booking confirmation by the board might be taken as a firm and unequivocal statement that the traveller had a seat reserved on the flight in question, and that a subsequent overbooking which resulted in his losing the seat was an offence under section 14.

A proprietor or travel agent will still be liable under section 14 even if the offence is actually committed by one of his staff, provided that it is in the course of the latter's employment. However, the fact that an offence has been committed under section 14 does not automatically invalidate the contract; the party who has suffered must bring his civil action in the normal way if he wishes to avoid his duties under the contract.

The 1968 Act has also had considerable impact on the law relating to the service of food and drink, and further details may be found in the appropriate section of Chapter 15.

2. The guest in residence

Registration

Under the Immigration (Hotel Records) Order 1972, every guest over 16 years of age must, on arrival at an hotel, register his full name and nationality, or have it registered for him. This need not be done in any special book, but the hotelier is required to keep some record of this information which may be inspected by the police, if required, at any time during the following 12 months.

British subjects need not give their address. Commonwealth citizens enjoy the same privilege. Details of each guest must be entered separately (not just "Mr. and Mrs."), and any guest who spends a night away from the hotel during the period of his stay should ensure that the fact is recorded.

Guests who are neither British, or Commonwealth citizens, and who are therefore classed under English and Scots law as aliens, must give not only their names and nationalities, but also the details of their passports, the date of leaving the hotel, and the address to which they are proceeding. However, persons, who are covered by the Diplomatic Privileges Act 1964 (*i.e.* ambassadors, their staff and their families) need not register at all, while those persons who are citizens of a British protectorate, or who are serving in either the U.K. or NATO armed forces, may register as if they were British subjects.

Registers are sometimes required as evidence in cases which do not involve the police, *e.g.* matters arising from private inquiries. No register need be produced under such circumstances unless there is a court order to that effect. Members of hotel staffs may also be required as witnesses, in which case they will normally be paid their expenses, but nothing more.

The behaviour of the guest

There is not much which can be written on this subject, since it consists largely of rules of common sense and diplomacy, tempered by individual managerial policy. There are, however, certain guidelines which may be laid down.

A guest is not legally entitled to a key to his room, although a failure to provide one may render the proprietor liable to make full compensation to the guest should any of his property be stolen or simply lost; see Chapter 13. Even where the guest *is* given a key, he is not entitled to lock the door against the proprietor or his staff; merely against his fellow guests.

It has already been noted that a guest who proves to be objectionable to other guests has no right to remain even at an inn, and he may be asked to leave. Once he has refused a reasonable request by the proprietor that he leave, he becomes a *trespasser* in the eyes of the law, and may be ejected, if necessary by force. In Scotland, however, each alleged "trespass" is considered on its merits. However, the absolute minimum amount of force should be used, and preferably none at all. The police have no authority to intervene in a civil matter such as a trespass, but they may be called where a breach of the peace is either being committed or expected to occur. Any damage wilfully or negligently caused by the guest may be charged to him.

Lost property in an hotel should be handed initially to the management, who should then attempt to identify the owner. After a reasonable length of time has passed (and this is always a question of fact in the circumstances), the property may either be retained by the management, or returned to the finder. The law is still unclear as to whether or not the proprietor has a better claim to the property than the finder. Articles of great value should ideally be handed to the police, since a person who "finds" property without making sufficient effort to trace the true owner may be found guilty of theft, and one should never risk such an accusation. All the above rules apply equally to the property of a guest who has left the hotel after paying his bill; such persons are in any case often traceable.

No guest has the right to demand to be allowed to pay by cheque, although travellers' cheques may be regarded as being equivalent to cash. Any guest wishing to pay by cheque should present it before he leaves, in order that it may be cleared while he is still on the premises.

The safety of the guest

We have already dealt at some length with the liability of an hotelier for the safety of the guest's property. Needless to say, the law also makes the hotelier to some extent responsible for the safety of the guest himself, and this is the most convenient place at which to discuss this responsibility.

Section 2 of the Occupiers Liability Act 1957, (in Scotland, an equivalent Act of 1960) which embodies most of the present law on the subject, makes the occupier of premises (*i.e.* for our purposes the proprietor) liable for the physical safety of all persons lawfully entering his premises. More specifically, he is under a duty of care to all lawful visitors to ensure that the premises are *reasonably* fit for the purpose for which such visitors are invited to use them. To use the language of one High Court judge:

> "Where the occupier of premises agrees for reward that a person shall have the right to enter and use them for a mutually contemplated purpose, the contract between the parties (unless it provides to the contrary) contains an implied warranty that the premises are as safe for that purpose as reasonable care and skill on the part of anyone can make them."

This duty of care extends to everyone (*e.g.* it would include the tradesman at the kitchen door, or the cabaret artist in a dressing room) and the more hazardous the purpose to which the premises are being put, the safer they must be. Most normal catering establishments, of course, are used solely or mainly for the accommodation of guests, and therefore the duty of the proprietor covers such matters as firm handrails, secure staircarpets, clean surfaces, unobstructed passageways, well-maintained lifts, adequate lighting and secure brickwork.

It makes no difference that lack of care is the fault of a member of staff, since, as was noted in Chapter 9, an employer is vicariously liable for the negligence of his servants in the normal course of their duties. It makes no difference even that the employee in question is acting contrary to express instructions, provided that the injured guest is not aware of the fact (see *Stone* v. *Taffe*, at p. 132). Where the defect is the result of careless work on the part of an independent contractor, the proprietor will still only escape liability if he can show that he made every reasonable effort to check that the job had been done properly, and that the defect was one which could only be discovered by an expert. The guest must, in such a case, sue the contractor.

The duty of care owed by the proprietor to each and every one of his guests extends only to those parts of the premises to which the guest is normally allowed access, or to which he is likely to go. Therefore, if the proprietor takes no steps to prevent a guest from using certain parts of the premises which are not strictly provided for him, he may still be liable if that guest meets with any accident; thus, in the case of *Campbell* v. *Shelbourne Hotel Ltd.* (1939), the plaintiff was a guest staying at the defendant's hotel; in the act of searching for a toilet at 11.20 p.m., the plaintiff wandered down an unlit passage, went through the wrong door, fell down stairs and was injured. It was held that the guest was entitled to damages from the defendant, since 11.20 p.m. was a reasonable time to expect lighting in any corridor into which a guest is likely to wander.

The duty to ensure that the premises are reasonably safe goes beyond the mere structure of the premises, and extends to the provision of emergency exits and warning notices. In addition, the proprietor must take reasonable steps to acquaint the guest with the layout of the premises, and emergency procedures, as in *MacLenan* v. *Segar* (1917), in which a guest arrived at an hotel late at night, and was taken straight to her room by lift. A fire broke out during the night, and the lady, knowing nothing of the layout of the hotel, panicked, attempted to leave by a second-floor window, and fell. Reference should also be made to the case of *Hallet* v. *Nicholson* at p. 40, above.

Children present a special problem, since not only are they more likely to be injured as the result of a trivial accident, but they are also more curious by nature, and are more likely to wander about. The proprietor does in fact owe a higher duty of care to a child than he does to an adult, and all potential attractions such as machinery and open cellar doors must be carefully guarded. It is not enough to warn a child by notice that he is out of bounds.

The proprietor of an hotel is also liable for all activities which are carried out on his premises, both by his staff, and by those whom he allows onto the premises. One example of this is his liability for the negligence of his staff, dealt with in an earlier chapter. Other examples might be dangerous activities such as a knife-throwing cabaret act, or a fireworks display in the grounds, even if these are organised solely for the amusement of the guests. He will not, however, normally be liable for an act of negligence by one guest which results in injury to another guest, unless it may be said that the proprietor was himself negligent in allowing the guest to carry out the activity in the first place (*e.g.* practising golf swings in a corridor). The injured guest may always, of course, sue the guest at fault. Section 1 of the Occupiers Liability Act 1984 makes an hotelier (like any other occupier) liable even to a trespasser in respect of dangers which it was reasonable to expect him to have been aware of, when at the same time he ought reasonably to have appreciated the presence of such persons near the danger and taken steps to warn or protect the trespasser. Obvious examples are "allurements" such as swimming pools left unguarded and unattended when it is known that children or young persons make use of them at night.

Brief mention should be made at this stage of the liability of the hotelier or restaurateur for the wholesomeness of the food and drink served on his premises; full details appear in Chapter 15 in which the effect of the Supply of Goods and Services Act 1982, is also considered. In this Act there is an implied term in the contract with each guest by virtue of which the hotelier undertakes to supply his service with reasonable care and skill.

There are several defences available to an hotelier who is sued for damages by a guest who has been injured on his premises, apart from the obvious one that he took "reasonable" care in the first place. First, he may be able to show that the guest was, at the time of the accident, doing something for the purposes of which he was not invited onto the premises. As was mentioned above, the liability of the proprietor extends only to those purposes for which a guest is invited to enter and make use of the premises. Thus, the guest may be invited to use the roof for sunbathing; if he uses it to play football, he may well be doing so at his own peril.

Secondly, it may be argued that the guest volunteered for the risk, in that he exposed himself to the danger in full knowledge of its existence. Cases of this type are, however, rare, and the courts do not look sympathetically at claims by the management that the guest was "warned" of the risk. The proprietor has a duty to make the premises safe, not to warn that they are unsafe.

A third, and more likely defence, is that the guest was contributorily negligent, in that he failed to take reasonable care for his own safety, and was thus the part-author of his own misfortune. Examples might be those of a guest who attempts to open a window, the catch of which is obviously broken, or a guest who, in a state of inebriation, trips over a flex from a carpet sweeper which has been left stretched across the hallway. In such cases, the damages payable by the proprietor will be reduced by the proportion to which the guest may be said to have been at fault.

Finally, the proprietor may seek to escape liability by means of an exemption clause which is made a term of the contract of booking, in the manner outlined earlier in the chapter. The courts tended to lean against such clauses in contracts anyway, but the matter has now been placed on a statutory footing by the Unfair Contract Terms Act 1977, which states that a person cannot, by means of a contractual term, seek to exclude or restrict his liability for death or personal injury arising out of negligence. It will be noted, however, that the Act does not make the hotel proprietor any *more* liable for negligence than he is already under the law—it merely states that he may not seek to exclude or reduce that liability by means of a clause in a contract.

The same Act states that a person may not, so far as *other* loss or damage is concerned, exclude or limit his liability by means of a contractual clause, except insofar as it is "reasonable" to do so. "Reasonable" is defined in the Act so as to have regard for "the circumstances which were, or ought reasonably to have been, known to or in the contemplation of the parties to the contract at the time the contract was made."

The Act states that even if a person is aware of a contractual term which seeks to exclude or limit liability for negligence, this in itself is not to be taken as an indication of his voluntary acceptance of any risk.

In addition to all this, the hotelier who allows a dangerous situation to arise in his hotel may be committing an offence under the Health and Safety at Work etc. Act 1974, section 3 of which makes him responsible for the safety of all persons who may be affected by his activities (*e.g.* hotel guests).

CHAPTER FIFTEEN

The sale of food and drink

ONE of the prime functions of a caterer is to provide food and drink for his customers, and it is hardly surprising to learn that the law has intervened in several ways to ensure that the consumer receives a product of reasonable quality. This intervention is justified, not only on the ground of justice to the consumer, but also on the ground of public health. The law on this subject is both complex and lengthy, and only a bare outline may be given in a book of this length.

Broadly speaking, the law relating to food and drink falls into three distinct categories, which will be dealt with in turn. These are: (1) duties imposed by the criminal law; (2) duties imposed by contract; (3) duties imposed under the laws of negligence.

1. Criminal liability

Parliament has, with the aid of the criminal law, imposed many heavy duties on the caterer, in an effort to ensure that what he produces complies with at least a minimum standard. The ways in which it has done this are laid out below; in all cases, unless the contrary is indicated, the term "food" also includes drink of all types.

The Food Act 1984

This Act, which brings together all the previous law on the subject, establishes a system whereby the consumer is protected against inferior food products, and whereby ministerial control is exercised over the preparation and service of food, and its contents. It replaces the Food and Drugs Act 1955 and the Food and Drugs (Scotland) Act 1956, and the following are among its main provisions.

Food unfit for human consumption

It is a criminal offence for any person to sell, offer or expose for sale, or have in his possession for the purposes of sale, any food which is intended for human consumption, but which is in fact unfit for that purpose. This is the effect of section 8 of the Act, and a separate offence is committed with each item of food which is so offered, sold or exposed. It is even an offence to "deposit" with or "consign" to any person, for the purpose of selling, or preparing for sale, any food intended for human consumption which is unfit for that purpose. Thus, for example, the delivery of such food by a wholesaler to a hotel kitchen would be an offence, whether it reached the dining room or not.

In order to be convicted of this offence, it is not necessary for the caterer to be proved to have *known* of the defect in his food, or even to have been careless. The offence is committed as soon as the food which is not fit is prepared for human consumption, and the caterer's ignorance is irrelevant. *Hobbs* v. *Winchester Corporation* (1910), was a case heard under an earlier statute which contained a provision identical to section 8. Hobbs was a butcher whose meat had been confiscated because it had been unfit for human consumption. He attempted to claim compensation on the grounds that since he had not known of the defect, he was not guilty. It was held that he was guilty, even though the impurity had not been discovered until it had been professionally analysed, and he could not possibly have known about it beforehand.

Also, an employer will be liable for acts committed by his employee. Thus, if a member of the kitchen staff allows impurities to enter food, and as a result it is deemed to be unfit for human consumption, the employer may be prosecuted. The only requirement is that the member of staff concerned be acting in the normal course of his employment; even if he is disobeying specific instructions, the employer will still be liable.

In order to prove that food was unfit for human consumption, it is not necessary to show that it was injurious to health. Thus, in *Greig* v. *Goldfinch* (1961), a pork pie was sold with a mould under the crust, and even though expert evidence was given to the effect that such a mould would not normally cause illness, it was held nevertheless that the pie was unfit for human consumption.

There are several defences open to a person charged with an offence against section 8 of the Act. First of all, it is a defence to show that the purchaser was given adequate notice of the fact that the food in question was not intended for human consumption, as for example where a butcher sells meat for dogs. It will, of course, always be a question of fact in each case, and it is for the accused to prove his claim to the satisfaction of the court.

A second possible defence is where the accused can show that he used all due diligence to prevent the commission of the offence; however, in the light of what happened in *Hobbs* v. *Winchester Corporation*, above, it would seem unwise to place too great a reliance on this defence.

The general defences provided under sections 100 and 102 of the Act, and mentioned below, also apply to charges under section 8.

Food not of the nature or quality demanded

By virtue of section 2 of the Act, it is an offence for any person to sell, to the prejudice of the purchaser, any food which is not of the nature, substance or quality demanded. A simple example might be the sale of bread and margarine as "bread and butter" or, as in *McDonalds Hamburgers* v. *Windle* (1987) selling a customer ordinary "Coke" instead of "Diet Coke." As with section 8, the caterer can commit an offence under section 2 without knowing it, and once again, he will be liable for the acts of his staff, or of an authorised agent. An offence under section 2 of the Act may, in relation to the same consignment of goods, be committed by both the retailer and the wholesaler.

Once again, the accused may use the defence that the purchaser was sufficiently informed of what he was getting, and was not therefore prejudiced. But this must be fully proved, as was illustrated in the case of *Preston* v. *Grant* (1925), in which a licensee was prosecuted for selling whisky at 42 per cent. under proof, when the law required that it be only 35 per cent. under proof at maximum. It was argued that, since there was a notice on display in the bar, informing purchasers that spirits were diluted and that their strength could not therefore be guaranteed, the purchaser in question had been sufficiently informed. It was held that since the licensee could not prove that the purchaser had actually read the notice, he could not rely on the defence.

It is worth noting in this context that the display of an appropriate notice on the wrapper or container will normally be deemed sufficient while, in a situation similar to *Preston* v. *Grant*, above, by section 3 of the Act, the dilution of spirit with water only is perfectly permissible provided that the strength does not fall below 37.2 per cent. by volume. In Scotland, whisky diluted to a strength below 35 per cent, under proof cannot, in fact, be called whisky: see *Brander* v. *Kinnear* (1923) and *Patterson* v. *Findlay* (1925).

A second defence arises where the charge has been brought

because of the presence of some extraneous matter in the food in question, and the accused can show that its presence was the unavoidable consequence of the process of collection or preparation of the food. However, two more recent cases have raised serious doubts concerning the availability of this defence. In *Smedleys Ltd.* v. *Breed* (1974), S were prosecuted under section 2 of the 1955 Act in respect of a caterpillar discovered in a tin of their peas. In the course of the season, S had canned three and a half million tins of peas, and only three other tins out of the whole of this number had been found to contain foreign bodies. S therefore put forward the defence that it was totally impracticable to collect peas in such a way as to avoid the occasional extraneous substances, and that the caterpillar's presence was therefore the "unavoidable consequence" of the process of manufacture. It was held by the House of Lords that steps could have been taken to ensure that the caterpillar did not enter the tin of peas, and that S were therefore liable.

In *Greater Manchester Council* v. *Lockwood Foods Ltd.* (1979), the same decision was arrived at when a black beetle found its way into a tin of strawberries, and the manufacturers had used all possible care and skill to avoid it. They were convicted on the grounds that the presence of the beetle was not the "inevitable consequence" of the process of canning (it was not even a *consequence* of it), and the comment was made that the defence previously available under section 3 of the Act (*i.e.* the "unavoidable consequence" defence) is now "virtually a dead letter." It is not necessary for the extraneous matter to be harmful to health before it will be held that an offence has been committed. In *Barber* v. *C.W.S.* (1983), for example, a conviction resulted from the presence of a straw in a bottle of milk.

Where the food has been submitted to some extraction or addition process, the display of an explanatory statement on the container or wrapper will suffice to absolve the caterer from any liability under section 2. It is still possible, of course, that an offence is being committed under section 8.

The defence of purchase under warranty applies here, as does the general defence under section 100, and they may now both be examined in more detail.

General defences under sections 100 and 102

Section 100 of the Act provides a general defence to any person charged with any offence under either the Act or the Hygiene Regulations made thereunder (for which see below). If the person charged can show that the offence was actually committed by some other person, and that he himself used all due diligence to prevent the commission of an offence, he may request that the prosecution be directed towards that other person, and that the charges against him be dropped. The new accused may himself make use of section 100, and so on, until the real culprit is identified.

Alternatively, by means of section 100, it may be found that more than one person is criminally liable, as in *Meah* v. *Roberts* (1977), in which a fitter employed by a firm which specalised in installing draught beer and lager equipment visited an Indian restaurant and cleaned the lager pipes with a caustic soda solution. He tried to explain to the Indian waiter what he was doing and why, but with little success. The fitter then placed the remainder of the caustic solution into an empty lemonade bottle, wrote "cleaner" on the label, and left the bottle on the bar counter. Bottles of lemonade for customers were also left in the same place, and the fitter did not tell any of the other staff what he had done.

A customer visited the restaurant with his family and ordered glasses of lemonade for the children. By mistake, the children were served with the caustic soda, and became ill as a result. M, the manager of the restaurant, was charged under sections 2 and 8 of the 1955 Act, and he claimed the defence under section 113, namely that the offence had occurred through the act or default of the fitter, and that he, M, had used all due diligence to prevent the offence. It was held that both M and the fitter should be convicted, since both had been guilty of default in allowing the incident to occur.

The accused may also be able to escape conviction if he can show (per section 102 of the Act) that he brought the food under a warranty that it was fit for human consumption, that he had no reason to suspect otherwise, and that the food in question was in the same state at the time of the alleged offence as it had been at the time of the giving of the warranty.

In *Walker* v. *Baxters' Butchers Ltd.* (1977), it was held that where packets of puff pastry were delivered in a refrigerated condition to a shop, and there placed on a shelf over a chilled display cabinet so that they would thaw out more quickly, the packets were in the "same state" when they thawed out as they had been when delivered. Such items, said the court, will always be in the "same state" unless the purchaser "physically tampers" with them, which will not happen where they are simply frozen or thawed out.

It also seems from the recent case of *Rochdale Metropolitan Council* v. *FMC (Meat) Ltd.* (1980) that a brand name can be a sufficient warranty in such a case, being a guarantee that the article in question (i.e. in the present case, a frozen chicken) may be sold under its brand name without infringing any section of the Act. By using this argument, the supplier of a chicken to a local authority, which he in turn had bought from a wholesaler, escaped liability under section 8.

Food labelling and pricing

Section 7 of the Act gives to the Department of Agriculture and the Secretary of State for Health and Social Services or the Secretary of State for Scotland the power to issue regulations concerning the labelling, marking or advertising of food which is intended for human consumption, and the description which may be applied to such food.

From 1st January, 1983, the laws of the U.K. were required to fall in line with those for the rest of the EEC as regards the labelling, presentation and advertising of foodstuffs for sale to the ultimate consumer, with the exception of milk and certain food additives. The Regulations which brought this about were the Food Labelling Regulations of 1980, and their Scottish equivalents dated 1981; lack of space prohibits further detailed explanation.

The Price Marking (Food and Drink on Premises) Order 1979 requires that every person who advertises, by any means, that he is, or may be, selling food or drink for human consumption on any premises must give an "indication" of the price of that food and drink, and any charge which is payable in addition. Where the food or drink is sold by reference to a quantity or a unit of measurement (*e.g.* $\frac{1}{5}$ gill), then the price indicated must be the price per specified quantity or unit(s) of measurement; otherwise, the price indicated must be the price for the food or drink (*e.g.* a "portion of chips," or "three course lunch").

Where there are not more than 30 separate items for sale, an indication of price must be given for each of the 30; where more than 30 items are on offer, an indication of price must be given for not less than 30 items. Where the items are divided into "categories" (*e.g.* starters, fish courses, sweets), then not less than 5 items within each category must be priced. Where the meal is a table d'hôte meal, it is sufficient to indicate the price for each meal, regardless of the number of items in it.

In the case of table wine, supplied for consumption with food, not less than six items must be priced (less, if less than six table wines are available, but then *all* items must be priced). Where the proprietor supplies more than one "kind" of wine (*i.e.* red, white and rosé), then it is sufficient if he indicates the price of at least two in each category.

All prices quoted must be inclusive of VAT, and the price indication must be legible and easily read by an intending purchaser, at or near the entrance to the "eating area," or, in the case of a "supply" area (presumably, for example, the counter of a self-service unit), at the point where the intending consumer chooses the food. Any service charge or "minimum order" limit must be displayed equally prominently.

The Order extends to all catering establishments (including public houses and snack bars), but does not apply in bona fide clubs, staff canteens, canteens in educational establishments, or residential establishments in which food and drink are served only to those who have engaged sleeping accommodation. Nor does the Order apply to food and drink prepared by special request or for which a price has been agreed in advance (*e.g.* outside catering for a wedding reception).

The Order arises under the Prices Act, 1974, and the penalty for failing to observe it is criminal prosecution. Under s.20 of the Consumer Protection Act 1987, it is a criminal offence to give a misleading price indication in respect of goods for sale, or to fail to take steps to correct a price indication which has become misleading.

Food hygiene regulations

Section 13 of the Act gives power to the appropriate Secretary of State to make regulations in respect of hygiene in those premises upon which food is stored, prepared or served. The Food Hygiene (General) Regulations 1970 (in Scotland, the Food Hygiene (Scotland) Regulations 1959, as amended) are the latest to be issued, and they lay down hygiene standards for all food businesses, which in this context includes not only cafés, restaurants, hotels, etc., but also schools, hospitals and canteens. Even registered clubs are covered. The following are the main points:

1. no food business may be carried on in or at any insanitary premises;
2. all items of equipment with which food or drink is likely to come into contact shall be kept clean, and shall be so designed as to enable them to be thoroughly cleaned, and so as to prevent contamination;
3. all food containers shall be kept free from contamination;
4. all food itself shall be kept free from contamination;
5. no food shall be kept less than 18 inches from the ground, unless special precautions are taken to guard against contamination;
6. all persons handling food shall make every attempt to remain clean while working; this includes both the persons themselves and the clothes they are wearing. They must cover all cuts and abrasions, and refrain from spitting, smoking or handling snuff while in the same room as open food;
7. clean food wrappers must be used; under no circumstances may open food be wrapped in printed paper;
8. no member of staff suffering from certain infectious diseases may be allowed to work near food;
9. the employer must provide suitably clean sanitary facilities which are close at hand, but completely away from food

rooms. There must be no handling of open food anywhere near these sanitary facilities, and the employer must display notices requiring staff to wash their hands after visiting the toilet;

10. the employer must provide an adequate supply of clean water, wash-hand basins, soap, nailbrushes, towels, drying facilities, first-aid kits, accommodation for clothing away from food areas, and washing facilities for both food and equipment;
11. there must be adequate lighting and ventilation in all food rooms, and these rooms must be in a good state of repair;
12. there may be no more accumulation of refuse upon food premises than is reasonably necessary;
13. the employer must observe any maximum or minimum temperature requirements in respect of certain items of food;
14. before any food is offered for sale, adequate precautions must be taken to ensure that any food which is unfit for human consumption is separated from food which is so fit;
15. open food must, wherever reasonably necessary, be effectively screened from possible contamination while it is being exposed for sale, or during actual sale or delivery. Food may still presumably be displayed, *e.g.* on an hors d'oeuvres trolley, provided that it is adequately covered;
16. persons engaged in the handling of open food must wear "sufficient clean and washable over-clothing." This will not include waiting staff, but it will include bar staff handling open food.

Further force has been added to the Food Hygiene Regulations by the passing of the Food Act 1984 (formerly the Food and Drugs (Control of Food Premises) Act 1976, and its Scottish equivalent, passed in 1977). The effect of the Act is that where a person is convicted of an offence under the Food Hygiene Regulations which involves the carrying on of food business at any insanitary premises or stall, or at any premises or stall which is so situated or designed or in such a condition that food is exposed to the risk of contamination, the court hearing the case may, upon the application of the local authority, order the premises to be closed.

The court must be satisfied that the continuation of activities at the premises would be injurious to health, but if the order is granted it will be effective until the danger has been removed to the satisfaction of the local authority, in that the specific measures ordered by the court have been carried out.

An emergency order may be granted pending the hearing of the main complaint under the Food Hygiene Regulations; wrongful use of this facility by the local authority may result in the authority being required by the court to pay compensation to the proprietor.

By virtue of Regulations issued in 1979, the 1976 Act has been extended to cover ships in inland and coastal waters which contain a catering business.

General

The enforcement of the provisions of the 1984 Act and the various Regulations made under them is in the hands of the local authority, whose Trading Standards Officers may enter any catering premises at any reasonable time (with force, if they have a warrant), inspect the premises, question the staff and take away portions of food for sampling.

Penalties under the Act are fines and/or imprisonment.

The Trade Descriptions Act 1968

The Trade Descriptions Act 1968 was something new in the field of consumer protection in that it made provision for the *criminal prosecution* of any person who misdescribes the goods or services which he has available. The effect of section 14 of the Act on the provision of hotel services and facilities has already been noted in Chapter 14; we are concerned here solely with the effect of the Act upon the provision of food and drink.

The Act does not apply to the Crown, so that, while industrial canteens within the nationalised industries will be covered by it, catering units such as NAAFI canteens and hospital kitchens will not be. Also, as the result of a High Court decision in 1970, it would appear that the Act does not apply to registered clubs.

Section 1 of the Act makes it a criminal offence for any person, in the course of any trade or business, to apply a "false trade description" to any goods, or to supply or offer to supply goods which have been falsely described. The term "false trade description" means "any materially false or misleading statement which is in any way displayed so that it is associated with the goods in the mind of the consumer." Such a statement may be either oral or in writing, and it may relate to the quality, quantity, composition, fitness for the purpose offered, or safety of the goods.

An "offer to supply" may be inferred from the mere possession of the goods, and the offence may be committed in an advertisement. A person may be found not guilty of an offence under section 1 even though he did not intend to commit the offence, unless he can make use of one of the defences provided by section 24, below. The person charged may be either a private individual or a company, and in theory, an employer may be held liable for the acts of this staff, although the case of *Beckett* v. *Kingston Bros.*, below, seems to provide a way out for an employer who finds himself in this situation.

Section 6 of the Act gives the Department of Trade and Industry the power to require persons who supply certain goods to give a definite meaning to certain expressions which they use, while section 8 gives the Board the power to insist that certain goods be marked in certain ways.

Section 11 of the Act makes it an offence to make any false or misleading statement concerning the price of any goods. This would include, for example, imposing a service charge which was not specified in advance. See also the provisions of s. 20 of the Consumer Protection Act 1987, at p. 221.

Section 24 of the Act provides a series of defences to anyone who is charged with an offence under the Act. These defences are as follows:

(1) That the offence was committed as a result of a pure mistake on the part of the person charged. It would appear from decided statements that this last phrase is to be interpreted strictly, and that it will be no defence for the person charged to prove that the offence was committed by his servant or agent. In *Butler* v. *Keenway Supermarkets Ltd.* (1974), for example, the management were not allowed to use the defence where a junior clerk at Head Office issued the wrong price tickets for a "reduced" item, with the result that instead of paying 1½p. less per item, as they believed, customers were in fact paying 8½p. more.

(2) That at the time when the offence was committed, the person charged was relying upon information supplied to him by someone else.

(3) That the offence was committed through the act or default of some other person. It seems that this other person may be an employee of the person charged: thus, in the case of *Beckett* v. *Kingston Bros.* (1970), the defendants had bought turkeys from Denmark, which carried a label stating that they were "Norfolk King Turkeys." The defendants instructed the managers of all their shops to stick a new label on each turkey so as to correct the misdescription. One of their managers did not, and the defendants were charged with an offence under section 1 of the 1968 Act. They claimed the defence laid down under section 24 of the Act that the offence was committed due to the act or default of some other person, and the court held that they were entitled to do so, and could not therefore be convicted. If the person responsible had been a junior employee under the direct control of the defendants, then they might still have been liable.

(4) That the offence was committed due to some accident or other cause beyond the control of the person charged.

(5) That the person charged could not reasonably be expected to know that the goods did not correspond with the description applied to them.

In all these cases, the person charged must prove, in addition to one or more of the above, that he took all reasonable precautions, and exercised all due diligence. Finally, as was mentioned in Chapter 14, it should be noted that the fact that an offence has been committed under the 1968 Act does not bring the contract to an end; the aggrieved party should bring an action on the grounds of misrepresentation in the normal way. It is, however, open to the court convicting the offender to award compensation to his "victim."

The enforcement of the 1968 Act is left in the hands of the Trading Standards Officers employed by each local authority, who may enter premises, seize and examine goods, make test purchases and bring prosecutions in their own name, with the approval of the Board of Trade. It is a separate offence to obstruct such an officer in the execution of his duty.

The procedure is different in Scotland, where the local Officers are expressly denied the authority to bring prosecutions in their own name by virtue of section 26(5) of the 1968 Act. Breaches of the Act will be reported to the Procurator Fiscal, as with all criminal prosecutions in Scotland.

2. Contractual liability

Any person who sells food and drink enters into a *contract* with the purchaser, and his contract is regarded in the eyes of the law as a contract for the sale of goods. Such sales are subject to the Sale of Goods Act 1979, s.14 of which states that where the purchaser, either expressly or by implication, makes known to the seller the purpose for which the goods are required, and the goods in question are sold in the course of a business, then there is an implied term in the contract that the goods shall be reasonably fit for the purpose for which they are supplied.

In *Frost* v. *Aylesbury Dairies* (1905), for example, a dairy sold a bottle of milk to F for consumption by himself and his family. The milk was in fact infected with typhoid germs, and was not "reasonably fit" for human consumption. Mrs. F died as a result of drinking some of the milk, and F sued the dairy under the Sale of Goods Act 1893, the forerunner of the 1979 Act. It was held that it was reasonable to assume that when the milk was purchased, it was intended for human consumption, for which it was not fit. Although it was accepted on behalf of the dairy that no amount of "skill and judgment" would have prevented what happened, and that they were therefore not morally at fault, they were nevertheless liable under the Act.

Thus, if a customer seats himself in a restaurant, and orders certain of the items on the menu, it is obvious that he requires them for consumption; since it is the restaurateur's business to supply such items for consumption, an implied term immediately enters the contract to the effect that the items in question shall be fit for human consumption; if it later transpires that the items in question are *not* fit for that purpose, then there has been a breach of contract for which the restaurateur may be sued. It makes no difference that the latter has not been negligent; he will still be liable for the breach of contract whether the defect was discoverable or not.

The fact that the goods were purchased under a brand name or trade mark will make little difference to the caterer's position, since if he normally trades in such goods under such a brand name or trade mark, there is still an implied term in the contract to the effect that the goods are of merchantable quality. Thus, the café owner who regularly sells a certain brand of chocolate will still be liable for breach of contract if that chocolate is not fit for human consumption. The fact that the real culprit may be the manufacturer will make no difference to him, since the customer is making the contract of sale with *him* and not the manufacturer. The retailer may, of course, sue the manufacturer in his turn.

The only possible way in which the caterer might absolve himself from liability under the contract would be for him to introduce a suitably worded exemption clause into the contract. Section 14 only impose an *implied* term, and this may in theory be defeated by a clear *express* term to the contrary. This course of action has, however, been made virtually impossible by the Unfair Contracts Terms Act 1977, which makes such clauses virtually worthless where the customer is a private "consumer." In the case of a breach of contract which causes death or personal injury, liability may not, of course, be excluded at all—see page 213, above.

See also the Supply of Goods and Services Act 1982, considered below.

3. Liability for negligence

The manufacturer of any goods is under a legal duty to the eventual consumer (whoever he may be) to ensure that the goods which he produces are reasonably safe for the purposes for which they were produced. In other words, a caterer is under a duty of care to his customers to ensure that the goods which he supplies are reasonably fit to be eaten. If, through the negligence of the caterer, they are not, and the customer suffers injury as a result, then the latter may sue for damages for negligence. This has nothing to do with any contract between the two parties; it is a separate issue entirely.

The most famous case on this subject was *Donoghue* v. *Stevenson* (1932), in which a lady entered a café, and sat down with a bottle of ginger beer purchased for her by a friend. She emptied part of the contents of the bottle into a glass, and drank it. As she was in the act of pouring out the remainder, the remains of a snail floated out of the bottle, which was of dark glass, and which thus hid the contents from sight until they were poured out. As the result of the incident, the lady became ill, and brought an action against the manufacturer of the ginger beer. It was held that she had a right to sue the manufacturers for damages for negligence, for, as one judge put it:

> "A manufacturer of products, which he sells in such a form as to show that he intends them to reach the ultimate consumer in the form in which they left him, and with no reasonable possibility of intermediate examination, and with the knowledge that the absence of reasonable care in the preparation or putting up of the products will result in an injury to the consumer's life or property, owes a duty to the consumer to take that reasonable care."

The manufacturer is, however, only required to take reasonable care, and he will not be held liable for any extra-ordinary defect which he could not reasonably have been expected to foresee. The duty of care, extends to all stages of manufacture, and liability does not cease merely because the goods in question are placed in a sealed container; it *does* make a difference, however, when the goods are presented in such a way that they may be inspected by the consumer. When this happens, and the consumer fails to inspect them in the way that one would normally expect inspection to occur, the damages payable may be reduced by the proportion to which the consumer was careless. It is doubtful, however, whether the law would ever expect the consumer of food or drink to make a careful inspection beforehand.

In some circumstances, the retailer may be liable in negligence even though he is not the manufacturer. If, for example, the manufacturer gives the retailer a specific warning that the goods in question must be consumed within a certain period, and the retailer ignores this warning, or fails to pass it on to the consumer, the manufacturer has done all that the law requires of him, and it is the retailer who may be sued for negligence. Similarly, if the retailer ignores specific instructions concerning the storage of goods, and a consumer is injured as a result, it is the retailer who must bear the liability.

In practice, the consumer is more likely to attempt to sue for damages for negligence; in this case, the most likely defendant will be the manufacturer. If, on the other hand, the consumer sues for contractual breach, it is the retailer who will be liable. In the case of food prepared and served on the same catering premises, of course, the caterer is both the manufacturer and the retailer. Again, however, no exemption clause will exempt the guilty party from liability for causing death or personal injury.

The Supply of Goods and Services Act 1982 also imposes a duty upon those supplying food and drink to the public, in that, by virtue of section 13, where the caterer is supplying any service in the course of a business, there is an implied term that he will carry out the service with reasonable skill and care.

The section was really intended to cover services such as hairdressing and car repairs, but it could, for example, cover the provision of facilities for a wedding reception, and anyone suffering emotional distress as the result of a badly organised catering function might be able to make use of this section to recover damages.

Section 16 of the Act allows the caterer to cover himself by means of an exemption clause, but it will be subject to the terms of the Unfair Contract Terms Act 1977, in that it must be reasonable and cannot in any case exempt liability for death or bodily injury.

The Common Law rules laid down in *Donoghue* v. *Stevenson* are also now subject to the provisions of the Consumer Protection Act 1987, which implements EEC Directive 1985/374 on product liability. Section 2 of the Act imposes civil liability on the manufacturer of any product which is "defective" in the sense that it does not live up to the standard expected of it by the purchaser (i.e. in the case of food or drink, it is not fit for human consumption). The manufacturer need not have been negligent, and the consumer may simply sue the supplier (e.g. the café proprietor) in place of the manufacturer unless and until the supplier gives him full particulars of the manufacturer. This liability cannot be avoided by means of a contractual term or a notice displayed on the premises.

INDEX